PROGRAMMING TASK	FUNCTION/TOPIC
Geometric Operations *(Continued)*	
Prompt user for a point	Getpoint
Prompt user for a corner (with window)	Getcorner
Find sine of angle	Sin
Find cosine of angle	Cos
Find arctangent of angle	Atan
Find relative polar points	Polar
Find intersecting points	Inters
Find a point on an entity	Osnap
Translate one UCS to another	Trans
String Operations	
Prompt user for a string	Getstring
Prompt user for a string (restricted)	Getkword
Find length of a string	Strlen
Find substring of a string	Substr
Combine strings	Strcat
Change case of a string	Strcase
Data-Type Conversion	
Convert string to real	Atof
Convert string to integer	Atoi
Convert string to ASCII character code	Ascii
Strip quotation marks from string	Read
Convert ASCII character code to a number	Chr
Convert angle (real) to string	Angtos
Convert integer to string	Itoa
Convert real to string	Rtos
Test for data type	Type
Convert real to integer	Fix
Convert integer to real	Float

CARL RODOLF & ASSOCIATES, INC.
5345 Madison Avenue, Suite 200
Sacramento, CA 95841

The ABC's of AutoLISP

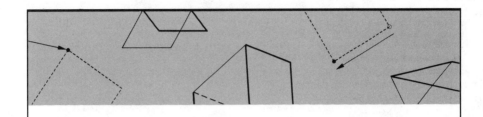

The ABC's of
AutoLISP

George Omura

SYBEX® *San Francisco • Paris • Düsseldorf • London*

Acquisitions Editor: Dianne King
Developmental Editor: Cheryl Holzaepfel
Copy Editor: Christian T.S. Crumlish
Technical Editor: Bob Callori
Word Processor: Scott Campbell and Deborah Maizels
Book Designer: Jeffrey James Giese
Chapter Art and Layout: Suzanne Albertson
Screen Graphics: Jeffrey James Giese
Typesetter: Elizabeth Newman
Proofreader: Lisa Jaffe
Indexer: Tom McFadden
Cover Designer: Thomas Ingalls + Associates
Cover Photographer: David Bishop

To Frank Plimier, MicroCADD pioneer

Acknowledgments

There can never be enough recognition given to the many people who are instrumental in creating a book such as this one. I would like to thank those people at SYBEX who gave their best effort to make *The ABC's of AutoLISP* a reality: Cheryl Holzaepfel, developmental editor, who gave much encouragement; Christian Crumlish, copy editor, who helped hammer out the details; Bob Callori, tech reviewer and colleague, whose insights helped mold the content of the book; Dianne King, acquisitions editor, who always seems willing to listen to my crazy ideas; and the people in the production department, who kept the book on track.

I would also like to thank Gloria Bastidas, Patricia Pepper, and Larry Knott at Autodesk for their continued help and information.

Contents at a Glance

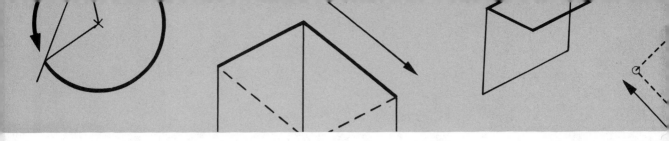

Table of Contents

4   *Prompting the User for Information*   *89*

5   *Making Decisions with AutoLISP*   *115*

10   *Editing AutoCAD Entities*   *245*

Introduction

One of AutoCAD's greatest assets is its adaptability. You can control just about every aspect of AutoCAD's operations, from the appearance of its drawing editor to its variety of menus. A key element of this adaptability is AutoCAD's built-in programming language, AutoLISP. With AutoLISP, you can virtually write your own commands and redefine others.

You can think of AutoLISP as a very sophisticated macro-building facility. (Simple macros are like scripts that automate repetitive keystrokes.) You don't need to be a programmer to use AutoLISP. In fact, AutoLISP is designed so that everyday users of AutoCAD can start working with it after a minimum of training. This book makes Auto-LISP accessible to AutoCAD users who are looking for a way to enhance and extend their use of AutoCAD.

Who Should Read This Book

This book introduces nonprogrammers to AutoLISP. If you are an intermediate-level AutoCAD user interested in learning about this powerful tool, then this is the book for you. If you are just beginning to learn AutoCAD, then you should probably become a bit more familar with AutoCAD before attempting to learn AutoLISP. This book assumes that you have at least an intermediate-level of expertise with AutoCAD and are acquainted with simple DOS operations.

This book also assumes that you are using version 9 or 10 of Auto-CAD on an IBM XT, AT, PS/2, or compatible, with MS- or PC-DOS version 2.1 or later. If you are using an earlier version of AutoCAD, most of the exercises and discussions in this book will still be relevant, but a few functions will be unavailable. Also, if you are using an operating system other than DOS, you should still be able to use this book, though the exercises were designed for use with DOS.

*H*ow This Book Is Organized

The book is divided into 11 chapters. The first three chapters give you an introduction to programming in AutoLISP. Chapter 1 shows you how to enter AutoLISP commands directly at the AutoCAD command prompt. Chapter 2 shows you how to create and save programs in a file. Chapter 3 discusses ways of organizing your programming projects and how to manage your computer's memory.

The next four chapters demonstrate how to apply AutoLISP to a variety of editing tasks. Chapter 4 discusses the functions that allow you to ask the user for input. Chapter 5 explains how to build decision-making capabilities into your programs. Chapter 6 shows you how to deal with geometric problems using AutoCAD. Chapter 7 discusses various ways to manipulate text.

The last four chapters show you how AutoCAD and AutoLISP interact. In Chapter 8, you will see how you can control many facets of AutoCAD through AutoLISP. Chapter 9 delves into lists, a fundamental component of all AutoLISP programs. Chapter 10 shows you ways of modifying AutoCAD entities by directly accessing the Auto-CAD drawing database. Finally, Chapter 11 looks at ways to dig deeper into the drawing database to get information on complex drawing entities like polylines and block attributes.

In addition, this book contains three appendices to be used as references. The first two cover AutoLISP error messages and group codes. (Group codes are used to access AutoCAD's drawing database.) The third appendix describes AutoCAD dimension variables and system variables.

*H*ow to Use This Book

Each chapter offers exercises and sample programs that demonstrate some general concept regarding AutoLISP. Through these exercises, the book shows you how to develop ideas into finished, running programs. The information you learn in one chapter will build on what you learned in the previous chapter. This way, your knowledge of AutoLISP will be integrated and cohesive, rather than fragmented.

For this reason, the best way to use this book is to read each chapter in order and do all of the exercises. Since topics are oriented toward accomplishing tasks rather than simply focusing on individual functions and capabilities, you will get a better grasp of how to use Auto-LISP in real-world situations if you read the chapters and do the exercises in the order in which they are presented.

How to Obtain a Program Disk

As a final note, if you are in a hurry and don't want to enter the programs presented in this book by hand, you can purchase a disk containing the programs. You will find an order form in the back of the book. In addition to the programs in the book, the disk contains a number of useful utilities you can take apart and examine, or load and use immediately.

1

Introducing AutoLISP

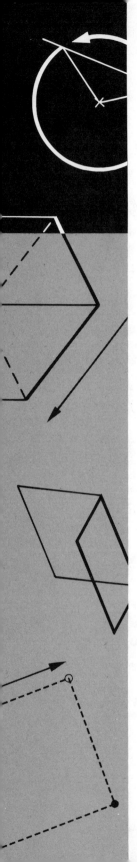

1

If you have never programmed a computer before, you may think that learning AutoLISP will be difficult. Actually, when you use a program such as AutoCAD, you are, in a sense, programming your computer to create and manipulate a database. As you become more familiar with AutoCAD, you may begin to explore the creation of linetypes and hatch patterns, for example. Or you may customize your menu to include your own specialized functions and macros. (Macros are like scripts that the computer follows to perform a pre-determined sequence of commands.) At this level, you are delving deeper into the workings of AutoCAD and at the same time programming your computer in a more traditional sense.

Using AutoLISP is really just extending your knowledge and use of AutoCAD. In fact, once you learn the basic syntax of AutoLISP, you only need to familiarize yourself with AutoLISP's built-in functions to start writing useful programs. AutoLISP's *syntax* is the standard order of elements in its expressions. You might look at AutoLISP functions as an extension to AutoCAD's library of commands. The more functions you are familiar with, the better equipped you are to use the program effectively.

AutoLISP closely resembles Common LISP, the most recent version of the oldest artificial-intelligence programming language still in use today. AutoLISP is essentially a pared down version of Common LISP with some additional features unique to AutoCAD. Many consider LISP to be one of the easiest programming languages to learn, partly because of its simple syntax. Since AutoLISP is primarily a subset of Common LISP, it is that much easier to learn.

In this chapter, you will become familiar with some of the basic elements of AutoLISP by using AutoLISP directly from the AutoCAD command prompt to perform a few simple operations. While doing this, you will be introduced to some of the concepts you will need to know to develop your own AutoLISP applications.

Checking Your Computer for the AutoLISP Facility

Before you can do anything with AutoLISP, you must ascertain whether AutoCAD's AutoLISP facility has been enabled. Follow these steps to check your system:

1. Start the AutoCAD program. When the Main menu appears, look at the top several lines (see Figure 1.1). You should see a line reading

   Advanced Drafting Extensions 3

If this statement does not appear on the Main menu, you do not have the AutoLISP capabilities. Nearly everyone who purchases Auto-CAD has the complete system, including the Advanced Drafting Extensions 3 (ADE-3 for short), and it is unlikely that you would not have such a system. However, it is possible that you have only ADE-1

```
            A U T O C A D
Copyright (C) 1982,83,84,85,86,87,88 Autodesk, Inc.
Release 10 (10/7/88) IBM PC
Advanced Drafting Extensions 3
Serial Number:  79-213123
NOT FOR RESALE

Main Menu

    0.   Exit AutoCAD
    1.   Begin a NEW drawing
    2.   Edit an EXISTING drawing
    3.   Plot a drawing
    4.   Printer Plot a drawing

    5.   Configure AutoCAD
    6.   File Utilities
    7.   Compile shape/font description file
    8.   Convert old drawing file

Enter selection:
```

Figure 1.1: The AutoCAD Main menu

or ADE-2. If this is the case, you should upgrade your AutoCAD program to a version that includes ADE-3.

2. Once you have determined that ADE-3 is present, choose option 5, Configure AutoCAD, from the menu. Do this by entering **5** at the prompt

Enter selection:

You will get a listing showing your current AutoCAD configuration.

3. Press ←. The Configuration menu will appear (see Figure 1.2).

4. Enter **8** to choose the Configure Operating Parameters option at the "Enter selection" prompt. The Operating Parameter menu will appear (see Figure 1.3).

This menu allows you to control some AutoCAD settings, such as the default plot file name and the location of temporary files. It also allows you to turn the AutoLISP facility on or off, and, in release 10, to control the use of AutoCAD's extended memory for AutoLISP.

```
          A U T O C A D
Copyright (C) 1982,83,84,85,86,87,88 Autodesk, Inc.
Release 10 (10/7/88) IBM PC
Advanced Drafting Extensions 3
Serial Number:  79-213123
NOT FOR RESALE

Configuration menu

   0.  Exit to Main Menu
   1.  Show current configuration
   2.  Allow detailed configuration

   3.  Configure video display
   4.  Configure digitizer
   5.  Configure plotter
   6.  Configure printer plotter
   7.  Configure system console
   8.  Configure operating parameters

Enter selection <0>:
```

Figure 1.2: The Configuration menu

```
          A U T O C A D
Copyright (C) 1982,83,84,85,86,87,88 Autodesk, Inc.
Release 10 (10/7/88) IBM PC
Advanced Drafting Extensions 3
Serial Number:   79-213123
NOT FOR RESALE

Operating parameter menu

    0.  Exit to configuration menu
    1.  Alarm on error
    2.  Initial drawing setup
    3.  Default plot file name
    4.  Plot spooler directory
    5.  Placement of temporary files
    6.  Network node name
    7.  AutoLISP feature

Enter selection <0>:
```

Figure 1.3: *The Operating Parameter menu*

5. Enter **7** for the AutoLISP Feature option at the "Enter selection" prompt to turn AutoLISP on. The following prompt appears:

Do you want AutoLISP enabled? <Y>

Usually the default is Y, for yes. Defaults appear between angle brackets and can be confirmed by pressing ←┘. If you are working on an unfamiliar system, this setting may be turned off, in which case the default would be N, for no.

6. Enter **Y**. The next prompt appears.

Do you want to use Extended AutoLISP? <N>

This default is usually set to N.

7. Enter **N** for no at this prompt.

If you are using a version earlier than 10, the Extended AutoLISP option is not available. We will discuss the use of extended memory with AutoLISP later. For now, just remember that you can control the use of Extended AutoLISP through this menu option.

8. Now return to the Main menu by pressing ← repeatedly to accept the default at each occurrence of the "Enter Selection" prompt. When exiting the Configuration menu, you will get the message

   If you answer N to the following question, all configuration changes you have just made will be discarded.
   Keep configuration changes? <Y>

   Press ← at this prompt to accept the yes default. You'll return to the AutoCAD Main menu.

9. Select option 1 to open a new file.

10. At the file-name prompt enter

    test =

This will open a new file called Test. The equal sign that follows the file name tells AutoCAD to give this file the standard AutoCAD settings. Use the equal sign here in case your system has a nonstandard AutoCAD template file. In any future exercises where you are asked to open a new file, always use the equal sign.

11. When the command prompt appears, press the F1 key to switch the display to Text mode.

Now you're ready to work with AutoLISP. As you read the following sections, perform the exercises at your keyboard.

Understanding the Interpreter and Evaluation

AutoLISP is accessed through the AutoLISP interpreter. When you enter data at the AutoCAD command prompt, the interpreter first reads it to determine if the data is an AutoLISP formula. If the data turns out to be intended for AutoLISP, then AutoLISP *evaluates* it, and returns an answer to the screen. In AutoLISP, the term evaluation means to find the value of something. This process of reading the command prompt, evaluating the data, and then printing to the screen, occurs whenever anything is entered at the command prompt and is an important part of how AutoLISP functions.

In some ways, the interpreter is like a hand-held calculator. Just as with a calculator, the information you wish to have AutoLISP evaluate must be entered in a certain order. For example, to add 0.618 and 1, you must enter the formula as follows:

(+ 0.618 1)

Try entering the above formula at the command prompt. AutoLISP evaluates the formula, (+ 0.618 1), and returns the answer, 1.618, displaying it on the prompt line.

This structure—(+ 0.618 1)—is called an *expression* and it is the basic structure for all AutoLISP programs. Everything intended for the AutoLISP interpreter, from the simplest expression to the most complex program, must be written with this structure. The result returned from evaluating an expression is called the *value* of the expression.

*T*he Components of an Expression

An AutoLISP expression must include an operator of some sort followed by the items to be operated on. An *operator* is an instruction to take some specific action. Examples of mathematical operators include the plus sign (+) for addition and the forward slash (/) for division.

We will often refer to the operator as a *function* and the items to be operated on as the *arguments* to the function or simply, the arguments. So, in the expression (+ 0.618 1), the + is the function and the numbers 0.618 and 1 are the arguments. All AutoLISP expressions, no matter what size, follow this structure and are enclosed by parentheses.

Parentheses are important elements of an expression. All parentheses must be balanced, that is, for each left parenthesis, there must be a right parenthesis. If you enter an imbalanced expression into the AutoLISP interpreter, you get the following prompt:

n>

where *n* is the number of parentheses required to complete the expression. If you see this prompt, you must enter the number of closing parentheses indicated by *n* in order to return to the command prompt.

Double quotation marks enclosing text must also be carefully balanced. If an AutoLISP expression is imbalanced, it can be quite difficult to complete it and exit AutoLISP. Figure 1.4 shows the components of the expression you just entered.

Note in Figure 1.4 that spaces are used to separate the function and arguments of the expression. Spaces are required between elements of the expression. Spaces are not required between the parentheses and the elements of the expression, but they can be helpful in improving the readability of expressions when they become complex. Spaces help both you and AutoLISP keep track of where one element ends and another begins.

Special care should be taken in placing spaces between single-character functions and their arguments. Math functions, such as + and /, can be especially troublesome. The order and type of arguments that follow a function may vary depending on the function. But the overall structure of expressions is always the function followed by its arguments, all enclosed in parentheses.

Using Arguments and Expressions

AutoLISP evaluates everything, not just expressions, but the arguments in expressions as well. This means that in the above example, AutoLISP evaluates the numbers 0.618 and 1 before it applies these numbers to the plus operator. In AutoLISP, numbers evaluate to themselves. This means that when AutoLISP evaluates the number 0.618,

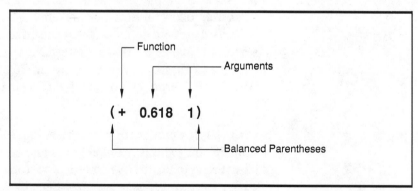

Figure 1.4: The parts of an AutoLISP expression

0.618 is returned unchanged. Since AutoLISP evaluates all arguments, expressions can also be used as arguments to a function.

For example, enter the following at the command prompt:

(/ 1 (+ 0.618 1))

In this example, the divide function (/) is given two arguments—the number 1 and the expression (+ 0.618 1). This type of expression is called a *complex* or *nested* expression because one expression is contained within another. So in our example, AutoLISP first evaluates the arguments of the expression, which are the expression (+ 0.618 1) and the number 1. It then applies the resulting value of the expression (1.618) and the number 1 to the divide function and returns the answer of 0.618047 (see Figure 1.5).

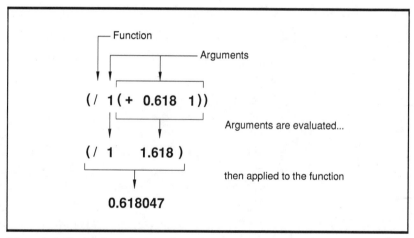

Figure 1.5: Evaluation of a nested expression

*U*sing Variables

Another calculator-like capability of the interpreter is its ability to remember values. A calculator with some memory can store the value of an equation for future use. In a similar way, you can store values using variables. A *variable* is like a container that holds a value. That value can change in the course of a program's operation. A simple analogy to this is the title of a government position. The position of president could be thought of as a variable. This variable can be assigned a value, such as Ronald Reagan or George Bush.

Understanding Data Types

Variables can take on several types of values or data types. Here is what some of these data types look like in AutoLISP:

Data Type	Example
Integer	24
Real number	0.618
String	"20 feet 6 inches"
List	(4.5021 6.3011 0.0)
File descriptor	<File: a620>
Entity name	<Entity name: 60000014c>
Selection set	<selection set: 1>
Symbols	Point1
Subrs	Setq

By separating data into types, the interpreter is better able to determine precisely how to evaluate the data and keep programs running quickly. Also, a computer stores different types of data differently, so the use of data types helps AutoLISP manage its memory more efficiently. Finally, data types help keep your programming efforts clear by forcing you to think of data as having certain characteristics. The following descriptions give you an idea of what each of these data types are.

Integers and Real Numbers

Integers are whole numbers from -32768 to $+32767$. The value of an expression containing only integers is always an integer. For example, the value of the expression (/ 25 2) is 12. AutoLISP drops the decimal portion from the resulting value.

Real numbers include decimal values. If the expression above is written using real numbers—(/ 25.0 2.0)—its value will be expressed as the real number 12.5. Integers have a black-and-white quality about them: 24 will always equal 24. Real numbers (sometimes referred to as *reals*), on the other hand, can be a bit less definite. For example, the two real values 24.001245781 and 24.001245782 are nearly identical but are not equal. But if you were to drop the last decimal place in both these numbers, then they would be equal values. This definitive quality of integers makes them more suited to certain types of uses, like counting, while real numbers are better suited to situations that require exacting values, such as determining coordinate values and angles. Also, computations performed on integers are faster than those performed on reals.

You may have noticed that in our previous examples, the real number 0.618 is preceded by a zero and is not written as .618. In Auto-LISP, real numbers with values between 0.1 and − 0.1 must begin with zero. If you do not follow this rule, you will get an error message. Enter the following at the command prompt:

(+ .618 1)

Though the above expression looks perfectly normal, the following error message appears:

error: invalid dotted pair

(We will look at what dotted pairs are later in this book.)

Strings

The term *string* refers to text. Strings are often used as prompts in AutoLISP expressions, but they can also be manipulated using Auto-LISP. For example, using the Strcat AutoLISP function, you could combine, or *concatenate*, two strings into one string. All strings are enclosed in double quotation marks. Try entering this:

(strcat "thirty seven feet" "six inches")

The following is returned:

"thirty seven feet six inches"

Lists

Lists are data elements enclosed in parentheses. They are the basic data structure in AutoLISP. A list can be made up of any number of integers, real numbers, strings, and even other lists.

There are two types of lists, those intended for evaluation and those intended as repositories for data. When a list contains a function as its first element, we can generally assume that it is an expression intended for evaluation. Such a list is often referred to as a *form*.

An example of a list as a repository of data is a list that represents a coordinate location. For example, the list

   (1.2 2.3 4.4)

contains three elements. The first element, 1.2, is the x coordinate; the second, 2.3, is the y coordinate; and the third, 4.4, is the z coordinate. Since the first element of this list is not a function, it cannot be evaluated.

File Descriptors

AutoLISP allows you to read and write text files to disk. *File descriptors* are used in a program to access files that have been opened for processing. You might think of a file descriptor as a variable representing the file in question. We will discuss this data type in more detail in Chapter 7.

Entity Names

Every object, or *entity*, in an AutoCAD drawing has a name. The name is an alphanumeric code unique to that object. This name can be accessed by AutoLISP and used as a means of selecting individual objects for processing. Entity names are provided by AutoCAD and are not user definable. Also entity names can change from one drawing session to another.

Selection Sets

Just as you can define a group of objects for processing using the AutoCAD Select command, you can also assign a group of objects, or a *selection set*, to a variable in AutoLISP for processing. Selection sets are given names by AutoCAD.

Symbols

AutoLISP treats everything as data to be evaluated. Therefore, *symbols*, or names given to variables and functions, are also a data type. Symbols are usually text, but they can also contain numbers, as in point1 or dx2. A symbol must, however, start with a letter. The terms symbol and variable are often used interchangeably, just as Joe Smith can be called a name or a person.

Subrs

Subrs are the built-in functions offered by AutoLISP. These functions perform tasks ranging from standard math operations such as addition and subtraction, to other more complex operations such as obtaining information from the drawing database about a specific object.

*A*toms

There are really two classes of data types, lists and atoms. You have already seen an example of a list. An *atom* is an element that cannot be taken apart into other elements. For example, a coordinate list can be "disassembled" into three numbers, the x value, the y value, and the z value, but the x, y and z values cannot be taken apart any further. In a coordinate list, the x, y, and z values are atoms. Symbols are also atoms because they are treated as single objects. So, in general, atoms are either numbers or symbols.

*A*ssigning Values to Variables with Setq

Variables are assigned values with the Setq function. As you have seen, a function can be a simple math operator such as one that performs addition or division. A function can also consist of a set of complex instructions to perform more than one activity, like a small program.

The Setq function tells AutoLISP to assign a value to a variable. Try the following exercise to assign the value 1.618 to the variable named Golden:

1. Enter the following at the command prompt:

   (setq golden 1.618)

You can obtain the value of the variable by preceding the variable name by an exclamation point. Now check the value of Golden.

2. Enter

!golden

The value 1.618 is returned. You might think of the exclamation point as another way of saying "Display the contents of."

Setq will assign a value to a variable even if the variable already has a value assigned to it. See what happens when Golden is assigned a new value.

3. Enter the following:

(setq golden 0.618)

Golden is reassigned the value 0.618 and the old value, 1.618, is discarded. You can even assign a new value to a variable by using the variable itself to increment the old value, as in

(setq golden (+ golden 1))

In this example, Golden is assigned a new value by adding 1 to its current value.

*P*reventing Evaluation of Arguments

But something doesn't seem quite right in the example above. Earlier, we said that AutoLISP evaluates the arguments in an expression before it applies the arguments to the function. In the above example, we might expect AutoLISP to evaluate the variable Golden before it is applied to the Setq function. Since Golden is a variable whose value is 0.618, it would evaluate to 0.618. AutoLISP would then try to set 0.618 equal to 1.618, which is impossible. The value returned by the argument (+ golden 1) cannot be assigned to another number (see Figure 1.6).

Here's why the above example works. Setq is a special function that is a combination of two other functions, Set and Quote (hence the name Setq). As with Setq, the function Set assigns the value of the second argument to the value of the first argument. The Quote function provides a means of preventing the evaluation of an argument. So,

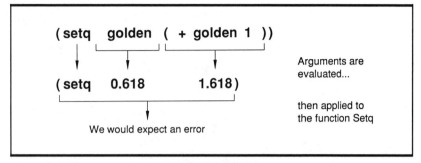

Figure 1.6: The expected outcome of using Setq

both Setq and Set Quote prevent the evaluation of the first argument, which in the above example is the variable Golden.

You could write the above example as

(set quote golden (+ golden 1))

and get the same answer. Or you could abbreviate the Quote function to an apostrophe, as in the following:

(set 'golden (+ golden 1))

and get the same answer. Figure 1.7 shows what happens when you use Set Quote. Any of these three forms work, but since Setq is the most concise, it is the preferred form.

To further illustrate the use of Quote, look at the following expression:

(setvar "snapunit" (12 12))

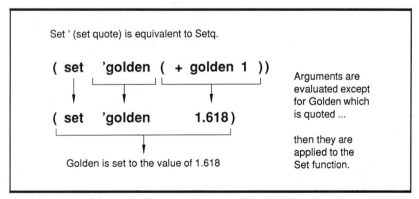

Figure 1.7: The Quote function prevents evaluation of an argument

The function in this expression is Setvar. Setvar performs the same function as the AutoCAD Setvar command—it changes the settings for system variables. Setvar accepts as its arguments a string value giving the name of the setting to change ("snapunit") and a value representing the new settings (12 12). Here we are attempting to use Setvar to change the snap distance setting to 12 by 12.

Remember, AutoLISP evaluates each argument before it is passed to the function. As with numbers, strings evaluate to themselves, so the string "snapunit" evaluates to "snapunit". But AutoLISP will also try to evaluate the list (12 12). AutoLISP always tries to evaluate lists as if they are expressions. As you saw earlier, the first element in an expression must be a function. Since the first element of the list (12 12) is not a function, AutoLISP will return the error message "error: bad function" (see Figure 1.8).

In this situation, we do not want the list (12 12) to be evaluated. We want it to be read "as is." To do this, we must add the Quote function, as in the following:

(setvar "snapunit" '(12 12))

Now AutoLISP will not try to evaluate (12 12), and Setvar will apply the list to the snapunit system variable setting.

Quote provides a means to prevent evaluations when they are not desirable. Quote is most often used in situations where a list must be used as an argument to a function. Remember that there are two types of lists, those intended for evaluation and those used to store data. The list (12 12) stores data, the width and height of the Snap distance. Because (12 12) does not have a function as its first element, it cannot

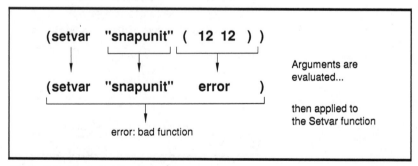

Figure 1.8: An error using Setvar

be evaluated. Since AutoLISP blindly evaluates everything, Quote is needed to tell AutoLISP not to evaluate (12 12).

Applying Variables

The variable Golden can now be used within an AutoCAD command to enter a value at a prompt, or within a function to obtain other results. To see how this works, you'll assign the value 25.4 to a variable called Mill.

1. Enter

    (setq mill 25.4)

    at the command prompt.

Now find the result of dividing Mill by Golden.

2. Enter

    (/ mill golden)

    This returns the value 15.698393.

Now assign this value to yet another variable.

3. Enter

    (setq B (/ mill golden))

Now you have three variables, Golden, Mill, and B, which are all assigned values that you can later retrieve, either within an AutoCAD command by entering an exclamation point followed by the variable, or as an argument within an expression.

Our examples so far have shown numbers being manipulated, but text can also be manipulated in a similar way. Variables can be assigned text strings that can later be used to enter values in commands that require text input. As you have seen, strings can be joined together, or concatenated, to form new strings. Strings and numeric values cannot be evaluated together, however. This may seem like a simple statement, but if you do not consider it carefully, it can lead to confusion. For example, it is possible to assign the number 1 to a variable as a text string by entering

(setq text1 "1")

Later, if you try to add this string variable to an integer or real number, AutoCAD will return an error message.

The examples used Setq and the addition and division functions. These are three functions out of many available to you. All the other usual math functions are available, plus the many functions that are used to test and manipulate variables. Table 1.1 shows some of the math functions available.

Table 1.1: A Partial List of AutoLISP Math Functions

FUNCTION	USED TO
Math functions that accept multiple arguments	
(+ *number number* ...)	add
(− *number number* ...)	subtract
(* *number number* ...)	multiply
(/ *number number* ...)	divide
(max *number number* ...)	find largest of numbers given
(min *number number* ...)	find smallest of numbers given
(rem *number number* ...)	find the remainder of numbers
Math functions that accept single arguments	
(1+ *number*)	add 1
(1− *number*)	subtract 1
(abs *number*)	find the absolute value
(exp *nth*)	*e* raised to the *nth* power
(expt *number nth*)	*number* raised to the *nth* power
(fix *real*)	convert *real* to integer
(float *integer*)	convert *integer* to real
(gcd *integer integer*)	find greatest common denominator
(log *number*)	find natural log of *number*
(sqrt *number*)	find square root of *number*

Table 1.1: A Partial List of AutoLISP Math Functions (Continued)

FUNCTION	USED TO
Functions for binary operations	
(˜ *integer*)	find logical bitwise NOT of *integer*
(logand *int. int. ...*)	find logical bitwise AND of integers
(logior *int. int. ...*)	find logical bitwise OR of integers
(lsh *int. bits*)	find logical bitwise shift of *int.* by *bits*

Since AutoLISP will perform mathematical calculations, you can use it as a calculator while you are drawing. For example, if you need to take a distance of 132 feet 6 inches and convert it to inches, you could enter

(setq inch1 (+ 6 (* 132 12)))

at the command prompt. The result of this expression is returned as 1590. The value 1590 is assigned to the variable Inch1, which can later be used as input to prompts that accept numeric values. This is a very simple but useful application of AutoLISP. In the next section, you will explore some of its more complex uses.

A ccessing Single Elements of a List

When you draw, you are actually specifying points on the drawing area in coordinates. Because a coordinate is a group of values rather than a single value, it must be handled as a list in AutoLISP. You must use special functions to access single elements of a list. Two of these functions are Car and Cadr. Car obtains the first element of a list, and Cadr obtains the second. The following example illustrates their use.

Suppose you want to store two point locations, 5, 6 and 10, 12, as variables called Pt1 and Pt2. You can construct a list representing these coordinates with the List function.

1. Enter the following two lines at the command prompt:

   (setq pt1 (list 5 6))
   (setq pt2 (list 10 12))

The List function in these expressions combines the arguments to form lists (see Figure 1.9).

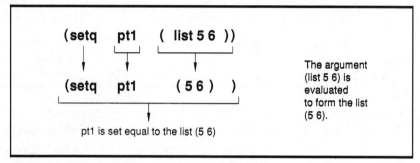

Figure 1.9: The List function

These lists are assigned to the variables Pt1 and Pt2. As we have just seen, variables accept not only single objects or atoms as their values but also lists. In fact, variables can accept any data type, even symbols representing other variables and expressions.

2. To see the new value for Pt1, enter the following:

   !pt1

   The list (5 6) appears.

3. Now suppose you want to get only the x coordinate value from this example. Enter

   (car pt1)

   The value 5 appears.

4. To get the y value, enter

   (cadr pt1)

   which returns the value 6. These values can in turn be assigned to variables, as in the line

   (setq x (car pt1))

Figure 1.10 may help you visualize what Car and Cadr are doing.

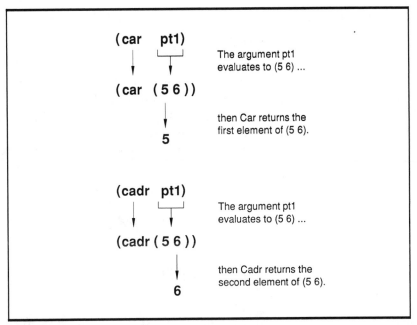

Figure 1.10: Car and Cadr of Pt1

Using the List function, you can construct a point variable using x and y components of other point variables. For example, you may want to combine the y value of the variable Pt1 with the x value of the point variable Pt2.

   5. Enter the following:

(list (car pt2) (cadr pt1))

   The list (10 6) is returned (see Figure 1.11).

These lists can be used to enter values during any AutoCAD command that prompts for points.

Actually, I have misled you slightly. The two primary functions for accessing elements of a list are Car and Cdr (pronounced "could-er"). The Cadr function we used earlier is really the contraction of Car and Cdr. You know that Car returns the first element of a list. Cdr, on the other hand, returns the value of a list with its first element removed.

   6. Enter the following at the command prompt:

(cdr '(A B C))

The list (B C) is returned (see Figure 1.12).

When Cdr is applied to the list (A B C) you get (B C), which is the list (A B C) with the first element, A, removed.

Notice that in the above example, the list (A B C) was quoted. If the quotation mark had been left out, AutoLISP would have tried to evaluate (A B C). Remember that AutoLISP expects the first element of an expression to be a function. Since A is a variable and not a function, you would get the following error message if you omitted the

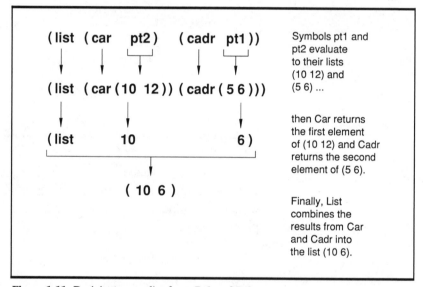

Figure 1.11: Deriving a new list from Pt1 and Pt2

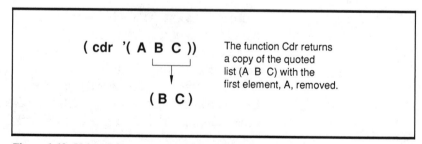

Figure 1.12: Using Cdr to remove the first element of a list

quote:

error: nul function
(A B C)

Now try using Cdr with the variable Pt1.

7. Enter

(cdr pt1)

The list (6) is returned.

Remember that anything within a pair of parentheses is considered a list; even ( ) is considered a list of zero elements.

Since the value returned by Cdr is a list, it cannot be used where a number is expected. Try replacing the Cadr in the earlier example with Cdr:

8. Enter

(list (car pt2) (cdr pt1))
(10 (6))

You get a list of two elements, 10 and (6) (see Figure 1.13). Though this is a perfectly legal list, it cannot be used as a coordinate list. The elements in a coordinate list must be numbers, not other lists.

So what exactly is Cadr then? Cadr is the contraction of Car and Cdr. You now know that Cdr returns a list with its first element

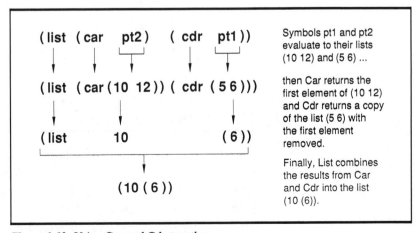

Figure 1.13: Using Car and Cdr together

removed and that Car returns the first element of a list. So to get 6 from the list held by the variable Pt1, you apply Cdr to Pt1 to get (6), and then apply Car to (6), as in the following example:

```
(car (cdr pt1))
6
```

This Car-Cdr combination is abbreviated to Cadr.

```
(cadr pt1)
6
```

Figure 1.14 shows graphically how this works. You can combine Car and Cdr in a variety of ways to break down nested lists. Figure 1.15 shows some examples of other Car and Cdr contractions. Any imaginable contraction is possible, but you are limited to four levels of nested expressions.

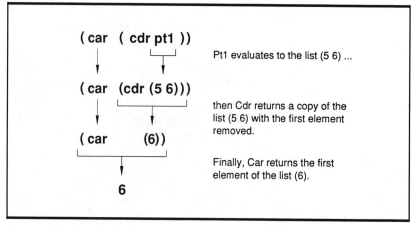

Figure 1.14: How Cadr works

Using Functions That Pause for Input

So far, you have been entering everything from the keyboard. However, you will most often want to get information from the drawing area of the AutoCAD screen. AutoLISP offers a set of functions that enable a pause to allow input for just this purpose. These functions are characterized by their Get prefix. Table 1.2 shows a list of these Get functions along with brief descriptions.

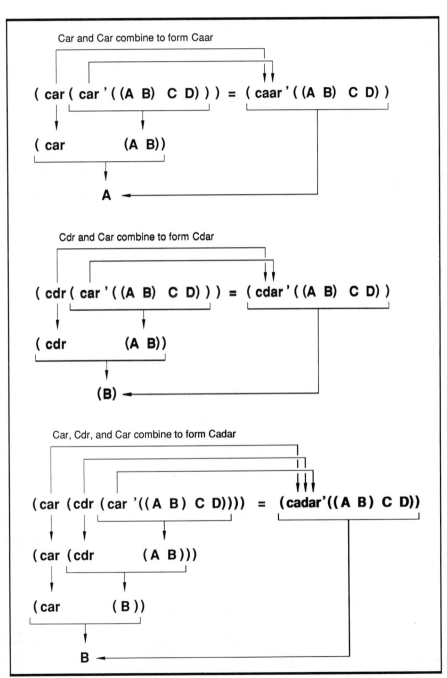

Figure 1.15: The Car and Cdr functions combined to extract elements of nested lists

Table 1.2: Get Functions That Allow Graphic Input

FUNCTION	DESCRIPTION
Getpoint	Allows key or mouse entry of point values. Returns values as lists of coordinate values.
Getcorner	Allows selection of the opposite corner of a window. Requires a point value defining the first corner of the window. The selected opposite corner defines the window.
Getorient	Allows key or mouse entry of angles based on Units command setting for angles. Returns values in radians.
Getangle	Allows key or mouse entry of angles based on the standard AutoCAD compass orientation of angles. Returns values in radians.
Getdist	Allows key or mouse entry of distances. Returns values as real numbers regardless of the unit format in use.

To see how one of these functions works, try the following exercise.

1. Turn Snap mode on by pressing the F9 function key.

2. Turn on the dynamic coordinate readout by pressing F6.

3. Enter the following at the command prompt:

(setq pt1 (getpoint))

This expression blanks the command line and waits until you enter a point. Just as with any standard AutoCAD command that expects point input, you can enter a relative or absolute point value through the keyboard, or pick a point on the drawing area using the cursor. The coordinate of the point you pick will become the value assigned to the variable Pt1, in the form of a list.

4. Move the cursor until the coordinate readout lists the coordinate 4,5 and then pick that point.

5. Check the value of Pt1 by entering the following:

   !pt1

   The value (4.0 5.0 0.0) or (4.0 5.0) is returned and the command prompt appears once again.

If you are using release 10, note that a z coordinate value of 0.0 was added. The system variable Flatland controls the inclusion of the z coordinate in functions that return coordinates. Normally, Flatland is set to 0, meaning the z coordinate will be included. If Flatland is set to 1, the z coordinate will not be included. All the elements of the coordinate list returned by Getpoint are reals.

Using Prompts with Get Functions

Each of these Get functions allows you to create a prompt by following the function with the prompt enclosed by quotation marks. The following exercise demonstrates the use of prompts in conjunction with these functions.

1. Enter this expression:

   (setq pt1 (getpoint "Pick the first point:"))

   The following prompt appears:

   Pick the first point:

2. Move your cursor until the coordinate readout shows 3,4 and then pick that point.

   The Get functions also allow you to specify a point from which the angle, distance, or point is to be measured.

3. Enter the following:

   (setq pt2 (getcorner pt1 "Pick the opposite corner:"))

   The following prompt appears:

   Pick the opposite corner:

   Pt1 is the point variable that holds the coordinate for the last point you picked. A window appears from the coordinate defined by Pt1.

4. Move the cursor until the coordinate readout shows 6.0000, 7.0000 and then pick that point.

You can also enter a relative coordinate through the keyboard in the unit system currently used in your drawing. Getangle and Getdist prompt you for two points if no point variable has been assigned a value. Getcorner always requires a point variable as a starting point (see Figure 1.16).

By using the Getpoint and Getcorner functions, you can easily store point and angle values as variables. You can then refer to a stored point by entering its variable in response to a command prompt that accepts point input.

5. Issue the Line command, and at the "From point" prompt, enter

   !pt1

   A rubber-banding line appears from the point previously defined as Pt1, just as if you had selected that point manually. (A *rubber-banding* line is a line whose endpoint dynamically follows the cursor as you move it.)

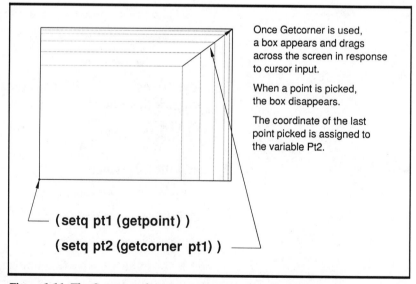

Once Getcorner is used, a box appears and drags across the screen in response to cursor input.

When a point is picked, the box disappears.

The coordinate of the last point picked is assigned to the variable Pt2.

(setq pt1 (getpoint))

(setq pt2 (getcorner pt1))

Figure 1.16: The Getcorner function as it appears on the drawing area

6. Now enter the following:

   !pt2

A line is drawn from the point stored by Pt1 to the point stored by Pt2.

*S*ummary

So far, you have been introduced to the AutoLISP interpreter, to some of the terms used, and to a few of the functions available in AutoLISP. You have also learned some basic rules for using AutoLISP:

- The expression or list is the fundamental structure of all Auto-LISP programs.

- All AutoLISP expressions intended for evaluation begin and end with parentheses, with the first element of the expression being an operator or function, and the rest the arguments to the operator.

- All parentheses, as well as double quotation marks enclosing strings, must be balanced within an expression.

- AutoLISP evaluates everything. When it evaluates expressions, it does so by evaluating the arguments before applying the arguments to the function.

- Numbers and strings evaluate to themselves.

- Variables evaluate to the last value assigned to them.

You have seen how you can store values as variables and how you can use AutoLISP to perform calculations. You may want to apply this knowledge to your everyday use of AutoCAD. Doing so will help you become more comfortable with AutoLISP and will give you further confidence to proceed with more complex programs.

You have also looked at how lists can be broken down and put together through the Car, Cdr, Quote, and List functions. List manipulation can be a bit hairy, so take some time to thoroughly understand these functions. You may want to practice building lists just to get a better feel for this unusual data type.

In Chapter 2 you will learn how to create an AutoLISP program. You will also learn how to store AutoLISP functions permanently so that they can be retrieved during subsequent editing sessions.

2

Storing and Running Programs

Featuring:

- Writing AutoLISP programs
- Loading and running AutoLISP files
- Using variables and argument lists
- Setting up programs to load automatically
- Using AutoLISP in menu and script files

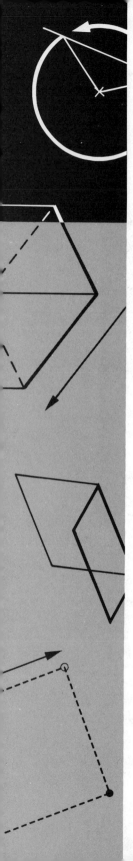

2

In the last chapter, you learned how to use the interpreter and, in the process, you were introduced to some of the basic concepts of Auto-LISP. You can now enter simple expressions into the interpreter to perform specific tasks. But once you exit the drawing editor, all of your work in AutoLISP is lost. AutoLISP would be difficult to use if there weren't some way of storing your programs for later retrieval. It would be especially difficult to create complex programs if you could only load them into the interpreter from the keyboard one line at a time. In this chapter, you will explore the development of programs through the use of AutoLISP files and in the process, review the Auto-LISP concepts you learned in Chapter 1.

Writing an AutoLISP Box Program

Instead of entering all of your programs directly into the interpreter, you have the option of writing them in a text file outside of AutoCAD. Later, when you want to use one of your programs, you can quickly load and run it using the AutoLISP Load function. Programs you store and load in this way will act just as if you had entered them into the interpreter manually. Since you can easily edit and review your functions in a word processor, you can begin to develop larger, more complex programs.

What You Need

Before you can create an AutoLISP file, you need a word processor that will read and write ASCII files. ASCII stands for American Standard Code for Information Interchange. As the name implies, the ASCII format was created to allow different computing systems to exchange data. Most word processors allow you to generate files in this format. WordStar, for example, uses what it calls a nondocument mode to read and write ASCII files. WordPerfect calls them DOS text files and uses special open and save options to handle them. Many utility programs such as Norton Commander, PC Tools, Xtree Pro, and SideKick offer text editors that handle ASCII files. You can also use the Edlin program that comes with DOS, though Edlin is rather difficult to use.

In this chapter and in the chapters that follow, whenever I have you open or create an AutoLISP file, I am asking you to open an ASCII file using your word processor. If you are using a word processor now, check to see if it handles ASCII files. If you don't have a word processor, you may want to purchase one of the utilities mentioned previously. Many of these utilities can be used under AutoCAD's Shell command so you don't have to exit AutoCAD to edit your AutoLISP files. Such a utility can save you a great deal of time when you are developing your programs.

*C*reating an AutoLISP File

The most common way to store an AutoLISP program is to save it as a text file with the extension .LSP. This file should contain the same information you would enter through the keyboard while using the interpreter interactively. I suggest that you create a directory called LSP in which you can store all of your AutoLISP programs. By keeping your programs together in one directory, you will be able to manage them as their number grows.

The program listed in Figure 2.1, which draws a box, combines many of the concepts you have learned in Chapter 1 into a single AutoLISP program. A *program* is a set of expressions that performs a

```
(defun c:BOX ( /  pt1 pt2 pt3 pt4 )
(setq pt1 (getpoint "Pick first corner: "))
(setq pt3 (getcorner pt1 "Pick opposite corner: "))
(setq pt2 (list (car pt3) (cadr pt1)))
(setq pt4 (list (car pt1) (cadr pt3)))
(command "line" pt1 pt2 pt3 pt4 "c" )
)
```

Figure 2.1: A program to draw boxes

task when entered at the AutoCAD command prompt. (Programs such as the one in Figure 2.1 can also be considered user-defined functions. You'll learn about these functions later.) You will create a file containing this program, and then load the program into AutoCAD and run it to see how it works.

If you have a word processor that works under the AutoCAD Shell command, start AutoCAD now and enter **1** at the Main menu to open a new AutoCAD file. At the "Enter name of drawing" prompt, enter:

box1 =

When you are in the drawing editor, issue the Shell command and then proceed with the exercise below. If your word processor is too large to run this way, exit to DOS for the exercise.

1. With your word processor, open an ASCII or nondocument file called BOX.LSP.

2. Carefully enter this first line from the program shown in Figure 2.1:

(defun c:BOX (/ pt1 pt2 pt3 pt4)

Be sure you have entered everything exactly as shown before you go to the next line. Pay special attention to the spaces between elements of the line. It's okay to have extra spaces but not okay to leave spaces out.

3. Press ⏎ to move to the next line.

4. Carefully enter the second line, again checking your typing and the spacing between elements before going to the next line.

5. Continue entering each line as described in the previous steps. When you are done, double-check your file for spelling errors and make sure the parentheses are balanced.

6. Print out your BOX.LSP file and compare it to Figure 2.1. It is often easier to spot errors on paper than it is to catch them on your screen.

7. Save and exit the BOX.LSP file.

You now have a program that you can load and run during any AutoCAD editing session.

L oading an AutoLISP File

To load an AutoLISP file, you use an AutoLISP function called Load. The Load function is used like any other AutoLISP function. It must be the first element of an expression, and it must be followed by an argument. The single argument to the Load function is always a string value. In the next exercise you'll use Load to load the BOX.LSP file you just created.

1. If you are not already in AutoCAD, start AutoCAD and enter **1** at the Main menu to open a new file. When you are prompted to enter a name, enter

   box1 =

2. When you are in the drawing editor, enter the following at the command prompt:

   (load "box")

   If the BOX.LSP file is in a directory other than the current directory, the LSP directory for example, you would enter

   (load "/lsp/box")

   You may also specify a drive letter when entering the name of an AutoLISP file. The box program is now available for you to run.

Notice that within the string in the above example, the forward slash is used to designate a directory instead of the usual backslash. This is important to keep in mind as it is a source of confusion to both novice and experienced AutoLISP users. AutoLISP uses the backslash to denote special codes within strings. Whenever AutoLISP encounters a backslash within a string, it expects a code value to follow. These codes allow you to control the display of strings in different ways, such as adding a carriage return or tab. You can use the backslash to designate directories, but you must enter it twice, as in the following example:

(load "\\lsp\\box")

3. Once the file is loaded, you will get the message

   C:BOX

   You may have noticed that Load uses a string data type for its argument. Just as with numbers, strings evaluate to themselves, so when AutoLISP tries to evaluate "/lsp/box" the result is "/lsp/box".

*R*unning a Loaded Program

Once you have loaded the Box program, you can run it at any time during the current editing session. However, when you exit Auto-CAD, the program will not be saved with the file. You must reload the program file in subsequent editing sessions to use it again. Now try running the program.

1. First, set the Snap mode and the dynamic coordinate readout on. The F9 key toggles the Snap mode and the F6 key toggles the dynamic coordinate readout.

2. Enter the word **box** at the command prompt. You should get the following prompt:

   Pick first corner:

3. If your screen is still in Text mode, use the F1 key to shift to the graphic screen. Move the cursor so that the coordinate readout shows 2.0000, 3.0000 and pick that point. The next prompt appears:

   Pick opposite corner:

4. Now move the cursor. Notice that a window follows the cursor's motion. The arrow in Figure 2.2 shows how the window grows. Move the corner of the window so that the coordinate 8.0000, 6.0000 is displayed on the coordinate readout and then pick that point. The box is drawn and the command prompt returns.

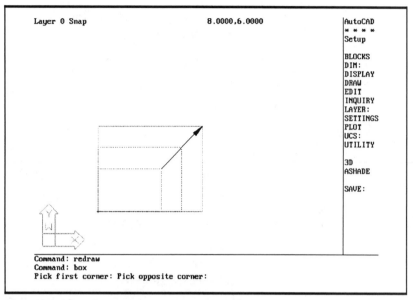

Figure 2.2: *How the window grows on the screen*

In the next section is a line-by-line description of how the Box program works.

If your program does not work, double-check your BOX.LSP file against Figure 2.1. As you progress through the book you will be asked to copy many programs. Whenever you find that one doesn't work, you should print out the file and compare it to the program listing in the book.

*H*ow the Box Program Works

Up until now, you have been dealing with very simple AutoLISP expressions that perform simple tasks such as adding or multiplying numbers or setting system variables. Now that you know how to save AutoLISP *code* (written instructions saved in a program file) in a file, you can begin to create larger programs. A program is really nothing more than a collection of expressions that are designed to work together to obtain specific results. In this section, we will examine the Box program to see how it works.

The Box program draws the box by first obtaining a corner point using Getpoint (see Figure 2.3):

(setq pt1 (getpoint pt1 "Pick first corner: "))

The user will see only the prompt portion of this expression:

Pick first corner:

Next, the program obtains the opposite corner point using Getcorner (see Figure 2.3):

(setq pt3 (getcorner pt1 "Pick opposite corner: "))

Again, the user only sees the prompt string:

Pick opposite corner:

In the previous exercise, you saw that Getcorner displays a window as the user moves the cursor. In the Box program, this window allows the user to see the shape of the box before the opposite corner is selected.

Once the second point is selected, the Box program uses the point coordinates of the first and opposite corners to derive the other two corners of the box. This is done by manipulating the known coordinates using Car, Cadr, and List (see Figure 2.4).

(setq pt2 (list (car pt3) (cadr pt1)))
(setq pt4 (list (car pt1) (cadr pt3)))

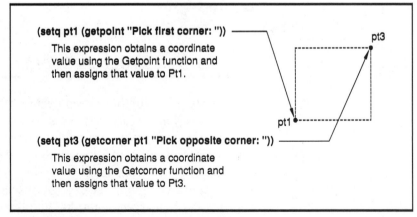

Figure 2.3: *How the Box program obtains input*

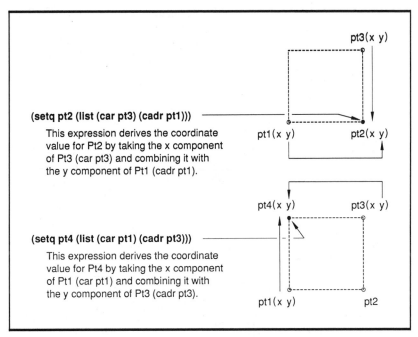

Figure 2.4: *Using Car, Cadr, and List to derive the remaining box corners*

Pt2 is derived by combining the x component of Pt3 with the y component of Pt1. Pt4 is derived from combining the x component of Pt1 with the y component of Pt3 (see Figure 2.5).

Using AutoCAD Commands in a Program

The last line in the box program

(command "line" pt1 pt2 pt3 pt4 "c")

shows you how AutoCAD commands are used in AutoLISP expressions (Figure 2.6)

Command is an AutoLISP function that calls standard AutoCAD commands. The command to be called follows the Command function and is enclosed in quotation marks. Anything in quotation marks after the Command function is treated as keyboard input. Variables

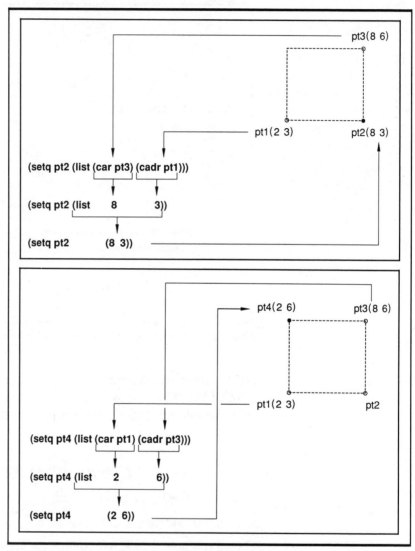

Figure 2.5: *Using the x and y components of points 1 and 3 to derive points 2 and 4*

follow, but unlike variables entered at the command prompt, they do not have to be preceded by an exclamation point. The *c* enclosed in quotation marks at the end of the expression indicates the Close option for the Line command (see Figure 2.7).

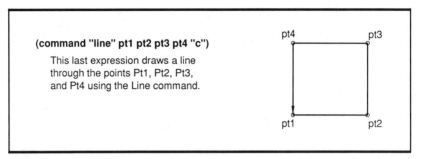

Figure 2.6: The program draws the box.

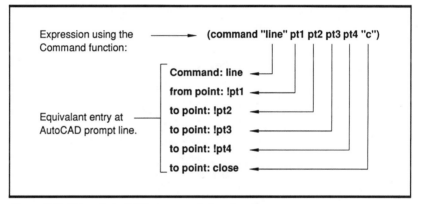

Figure 2.7: Using AutoCAD commands in a function

Using Variables and Argument Lists in a Program

Variables are like the messengers of your programs. They store and convey all forms of data. They are actually pointers to locations in your computer's memory where a value is stored. The names given to variables are symbols representing that location. The main processor in your computer takes care of the details of memory allocation and variable assignment. To you, the variable has a name and a value and that's about all you need to know.

You do, however, need to manage variables in order to make efficient use of the small amount of memory you have for AutoLISP. We can do this through the use of argument lists. In the following section you will learn how to use argument lists to both help transfer data from one function to another and to keep your memory usage to a minimum.

*U*sing Variables in an Expression

The Box program is a collection of expressions working together to perform a single task. Each individual expression performs an operation whose resulting value is passed to the next expression through the use of variables (see Figure 2.8).

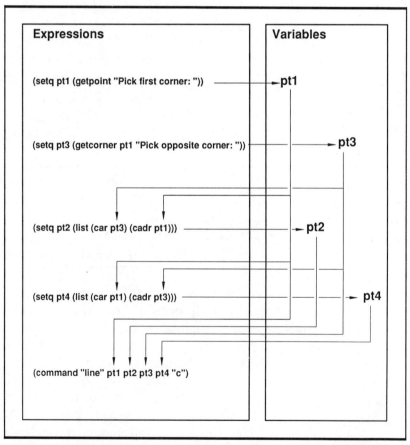

Figure 2.8: Variables help move information from one expression to another.

The first line in the Box program

(defun c:BOX (/ pt1 pt2 pt3 pt4)

ties the collection of expressions that follow into a command called Box. Defun is a special function that allows you to define your own programs and functions. The arguments to Defun are first the function name, in this case, c:BOX, and then the argument list. Defun suppresses the evaluation of its first argument much like Setq. The *c:* in the name tells AutoLISP that this program is to act like an AutoCAD command. This means that if the program name is entered at the AutoCAD command prompt, it will be executed as an AutoCAD command. The name following *c:* should be written in uppercase letters to help keep your program code readable.

You should take care not to give your programs names reserved for AutoLISP's built-in functions and atoms. If, for example, you were to give the Box program the name Setq, then the Setq function would be replaced by the Box program and would not work properly. Below is a list of AutoLISP function names that can easily be mistaken for user-defined variable names.

abs	if	or
and	length	pi
angle	list	read
apply	load	repeat
atom	member	reverse
distance	nil	set
eq	not	T
equal	nth	type
fix	null	while
float	open	

*T*he Argument List

In the example above, the list that follows the name Box is an *argument list*. An argument list is used for two purposes. It is used when one program is called from another program and variable values must be passed between them. It is also used to determine local and global variables. You'll look at both of these uses in this section.

First let's use an argument list to pass values to a function that adds the squares of two variables. In the following exercise you'll enter this function directly into the AutoLISP interpreter:

```
(defun ADSQUARE (x y)
( + (* x x) (* y y))
)
```

1. Carefully enter the first line, as follows (pay special attention to the parentheses and spaces):

   ```
   (defun ADSQUARE (x y)
   ```

2. When you are sure everything is correct, press ←. You will see the following prompt:

   ```
   1>
   ```

   This tells you that your expression is missing one closing parenthesis. This demonstrates what occurs when you leave out a parenthesis while entering expressions through the keyboard. You'll add the parenthesis in a moment.

3. Enter the second line of the function at the 1> prompt, again checking your typing before pressing ←.

4. Enter the closing right parenthesis at the "1" prompt. The command prompt will return.

In this example, the *c*: is left out of the Defun line. By doing this, you create what is called a *user-defined function* that can be used in other programs or during an AutoCAD command. Note that the variables X and Y are included in the parentheses after the name of the function, Adsquare. This is the argument list.

Now let's use this new function.

1. Enter the following at the command prompt:

   ```
   (adsquare 2 4)
   ```

   AutoLISP returns 20.

The variables X and Y in the Adsquare function take on the arguments 2 and 4 in the order they are listed (see Figure 2.9).

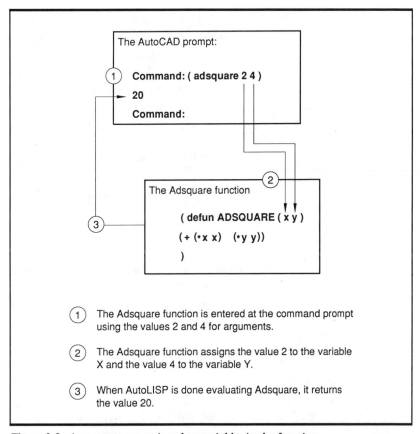

Figure 2.9: Arguments are assigned to variables in the function.

Variables can also be used to pass values to functions. For example, if you have a variable called A whose value is 2 and a variable B whose value is 4, you could use A and B in place of the 2 and 4.

2. Enter the following:

```
(setq a 2)
(setq b 4)
(adsquare a b)
```

AutoLISP returns 20.

Remember that AutoLISP evaluates the arguments before applying them to the function. This rule applies even to functions that you create yourself. In this case, A is evaluated to 2 before it is passed to the X variable and B is evaluated to 4 before it is passed to the Y variable.

The second use for the argument list is to determine global and local variables. A *global variable* maintains its value even after a program has finished executing. In Chapter 1, you assigned the value 1.618 to the variable Golden; Golden will hold that value no matter where it is used. Any function can evaluate Golden to get its value.

1. Enter the following:

   (setq golden 1.618)
   (adsquare 2 golden)

   The value 6.61792 is returned.

A *local variable*, on the other hand, holds its value only within the program or user-defined function it is found in. For example, the variable X in the Adsquare function above holds the value 2 only while the function is being evaluated. Once the function has finished processing, X's value of 2 is discarded.

2. Enter the following:

   !x

   Nil is returned. The variables A, B, and Golden, however, are global and will return values.

3. Enter the following:

   !golden

   The value 1.618 is returned.

This temporary assigning of a value to a variable with a program or function is called a *binding*. This term should not be confused with the term *bound*, which often refers to the general assignment of a value to a variable. In the example of X above, we say that a binding is created for the value X within the function Adsquare. Bindings only take place for variables in the argument list of a function. Global variables cannot have bindings since, by definition, they are not confined to individual functions (see Figure 2.10).

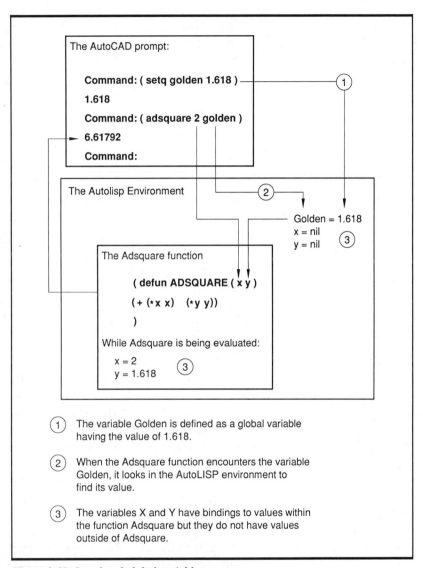

Figure 2.10: Local and global variables

Since local variables only exist within the program or user-defined function that uses them, they do not take up system memory permanently. With more memory available, you are free to use a greater number of programs.

Since an argument list is used for two purposes, the forward slash symbol is used to separate two types of local variables. The slash appears between function arguments to which values are passed when the function is called and the list of variables that receive values during the execution of the function:

```
(defun square2 (x y / dx dy)
(setq dx (* x x))
(setq dy (* y y))
( + dx dy)
)
```

You must include a space before and after the slash sign in the argument list. If these spaces are not present, you will get an error message.

X and Y are variables that will be assigned values when the function is called initially, as in the Adsquare function given earlier. Dx and Dy, on the other hand, are variables assigned values within the function, so they follow the slash sign. In either case, the variables are local. Variables left out of the list become global. If, for example, Dy were left out of the argument list, its value would remain in the AutoLISP system memory for as long as the current editing session lasted, and could be retrieved through evaluation by any other function. However, all of the functions and variables you have created in this session will be lost as soon as you exit the drawing editor.

In both the Adsquare and Square2 functions above, we left out the *c:*. As we mentioned, this allows the function to be used by other programs like a subprogram. You can also use functions defined in this way in the middle of other commands by entering the name of the function enclosed by parentheses at the command prompt. For example, this exercise defines a function that converts centimeters to inches.

1. Carefully enter the following function:

    ```
    (defun CMTOI (cm)
    (* cm 0.3937)
    )
    ```

2. Issue the Insert command to insert the border file into your current drawing. The border file is a drawing of a 1×1 rectangle used by the AutoCAD Setup function to place a border in a drawing.

3. When the prompt

    Block name (or ?):

    appears, enter **border**.

4. When the next prompt

    Insertion point:

    appears, enter the coordinate pair **1,1**.

5. When the prompt

    X scale factor (1) / Corner / XYZ:

    appears, enter

    (cmtoi 20)

    to signify that your symbol is to be given the scale of 20 centimeters. The AutoLISP function Cmtoi will convert the 20 to 7.8740 and enter this value for the X scale factor prompt.

6. Press ⏎ twice to accept the default y scale factor and 0 rotation angle. The square border appears with a width and height of 7.8740 units.

Cmtoi can be quite useful where a value conversion or any other type of data conversion is wanted.

Loading Programs Automatically

Eventually, you will find that some of your AutoLISP programs are indispensable to your daily work. You can have your favorite set of AutoLISP programs loaded automatically at the beginning of every editing session by collecting all of your programs into a single file called ACAD.LSP. Be sure that ACAD.LSP is in your AutoCAD directory. By doing this, you won't have to load your programs every time you open a new file. AutoCAD looks for ACAD.LSP whenever it opens the drawing editor, and will load it automatically if it exists.

In this exercise you'll rename the Box program file as ACAD.LSP and place it in your AutoCAD directory.

1. Exit AutoCAD and check to see if you already have a file called ACAD.LSP in your Acad directory. If so, change its name to ACADTEMP.LSP.

2. Next, rename the BOX.LSP file as ACAD.LSP. Place the ACAD.LSP file in your AutoCAD directory if it isn't there already.

3. Start AutoCAD and open any file. When the drawing editor loads, notice the following message in the prompt area:

   Loading acad.lsp...

   Now the Box program is available to you without you having to load it manually.

Though the ACAD.LSP file only contains the Box program, you could have included several programs and functions in that single file. Then you would have access to several AutoLISP programs by loading just one file. Since each program and function is a complete, self-contained expression, you needn't take special steps to separate them though you should leave some lines as space between programs for readability.

Before you continue, exit from AutoCAD and change the name of your ACAD.LSP file back to BOX.LSP. Then change the file name ACADTEMP.LSP back to ACAD.LSP.

*A*utomatically Loading a Single ACAD.LSP File

As you begin to accumulate more AutoLISP functions in your ACAD.LSP file, you will notice that AutoCAD takes longer to load them. This delay in loading time can become annoying, especially when you want to quickly open a small file to make a few simple revisions.

Fortunately, there is an alternative method for automatically loading programs that can reduce AutoCAD's start-up time. Instead of placing the program's code in ACAD.LSP, you can include a function that loads and runs the program in question. For example, you could have the following line in place of the Box program in the ACAD.LSP file:

```
(defun c:BOX ( ) (load "/lsp/box") (c:box))
```

We will call this the *box-loader* program. Once the above program is itself loaded, it can be started by entering **box** at the command prompt. This box-loader program then loads the real Box program, which in turn replaces this box-loader program. The (c:box) in the box-loader program is evaluated once the actual Box program has been loaded. The symbol *c:box* represents the program Box, so when it is evaluated, like any program or function, it will execute.

As you can see, this program takes up considerably less space than the actual Box program and will therefore load faster at start-up time. You can have several of these loading programs, one for each user-defined AutoLISP function or program you wish to use on a regular basis. Imagine that you have several programs equivalent in size to the Box program. The ACAD.LSP file might be several pages long. A file this size can take several seconds to load. If you replace each of those programs with one similar to the box-loader program above, you substantially reduce loading time. If you imagine that each of the original programs is several lines long, then you can see that you will save even more space as the list of programs in ACAD.LSP grows. You also save memory by setting your ACAD.LSP file in this way, since the programs are loaded only as they are called.

Finally, if you want an AutoLISP program to execute automatically when the ACAD.LSP file is loaded, give it the name **S::Startup** and do not include any arguments in its argument list. This is a special program name reserved for this purpose.

Using AutoLISP in a Menu

There are two reasons why you might write AutoLISP code directly into the menu file. The first is to selectively load external AutoLISP programs as they are needed. The second is to reduce the amount of time required to load and run a program. You'll take a look at both uses in this section. We are assuming that you are familiar with the AutoCAD menu system. If you are not, you may want to refer to *Advanced Techniques in AutoCAD* (SYBEX, 1989) before continuing.

Loading a Selected Program

You may have several useful but infrequently used programs that take up valuable memory. You might prefer not to load these programs at start-up time. If you place them in the menu file, they will only be loaded when they are selected from the menu. In fact, this is what the AutoShade and 3dobjects menu options do. When you pick Ashade from either the screen or pull-down menu, and Auto-Shade is present on your computer, an AutoLISP program called ASHADE.LSP is loaded.

You can include the code of the program in the menu file or you can use a method similar to the one described earlier to load external AutoLISP files. The method for the menu system is slightly different.

In the example for loading programs from an external AutoLISP file, the loader program is replaced by the fully operational program of the same name. But if you were to place the following expression in a menu, the program would load every time the menu option was selected:

```
[box]^C^C(load "box");box
```

There is nothing wrong with loading the program each time it is run, but if the AutoLISP file is lengthy, you may get tired of waiting for the loading to occur every time you select the item from the menu. A better way to load a program from the menu is to use the If function, as in the following:

```
[box]^C^C(if (not c:box)(load "box"); +
(princ "Box is already loaded. "));box
```

This example demonstrates three new functions—If, Not, and Princ. The If function checks to see if certain conditions can be met, and then evaluates an expression depending on the result. The first argument to the If function tests the condition that is to be met. The second argument is the expression to be evaluated if the condition is true. Optionally, a third expression can be added to be evaluated when the test condition returns nil.

The Not function returns T, for true, if its argument evaluates to nil; otherwise it returns nil (see Figure 2.11).

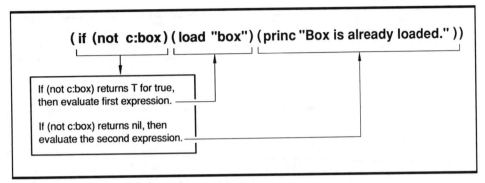

Figure 2.11: *Using the If function*

So, in the menu sample above, if c:Box has not been loaded yet, Not will return T for true and the If program will evaluate the (load "box") expression and load the Box program. If c:box has already been loaded, then Not will return nil and BOX.LSP will not be loaded again. Instead, the second argument will be evaluated. This expression

 (princ "Box is already loaded.")

simply displays the string

 Box is already loaded.

on the command prompt.

 Princ is a function that prints the value of its argument to the command prompt. It also serves other functions which we will cover later in this book.

 You may have noticed that the If function does not conform to the standard rules of evaluation. When If is used, the second or third argument is evaluated depending on the value of the first argument.

Speeding Up Program Execution

 The second reason for placing code in the menu is to increase loading speed. Instead of creating a function using Defun, you can set up a program to be read and executed line by line. This saves time since the interpreter reads and executes each expression of your program as it occurs in the menu listing, instead of reading the entire set of expressions and then executing the program. Figure 2.12 shows how the Box

```
[BOX]^C^C(setvar "menuecho" 1);+
(setq pt1 (getpoint ``Pick first corner: ``));\+
(setq pt3 (getcorner ``Pick opposite corner: ``));\+
(setq pt2 (list (car pt3) (cadr pt1)));+
(setq pt4 (list (car pt1) (cadr pt3)));+
line;!pt1;!pt2;!pt3;!pt4;C;
```

Figure 2.12: The Box program written as a menu option

program from Chapter 1 would look if written as a menu option. In a moment you'll enter this program.

Note that the Defun function is absent from the listing. When the Box option is picked from the menu, AutoCAD reads the associated text just as it would any menu option. Since the text in this case is AutoLISP code, the AutoLISP interpreter evaluates each expression as if it were entered through the keyboard.

Note that the semicolon is used to indicate the Enter key at the end of each expression. A backslash is used to pause for input, just as you would use a backslash in other commands that require mouse or keyboard input. Also note the use of the plus sign at the end of the lines, indicating the continuation of the menu item. Finally, note that the last line of the menu item uses the exclamation point to enter the values of the variables as responses to the Line command. The *C* at the end of the line is the Close option of the Line command.

You also may have noticed a new expression in the first line:

(setvar "menuecho" 1)

The Setvar function in the above expression does the same thing that the Setvar command in AutoCAD does. In this case, it sets the Menuecho system variable to 1. System variables are AutoCAD settings that give you control over the many functions of AutoCAD. The Menuecho system variable is a setting that controls the display of commands placed in the menu file. When it is set to 1, commands placed in the menu are not echoed to the command prompt.

Let's write a menu file that places the Box program as an option on the screen menu.

1. Using your word processor, copy the listing shown in Figure 2.12 into a file called BOX.MNU, again being careful to input the listing exactly as shown.

2. Get back into the AutoCAD drawing editor and then at the command prompt, enter **menu**.

3. At the prompt

   Menu file name or. for none <acad>:

   enter **box**.

4. Pick the Box option from the menu, and you will see the prompts you entered when you created the Box menu above. This program will work in the same way as the BOX.LSP program.

5. To get the AutoCAD menu back, enter **menu** and then **acad** when prompted for a menu name.

Since Defun is not used in this example, no argument list is needed. Any variables used in the listing become global. For this reason, when you use menus for AutoLISP programs, it is especially important to keep track of variable names so they do not conflict with variables from other programs. You might want to include some additional code to set any variables used to nil, as in the following:

(setq pt1 nil pt2 nil pt3 nil pt4 nil)

As you can see here, you can assign values to several variables at once with a single Setq command.

*U*sing Script Files

AutoCAD has a useful feature that allows you to write a set of predefined command sequences and responses stored as an external text file called a *script file*. This scripting ability is similar to writing a macro in the menu file. The main difference between menu macros and scripts is that scripts do not allow you to pause for input. Once a script is issued, it runs until it is completed. Also, unlike menu macros, scripts can exist as independent files that are called as they are needed from the command prompt.

There may be times when you want to embed AutoLISP code into a script. You can either write the code directly into the script file or use the Load function to load an AutoLISP file from the script.

You can convert an AutoLISP program file directly to a script file simply by changing the file extension from .LSP to .SCR. To load a script, you use the AutoCAD Script command.

*S*ummary

You have been introduced to some new ways to use AutoLISP.

- The function Defun allows you to create programs that can be invoked from the AutoCAD command line.
- Variables can pass information between expressions and functions.
- You can create functions that can respond to AutoCAD commands.
- You can store functions and programs as files on disk and easily retrieve them at a later date.
- You can store frequently used functions in a file called ACAD.LSP to be loaded automatically whenever you start AutoCAD.

Try your hand at writing some functions on your own. You may also want to try using the menu file to store programs, or you may want to keep each of your programs as separate files and load them as they are needed.

In the next chapter, you will be introduced to some of the ways you can plan, organize, and execute a programming project.

3

Planning and Organizing Programs

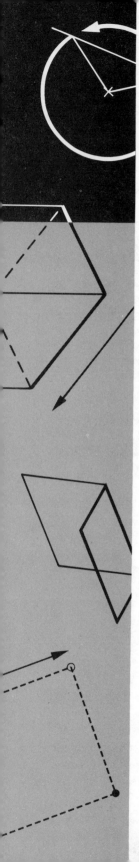

3

When you write a program, you are setting out to solve a problem. It is often helpful to begin by planning how you want to solve your problem. Your plan may need revisions along the way, but it can give you a framework for both an overall and a detailed understanding of the problem. Often the most monumental problem can be broken into parts that can be dealt with easily.

By taking some time to analyze your goals and writing down some preliminary plans, you can shorten your program development time considerably. In this chapter we will discuss some methods for planning your programming efforts and, along the way, you will get a more detailed look at how AutoLISP works.

You may encounter problems transcribing the programs from this book. It is very easy to make typographic errors and even easier to miss the errors when you are checking your files against the figures. If you encounter a problem, be patient. Check and double-check your files. The following points cover the most common transcription errors:

- Pay special attention to the spelling of variable names and the number and placement of parentheses.

- Be sure to space the elements of your code correctly.

- Problems can occur when lowercase *l*'s and *1*'s are confused. Uppercase *O*'s and *0*'s are also problematic. I will try to alert you to the use of 1's and 0's in the program listings wherever possible.

- When a program requires other functions to work properly, be sure all the functions needed are loaded at the time the main program is loaded.

Finally, I have included a list of error messages in Appendix A. These error messages can help you find errors in your code.

If you prefer, you can order the programs on disk from the author. This can save you some time and frustration. See the ordering information at the back of this book.

*L*ooking at a Program's Design

As simple as the BOX.LSP program is, it follows some basic steps in its design. These steps are as follows:

1. Establish the name of the program or function.

2. Obtain information by prompting the user.

3. Process the information.

4. Produce the output.

Let's look at a breakdown of the program to see these steps more clearly. The first line defines the program by giving it a name and listing the variables it will use:

(defun c:box (/dx dy pt1 pt2 pt3 pt4)

The second and third lines of the program obtain the minimum information needed to define the box:

(setq pt1 (getpoint "Pick first corner: "))
(setq pt3 (getcorner "Pick opposite corner: "))

The fourth and fifth lines process the information to find the other two points needed to draw the box:

(setq pt2 (list (car pt3) (cadr pt1)))
(setq pt4 (list (car pt1) (cadr pt3)))

The last line draws the box in the drawing editor:

(command "line" pt1 pt2 pt3 pt4 "c")

This four-step process can be applied to nearly every program you produce.

You should also consider how standard AutoCAD commands work. If you design your prompts and prompt sequences to match closely those of AutoCAD's, your programs will seem more familiar and therefore easier to use. For example, in AutoCAD, when a command requires editing of objects, you are first prompted to select the objects to be edited. So when you design a program that performs some editing function, you may want to follow AutoCAD's lead and have your program select objects first. (I will discuss functions that allow you to select objects later in this book.)

Outlining Your Programming Project

It is often helpful to think of how you would accomplish your programming task using AutoCAD without the aid of AutoLISP. Then think of how AutoLISP can automate the process. In the case of the Box program, we first consider how we normally draw boxes by selecting points, then we apply our knowledge of AutoLISP to accomplish the same results.

Before you actually start writing code, you will want to make a list describing what your program is to do. The Box program was planned as the following sequence of statements:

1. Get the location of one corner of the box. Save that location as a variable called Pt1.

2. Get the location of the other corner of the box. Save that location as a variable called Pt3.

3. Calculate the other two corners by using information about the known corner locations Pt1 and Pt3.

4. Draw the box.

The above list outlines the procedures needed to accomplish your task. This type of list is often called *pseudocode*. It is a plain-language description of the code your program is to follow. It acts like an outline of your program's code. Some programmers liken it to a recipe in a cookbook. Just as with an outline, you may have to go through several iterations of lists like this before actually hitting on one that is workable.

Along with the pseudocode of a program, you may also want to sketch out what your program is supposed to do, especially if your program is performing some graphic manipulation. Figure 3.1 shows

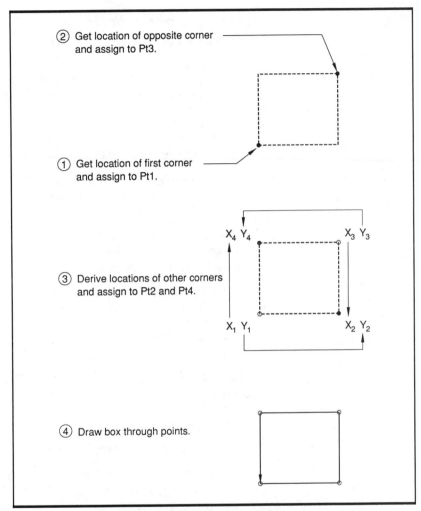

Figure 3.1: *A sample sketch used to develop BOX.LSP*

a sketch done as an aid to developing the Box program. The steps shown in the sketch correspond to the steps in the pseudocode mentioned earlier.

Using Functions

We have broken down the Box program conceptually into three processes—obtaining information, processing the information, and producing the output. We can also break it down physically by turning each process into a function, as in the following:

```
(defun getinfo ( )
(setq pt1 (getpoint "Pick first corner: "))
(setq pt3 (getcorner pt1 "Pick opposite corner: "))
)
(defun procinfo ( )
(setq pt2 (list (car pt3) (cadr pt1)))
(setq pt4 (list (car pt1) (cadr pt3)))
)
(defun output ( )
(command "pline" pt1 pt2 pt3 pt4 "c" )
)
```

You now have three functions that can be called independently. You now need a way to tie these functions together. You can write a main program that does just that:

```
(defun C:BOX1 (/ pt1 pt2 pt3 pt4)
(getinfo)
(procinfo)
(output)
)
```

Let's create this new version of the Box program and run it to see how it works.

1. Open a new AutoLISP file called BOX1.LSP.

2. Enter the above three functions, Getinfo, Procinfo, and Output.

3. Enter the main program above that ties the function together. Your file should look like Figure 3.2.

4. Start AutoCAD and, using option 1 from the Main menu, enter **chapt3=** to open a new AutoCAD file, and load the BOX1.LSP file.

5. Run the Box1 program. You will see that it acts no differently from the Box program in Chapter 1.

The Box1 program listed above acts as a sort of master organizer that evaluates each of the three functions, Getinfo, Procinfo, and Output, as they are needed. This modular approach to programming has several advantages.

```
(defun getinfo ()
 (setq pt1 (getpoint "Pick first corner: "))
 (setq pt3 (getcorner pt1 "Pick opposite corner: "))
)

(defun procinfo ()
 (setq pt2 (list (car pt3) (cadr pt1)))
 (setq pt4 (list (car pt1) (cadr pt3)))
)

(defun output ()
 (command "pline" pt1 pt2 pt3 pt4 "c" )
)

(defun C:BOX1 (/ pt1 pt2 pt3 pt4)
 (getinfo)
 (procinfo)
 (output)
)
```

Figure 3.2: The contents of BOX1.LSP

First, each function exists independently and can be used by other programs. This reduces the amount of overall code needed to run your system. In the above exercise, you increased the size of the Box program, but as you develop more and more programs, you will find that you can use certain functions in many programs. Functions you write this way can serve as the building blocks of other programs.

Second, while writing programs, you can more easily locate bugs because you will be able to trace them to one function or another. Whenever AutoCAD encounters an error, it displays an error message along with the offending expression.

Third, because smaller groups of code are more manageable, they make your problem-solving tasks seem less intimidating. The actual Box1 program represents the problem in general terms, and the functions take care of the details. You can get a clearer idea of how your programs work because clarity is built into the program by virtue of this modular structure.

Finally, you can add or modify features more easily by plugging other functions into the main program or the functions that make up the program.

*A*dding a Function

As great a program as AutoCAD is, it does have some shortcomings. One is the fact that it does not dynamically display relative x and y coordinates. It does display relative polar coordinates dynamically, but often it would be helpful to see distances in relative x and y coordinates. One example where this would be useful is in the creation of floor plans for which a dynamic display of relative x and y coordinates could help you size rooms in a building. This display would show your x and y coordinates relative to some specified point as you move the cursor. It would also be helpful if this dynamic display were to show the room's area as the cursor moved. With AutoLISP you can add functions to programs to overcome such shortcomings. Figure 3.3 shows a function that displays relative x and y coordinates in the status line. In the next exercise you'll enter this function, and then use it as you work with an AutoCAD file. Later you'll add this function to the Box program.

1. Exit AutoCAD temporarily with either the Shell command or the End command.

2. Open an AutoLISP file called RXY.LSP and copy the program listed in Figure 3.3. Check your file carefully against the listing to be sure it is correct. (Since this is a somewhat long program, you may want to make a printout of it and check the printout for typos.)

```
(defun RXY (/ pt lt x last pick lpt1)
(if (not pt1)(setq lpt1 (getvar "lastpoint"))(setq lpt1 pt1))
   (while (/= pick t)
      (setq pt (cadr (setq lt (grread t))))
      (if (= (car lt) 5)(progn
            (setq x (strcat
                  (rtos (- (car pt) (car lpt1))) " x "
                  (rtos (- (cadr pt) (cadr lpt1))) " SI= "
                  (rtos (*(- (car pt) (car lpt1))
                         (- (cadr pt) (cadr lpt1))
                      )
                  2 2)
               )
            )
            (grtext -2 x)
         )
      )
      (setq pick (= 3 (car lt))))
   )
(cadr lt)
)
```

Figure 3.3: The Rxy function

3. Return to the Chapt3 AutoCAD file.

4. Turn on Snap mode and the dynamic coordinate readout.

5. Load RXY.LSP.

6. Start the Line command.

7. At the prompt for the first point, pick the coordinate 2, 2.

8. At the next point prompt, enter the following:

   (rxy)

   Notice how the coordinate readout now dynamically displays the x and y coordinates relative to the first point you picked.

9. Move the cursor until the coordinate readout shows 6.0000, 7.0000, and then pick that point. A line is drawn with a displacement from the first point of 6, 7.

10. Press ⏎ to end the Line command.

I won't go into a detailed explanation of this function quite yet. Imagine, however, that you have just finished writing and debugging this function and you want to add it permanently to the Box program.

1. Exit AutoCAD temporarily.

2. Open the BOX1.LSP file and change the Getinfo function to the following:

```
(defun getinfo ( )
(setq pt1 (getpoint "Pick first corner: "))
(princ "Pick opposite corner: ")
(setq pt3 (rxy))
)
```

Your new BOX1.LSP file should look like Figure 3.4. The boldface print in the figure shows the code that is to be changed.

You have replaced the expression that obtains Pt3 with two lines, one that displays a prompt and another that uses the Rxy function to obtain the location of Pt3:

```
(setq pt3 (rxy))
```

```
(defun getinfo ()
  (setq pt1 (getpoint "Pick first corner: "))
  (princ "Pick opposite corner: ")
  (setq pt3 (rxy))
)

(defun procinfo ()
  (setq pt2 (list (car pt3) (cadr pt1)))
  (setq pt4 (list (car pt1) (cadr pt3)))
)

(defun output ()
  (command "pline" pt1 pt2 pt3 pt4 "c" )
)

(defun C:BOX1 (/ pt1 pt2 pt3 pt4)
  (getinfo)
  (procinfo)
  (output)
)
```

Figure 3.4: *The revised BOX1.LSP file*

Now when you use the Box1 program, the width, height, and area of the box are displayed on the status prompt.

3. Return to the Chapt3 file.

4. Load the RXY.LSP and BOX1.LSP files.

5. Run the Box1 program by entering **box1** at the command prompt.

6. Make sure the Snap mode and dynamic coordinate readout are both on.

7. At the "Pick first corner" prompt, pick the point with coordinates 2, 3.

8. At the "Pick opposite corner" prompt, move the cursor and note how the coordinate readout responds. If you move the cursor to the first point you picked, the coordinate readout will list 0, 0, telling you that you are at the first corner.

9. Now move the cursor until the coordinate readout lists 5.0000, 5.0000, and then pick that point. You have drawn a box exactly five units in the x direction by five units in the y direction.

In the above exercise, after you picked the first corner of the box, the window no longer appeared. Instead, the status line changed to display the height and width of your box as you moved the cursor. It also displayed the area of the box. By altering a function of the main Box1 program, you have added a new feature to it. Of course, you had to do the work of creating RXY.LSP, but the Rxy function can be used to dynamically display relative x and y coordinates for any command that reads point values.

Since you have added a call to the Rxy function in your Box1 program, you will have to load RXY.LSP every time you want to use it. You may want to include the Rxy function in the BOX1.LSP file so you don't have to think about loading RXY.LSP independently.

Using Existing Functions in New Programs

You have seen that after breaking the Box program into independent functions, you can add other functions to it to alter the way it works. In the following section, you will create two more programs, one to draw a 3-D box, and one to draw a 3-D wedge, using those same functions from the Box program.

Creating a 3-D Box Program

To create a 3-D box from a rectangle, all you really need to do is extrude your rectangle in the z direction with the Change command, and then add a 3dface to the top and bottom of the box. 3dfaces are AutoCAD entities that act like surfaces in three-dimensional space. Your program will also need a way to prompt the user for a height. We can accomplish these things by creating a modified version of the Box1 main program, as shown in Figure 3.5.

In the following exercise, you will add the 3-D Box program to the BOX1.LSP file and then run it.

1. Exit AutoCAD temporarily.

2. Open BOX1.LSP again. Add the program shown in boldface in Figure 3.5. Your BOX1.LSP file should look like Figure 3.5 when you are done.

```
(defun getinfo ()
(setq pt1 (getpoint "Pick first corner: "))
(princ "Pick opposite corner: ")
(setq pt3 (rxy))
)

(defun procinfo ()
(setq pt2 (list (car pt3) (cadr pt1)))
(setq pt4 (list (car pt1) (cadr pt3)))
)

(defun output ()
(command "pline" pt1 pt2 pt3 pt4 "c" )
)

(defun C:BOX1 (/ pt1 pt2 pt3 pt4)
(getinfo)
(procinfo)
(output)
)

(defun C:3DBOX (/ pt1 pt2 pt3 pt4 h)
(getinfo)
(setq h (getreal "Enter height of box: "))
(procinfo)
(output)
   (command "change" "Last" "" "Properties" "thickness" h ""
            "3dface" pt1 pt2 pt3 pt4 ""
            "3dface" ".xy" pt1 h ".xy" pt2 h
                     ".xy" pt3 h ".xy" pt4 h "")
   )
)
```

Figure 3.5: The BOX1.LSP file with the 3dbox program added

3. Return to the Chapt3 AutoCAD file and erase any objects on the screen.

4. Load BOX1.LSP again. If you had to exit AutoCAD to edit BOX1.LSP, load RXY.LSP also.

5. Toggle the Snap mode on and enter **3dbox** at the command prompt.

6. At the "Pick first corner" prompt, pick the point with coordinates **2, 3**.

7. At the "Pick opposite corner" prompt, move the cursor until the coordinate readout shows 7.0000, 5.0000, and then pick that point.

8. At the "Enter height of box" prompt, enter **6**. A box appears.

9. Issue the Vpoint command and at the prompt

   Rotate/<View point> <0.0000,0.0000,1.0000>:

   enter **−1, −1,1**. Vpoint is a command that allows you to see your drawing in three dimensions. Now you can see that the box is actually a 3-D box.

10. Issue the Hide command. The box appears as a solid object.

Let's take a closer look at the 3dbox program itself, and at how it runs. I mentioned earlier that one way of looking at your programming task is to consider how you would accomplish the task without AutoLISP. In the case of the 3dbox program, you can think of how you would draw a three-dimensional box manually. Figure 3.6 shows the steps you would take to draw a three-dimensional box without the aid of AutoLISP.

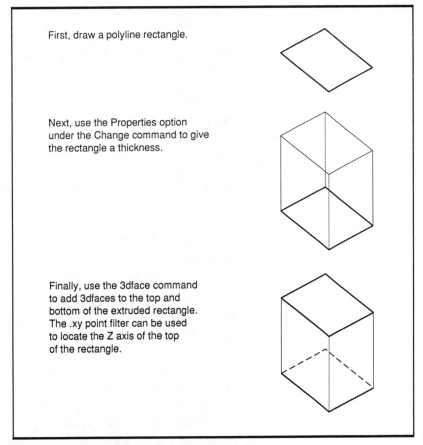

First, draw a polyline rectangle.

Next, use the Properties option under the Change command to give the rectangle a thickness.

Finally, use the 3dface command to add 3dfaces to the top and bottom of the extruded rectangle. The .xy point filter can be used to locate the Z axis of the top of the rectangle.

Figure 3.6: Drawing a three-dimensional box manually

Let's look at how this process is translated into an AutoLISP program. First, you draw the polyline rectangle using the Getinfo, Procinfo, and Output functions. You add a prompt to get the desired height from the user.

(setq h (getreal "Enter height of box: "))

This assigns the height value to the variable H. Next, the Command function is used to invoke the Change command:

(command "change" "Last" "" "Properties" "thickness" h ""

If this sequence was entered manually, it would look like this:

```
Command: change
Select object: L
Select object: ←
Properties/<change point>: P
Change what property (Color/Elev/LAyer/LType/Thickness) ? th
New thickness <0.0000>: !h
Change what property (Color/Elev/LAyer/LType/Thickness) ? ←
Command:
```

Remember that a pair of quotation marks translates into a ←. This sequence extrudes the polyline rectangle in the Z direction. (I spelled out Last, Properties, and Thickness in the program code for clarity, though I could have used just the *L*, *P*, and *th* shown in the manual example.) Then the command function continues by adding 3dfaces:

"3dfaces" pt1 pt2 pt3 pt4 ""

This line adds a 3dface at the base of the rectangle. The next two lines

```
"3dface" ".xy" pt1 h ".xy" pt2 h
         ".xy" pt3 h ".xy" pt4 ""
```

add a 3dface to the "top" of the extruded rectangle using the .xy point filter. The .xy filter allows you to enter a point in three-dimensional space by first entering a point's x and y coordinates using the cursor, and then entering the z coordinate value through the keyboard.

Figure 3.7 shows the entire process that the 3dbox program follows. You may have noticed that although you added the program 3dbox to the BOX1.LSP file, you still called up the program by entering its name, 3dbox. An AutoLISP file is only used as the vessel to hold your program code. AutoLISP makes no connection between the

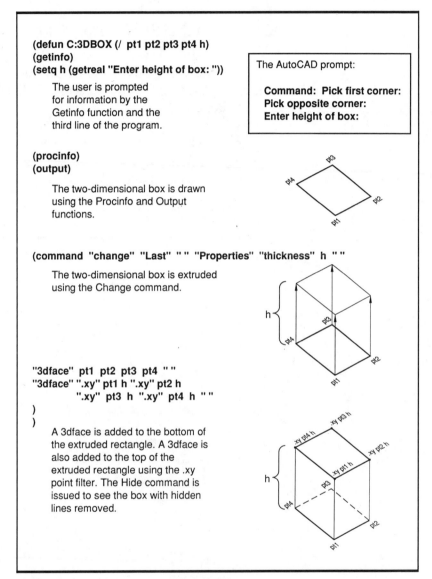

```
(defun C:3DBOX (/ pt1 pt2 pt3 pt4 h)
(getinfo)
(setq h (getreal "Enter height of box: "))
```

The user is prompted for information by the Getinfo function and the third line of the program.

The AutoCAD prompt:

Command: Pick first corner:
Pick opposite corner:
Enter height of box:

```
(procinfo)
(output)
```

The two-dimensional box is drawn using the Procinfo and Output functions.

```
(command "change" "Last" " " "Properties" "thickness" h " "
```

The two-dimensional box is extruded using the Change command.

```
"3dface" pt1 pt2 pt3 pt4 " "
"3dface" ".xy" pt1 h ".xy" pt2 h
        ".xy" pt3 h ".xy" pt4 h " "
)
)
```

A 3dface is added to the bottom of the extruded rectangle. A 3dface is also added to the top of the extruded rectangle using the .xy point filter. The Hide command is issued to see the box with hidden lines removed.

Figure 3.7: How the program draws a 3-D box

program name and the name of the file that holds the program. You could have called BOX1.LSP by another name like MYPROGM.LSP or MYBOX.LSP and the programs would still run the same. Of course, you would have to give the appropriate name when loading the file.

Creating a 3-D Wedge Program

Let's create a new program that draws a wedge shape based on information similar to that given for the 3-D box. Figure 3.8 shows the BOX1.LSP file with a three-dimensional wedge program added at the bottom.

1. Exit AutoCAD temporarily.

2. Open the BOX1.LSP file again and add the 3dwedge program shown in boldface at the bottom of Figure 3.8.

3. Return to the Chapt3 AutoCAD file.

```
(defun getinfo ()
(setq pt1 (getpoint "Pick first corner: "))
(princ "Pick opposite corner: ")
(setq pt3 (rxy))
)

(defun procinfo ()
(setq pt2 (list (car pt3) (cadr pt1)))
(setq pt4 (list (car pt1) (cadr pt3)))
)

(defun output ()
(command "pline" pt1 pt2 pt3 pt4 "c" )
)

(defun C:BOX1 (/ pt1 pt2 pt3 pt4)
(getinfo)
(procinfo)
(output)
)


(defun C:3DBOX (/ pt1 pt2 pt3 pt4 h)
 (getinfo)
 (setq h (getreal "Enter height of box: "))
 (procinfo)
 (output)
   (command "change" "Last" "" "Properties" "thickness" h ""
            "3dface" pt1 pt2 pt3 pt4 ""
            "3dface" ".xy" pt1 h ".xy" pt2 h
                     ".xy" pt3 h ".xy" pt4 h ""
   )
)


(defun C:3DWEDGE (/ pt1 pt2 pt3 pt4 h)
(getinfo)
(setq h (getreal "Enter height of wedge: "))
(procinfo)
(output)
   (command "3dface" pt1 pt4 ".xy" pt4 h
                     ".xy" pt1 h pt2 pt3 ""
            "3dface" pt1 pt2 ".xy" pt1 h pt1 ""
            "copy" "L" "" pt1 pt4
   )
)
```

Figure 3.8: A program to draw a 3-D wedge

4. Load BOX1.LSP again. If you had to exit AutoCAD to edit BOX1.LSP, load RXY.LSP also.

5. Erase the box currently on the screen.

6. Enter **3dwedge** at the command prompt.

7. At the "Pick first corner" prompt, pick the point with coordinates 2, 3.

8. At the "Pick opposite corner" prompt, pick a point so the wedge's base is 7 units by 5 units.

9. At the "Enter height" prompt, enter **6**. A wedge appears.

10. Issue the Hide command. The wedge appears as a solid object.

This program is nearly identical to the 3dbox program. Figure 3.9 shows the process involved in drawing a three-dimensional wedge manually.

Just like the 3dbox program, 3dwedge starts by drawing the base of the wedge using the Getinfo, Procinfo, and Output functions. The "Enter height" prompt is also used in 3dwedge. The most significant change between 3dbox and 3dwedge is the command function:

```
(command "3dface" pt1 pt4 ".xy" pt4 h
                  ".xy" pt1 h pt2 pt3 ""
         "3dface" pt1 pt2 ".xy" pt1 h pt1 ""
         "copy" "L" "" pt1 pt3
)
```

Here, 3dfaces are used to draw the wedge's surfaces. The .xy point filter is used to locate the high points of the wedge in three-dimensional space. Figure 3.10 shows the entire process.

Now you have three programs that use as their basic building blocks the three functions derived from your original Box program. You also have a function Rxy that can be used independently to dynamically display relative x and y coordinates.

*M*aking Your Code More Readable

The Box program is quite short and simple. As your programs grow in size and complexity, however, you will find that they become more

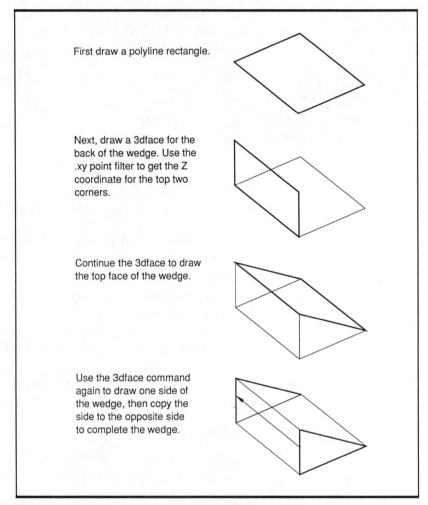

First draw a polyline rectangle.

Next, draw a 3dface for the back of the wedge. Use the .xy point filter to get the Z coordinate for the top two corners.

Continue the 3dface to draw the top face of the wedge.

Use the 3dface command again to draw one side of the wedge, then copy the side to the opposite side to complete the wedge.

Figure 3.9: *Drawing a three-dimensional wedge manually*

and more difficult to read. Breaking programs into modules helps to clarify your code. There are other steps you can take to help keep your code readable.

Using Prettyprint

The term *prettyprint* describes a way of formatting your code to make it readable. With prettyprint, indents are used to offset portions of code.

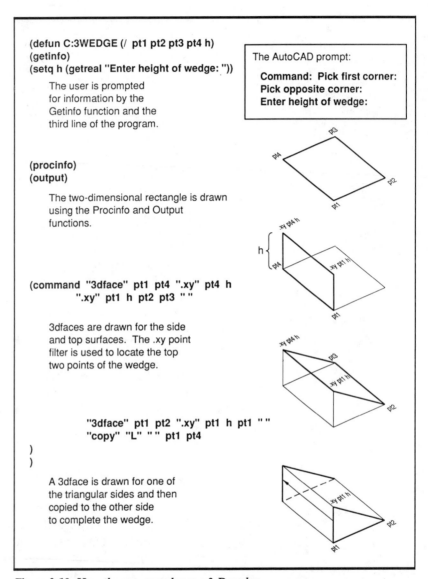

The AutoCAD prompt:

Command: Pick first corner:
Pick opposite corner:
Enter height of wedge:

```
(defun C:3WEDGE (/  pt1 pt2 pt3 pt4 h)
(getinfo)
(setq h (getreal "Enter height of wedge: "))
```

The user is prompted
for information by the
Getinfo function and the
third line of the program.

```
(procinfo)
(output)
```

The two-dimensional rectangle is drawn
using the Procinfo and Output
functions.

```
(command "3dface" pt1 pt4 ".xy" pt4 h
          ".xy" pt1 h pt2 pt3 " "
```

3dfaces are drawn for the side
and top surfaces. The .xy point
filter is used to locate the top
two points of the wedge.

```
          "3dface" pt1 pt2 ".xy" pt1 h pt1 " "
          "copy" "L" " " pt1 pt4
)
)
```

A 3dface is drawn for one of
the triangular sides and then
copied to the other side
to complete the wedge.

Figure 3.10: How the program draws a 3-D wedge

Figure 3.11 shows three examples of the 3dbox program. The first example is arranged randomly, the second lists each expression as a line, and the third makes use of prettyprint to organize the code visually.

```
(defun C:3DBOX (/ pt1 pt2 pt3 pt4 h) (getinfo)
(setq h (getreal "Enter height of box: "))(procinfo)(output)
(command "change" "Last" "" "Properties" "thickness" h
"" "3dface" pt1 pt2 pt3 pt4 "" "3dface" ".xy" pt1 h ".xy" pt2
h ".xy" pt3 h ".xy" pt4 h ""))



(defun C:3DBOX (/ pt1 pt2 pt3 pt4 h)
(getinfo)
(setq h (getreal "Enter height of box: "))
(procinfo)
(output)
(command "change" "Last" "" "Properties" "thickness" h ""
"3dface" pt1 pt2 pt3 pt4 ""
"3dface" ".xy" pt1 h ".xy" pt2 h ".xy" pt3 h ".xy" pt4 h ""))



(defun C:3DBOX (/ pt1 pt2 pt3 pt4 h)
   (getinfo)
   (setq h (getreal "Enter height of box: "))
   (procinfo)
   (output)
      (command "change" "Last" "" "Properties" "thickness" h ""
              "3dface" pt1 pt2 pt3 pt4 ""
              "3dface" ".xy" pt1 h ".xy" pt2 h
                       ".xy" pt3 h ".xy" pt4 h ""
      )
  )
```

Figure 3.11: Three ways to format the 3dbox program code

Notice how the listing is written under the Command function in the third example. Each new command to be issued using the Command functions is aligned with the last in a column. This lets you see at a glance the sequence of commands being used.

*U*sing Comments

It often helps to insert comments into a program as a means of giving a plain-language description of the code. Figure 3.12 shows the Box program from Chapter 1 with comments included. The comments start with a semicolon and continue to the end of the line. When AutoLISP encounters a semicolon, it ignores everything that follows it up to the end of the line. Using the semicolon, you can include portions of your pseudocode as comments to the program code. Excessive use of comments can cause slower loading of programs, so you should try to strike a balance between explaining your code and keeping your file to a minimum in size. You may even want to keep two versions of your programs, those with comments that you use to

```
;Function to draw a simple 2 dimensional box
;-------------------------------------------------------------------------


(defun c:BOX (/ pt1 pt2 pt3 pt4)                        ;define box function
 (setq pt1 (getpoint "Pick first corner: "))            ;pick start corner
 (setq pt3 (getpoint pt1 "Pick opposite corner: "))     ;pick other corner
 (setq pt2 (list (car pt3) (cadr pt1)))                 ;derive second corner
 (setq pt4 (list (car pt1) (cadr pt3)))                 ;derive fourth corner
 (command "line" pt1 pt2 pt3 pt4 "c")                   ;draw box
 )                                                      ;close defun




;Function to display relative XY coordinates in status line
;-------------------------------------------------------------------------


(defun RXY (/ pt lt x last pick lpt1)
(if (not pt1)(setq lpt1 (getvar "lastpoint"))(setq lpt1 pt1)) ;get last point
   (while (/= pick t)
      (setq pt (cadr (setq lt (grread t))))             ;read cursor
      (if (= (car lt) 5)(progn                          ;location
         (setq x (strcat
                    (rtos (- (car pt) (car lpt1))) " x " ;get X coord
                    (rtos (- (cadr pt) (cadr lpt1))) " SI= " ;get Y coord
                    (rtos (*(- (car pt) (car lpt1))     ;get area
                            (- (cadr pt) (cadr lpt1))
                          )         ;close mult
                  2 2)             ;close rtos
                  )               ;close strcat
              )                   ;close setq x
         (grtext -2 x)                                  ;display status
         )                 ;close progn
      )                    ;close if
   (setq pick (= 3 (car lt)))                           ;test for pick
   )                       ;close while
(cadr lt)                                               ;return last
)                                                       ;coordinate
```

Figure 3.12: *A sample of code using comments*

develop and debug, and those in their final debugged form without comments.

*U*sing Uppercase and Lowercase Letters

In programming, *case sensitivity* is a term that means the programming language distinguishes upper- and lowercase letters. Except where string variables occur, AutoLISP does not have any strict requirements when it comes to using upper- and lowercase letters in the code. However, you can help keep your code more readable by using uppercase letters sparingly. For example, you may want to use all uppercase letters for defined function names only. That way you can easily identify user-created functions within the code. You can also mix upper- and lowercase letters for variable names to help convey their meaning. This can help give the variable name more significance while still keeping the name short to conserve space. For example, you might give the name NewWrd for a variable that represents a new string value. NewWrd is more readable than, say, newwrd.

AutoLISP is only case sensitive when string variables are concerned. The string "Yes" is different from "yes", so you must take care when using upper- and lowercase letters in string variable types. We will cover this topic in more detail in the next chapter.

*A*ccessing Variables from the Calling Function with Dynamic Scoping

You may have noticed that in the functions Getinfo, Procinfo, and Output, the argument list is empty (see Figure 3.2). There are no variables local to those functions. The variables used in the programs Box1, 3dbox, and 3dwedge appear in their argument lists rather than in the functions called by these programs. A binding is created between variables and their values within these programs. When the program ends, the variables lose the values assigned to them.

On the other hand, there are no variable bindings created within the individual functions called by the main programs, so when the functions assign values to variables, the variables are freely accessible to all the functions used by the main program. This ability of a function to access variables freely from the calling function is known as *dynamic scoping*.

Whenever a function looks for a variable's value, it looks among its own local variables first. If it does not find the value there, it will then look to the calling function or program for the value. Finally, if it does not find the value there, the function will look at the global environment for a value.

The Adsquare function in Chapter 2 had to look in the AutoLISP global environment for the value of Golden since Golden was not an argument to Adsquare (see Figure 2.10).

All the variables used by the Box1 program and the functions it calls are included in its argument list. For this reason, variables have a binding within Box1 but are freely accesible to any of the functions called by Box1.

An interesting effect of dynamic scoping is the ability to maintain two variables of the same name, each holding different values. To see how this works, do the following.

1. Erase the wedge currently on the screen.

2. Enter the following expression:

   (setq pt1 (getpoint))

3. Pick a point near the coordinate 6, 1. This assigns the coordinate you pick to the variable Pt1.

4. Start the Box1 program.

5. At the "Pick first corner" prompt, pick a point near the coordinate 2, 3.

6. At the "Pick opposite corner" prompt, pick a point so the coordinate readout shows 7.0000, 5.0000. The 2-D box appears.

7. Issue the Line command, and at the "First point" prompt, enter

   !pt1

8. The line will start at the point you selected in step 3 of this exercise.

In the above example, you assigned a point location to the variable Pt1. Then you ran the Box1 program, which also assigns a value to a variable called Pt1. Pt1 in the Box1 program is assigned the coordinate of the first corner point you pick. After the box was drawn, you started the Line command and entered the variable Pt1 as the starting point. You might have expected the line to start from the corner of the box since that is the point last assigned to Pt1. Instead, the line began at the location you had assigned to Pt1 before you ran the Box1 program. Two variables named Pt1 existed, the global variable Pt1 you created before you ran Box1, and the Pt1 created by the Box1 program. The Box1 version of Pt1 lives and dies within that program and has no affect on the global Pt1 (see Figure 3.13).

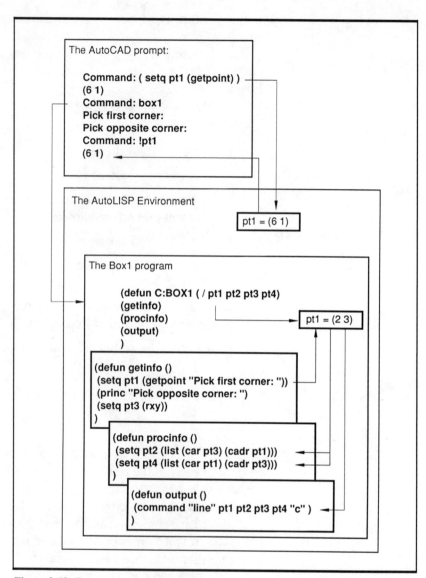

Figure 3.13: *Dynamic scoping allows two distinct variables with the same name.*

Dynamic scoping of variables can simplify your program coding efforts since you don't have to create an argument list for every function you write. It can also simplify your management of variables.

*A*utoLISP and Memory

Although you now know how to break a program into functions that perform discrete operations, you should not get carried away with creating functions and variables since they drain your memory resources. If you accumulate too many functions and variables, you will encounter the following message:

error: insufficient node space

When AutoLISP loads a function, it places the function in memory. Even more memory is used when you run the function to store temporary results from computations. The more complex the function, the more memory it will take to both load it and run it.

You can control the amount of memory AutoCAD allocates to AutoLISP by using the DOS SET command. SET allows you to set up special parameters for application programs that look for information in the DOS *environment*. The DOS environment contains the names and parameters established using the PATH, PROMPT, and SET commands. This information is stored in RAM and is available to any program that can access it. AutoCAD locates drawing files by looking at the PATH parameter, for example. AutoCAD also examines this environment to find other parameters such as the amount of memory to allocate for work space (ACADFREERAM) and the location of AutoCAD configuration files (ACADCFG).

*I*ncreasing the DOS Environment

For versions 3.2 and 3.3 of DOS, you may run out of environment space to store all the settings mentioned above. If this occurs, you will usually get the following message when trying to make the settings:

Out of environment space.

To increase the DOS environment size, start by using the DOS Shell function. The DOS environment is usually given 128 bytes. Using your DOS text editor, place the following line in your CONFIG.SYS file, which is found in the root directory of your hard-disk drive:

SHELL = c:\command.com /e:512 /p

This will increase the DOS environment size to 512 bytes, which is usually enough to store your AutoCAD settings along with any other settings you may need for DOS and other programs. You can specify a larger or smaller size by replacing the 512 in the example above with your desired setting. (For more information on the Shell function and the CONFIG.SYS file, refer to your DOS manual.)

If you do not have a CONFIG.SYS file, use DOS's COPY CON command or the Edlin line editor and create an ASCII file containing the following lines:

```
SHELL = c:\command.com /e:512 /p
FILES = 24
BUFFERS = 32
```

The FILES = 24 statement tells DOS to allow up to 24 files to be open at once. AutoCAD will open many temporary files in the course of its operation. This setting will improve AutoCAD's performance. The BUFFERS = 32 statement tells DOS to store in RAM the information most recently read from the hard disk. This setting improves overall disk access speed and therefore AutoCAD performance. The value 32 is somewhat arbitrary. You can try different values to see which one gives you the best results. The maximum value allowed is 99 but I suggest you try to keep the value as low as possible since the higher the value, the more memory is used for disk buffering.

*S*etting AutoLISP Memory

To set the amount of memory AutoCAD is to allocate to AutoLISP, you use the LISPHEAP and LISPSTACK parameters. For example, you can enter the following at the DOS prompt to set the LISPHEAP and LISPSTACK parameters:

```
SET LISPHEAP = 30000
SET LISPSTACK = 10000
```

LISPHEAP controls the amount of memory allocated to functions and symbols. This is the node space referred to in the "insufficient node space" error message. String space, the memory needed to store string data types, is also part of LISPHEAP. LISPSTACK controls the amount of memory allocated to arguments and partial results created while a program runs. You could think of LISPHEAP as storage space, and LISPSTACK as the workspace. The total of these two values cannot exceed 45,000. The default values for LISPHEAP and LISPSTACK are 40,000 and 3,000 respectively for version 10 of AutoCAD. For earlier versions, the values are 5,000 and 5,000.

The DOS environment settings are lost once you turn off your computer, so if you want to change these settings from their default values, you should include the SET LISPHEAP and SET LISPSTACK commands in your AUTOEXEC.BAT file. This way, LISPHEAP and LISPSTACK will be set automatically each time your computer starts up. Generally, the version 10 defaults are adequate for most beginning AutoLISP users, but if you are using version 9 or earlier, you may want to adjust the setting upward. You can start with the settings shown above.

Variable Names and Memory

As you write programs, you will want to give your variables meaningful names in order to help keep track of their purposes. However, in order to conserve memory, it is good practice to keep the variable name to six characters or less. For example, in the 3dbox program, we used the variable H to represent the height of the box. You could have given the variable the name Boxheight to help you remember what it represented, but Boxheight is over six characters long and would require extra LISPHEAP space for storage. A better name might be Boxht or just Height. Each of these names gives information about the variable without being too wasteful of memory or too cryptic. Also, whenever possible, revise variable names to conserve memory.

Reclaiming Node Space

If you find that you have run out of node space and you don't want to have to quit AutoCAD to reset LISPHEAP and LIPSTACK, you can reclaim node space used by previously loaded functions in one of three ways: redefine functions and variables to nil, use the Clean function, or use the virtual function pager. Let's look at all three methods.

Redefining Functions

Redefining functions to nil is done by entering the following:

(setq *oldfunction* nil)

Here, *oldfunction* is the name of a seldom-used function that has been loaded previously. By setting it to nil, you are recovering all the space AutoLISP used to store it. Of course, if you need to use that function later, you will have to reload it.

The Clean Function

Another method for reclaiming node space is to load the Clean function shown in Figure 3.14. Any node space taken by functions loaded after Clean can be recovered by entering Clean at the command prompt. Again, to use functions removed by Clean, you must reload them. Functions loaded before Clean are not affected. I will explain how this program works in Chapter 9.

The Virtual Function Pager

If you find that you need more memory for storing functions, you can use the Virtual Function Pager facility to store functions temporarily on disk or in expanded or extended memory. The Virtual Function Pager is initialized by entering the following expression:

(vmon)

```
;program to clean symbols and functions from atomlist and close open files
;-------------------------------------------------------------------------------
(defun C:CLEAN (/ i item)
 (setq i 0)                                                 ;set up counter
   ;while not at the end of atomlist do...
   (while (not (equal (setq item (nth i atomlist)) nil))
     (if (= (type (eval item)) 'FILE)                       ;if item is a file
       (close (eval item))                                  ;close the file
     ) ;end IF
   (setq i (1+ i) )                                         ;add 1 t counter
   ) ;end WHILE
 (setq atomlist (member 'C:CLEAN atomlist))                 ;redefine atomlist
 'DONE                                                      ;without symbols
 )                                                          ;previous to C:CLEAN
                                                            ;and print DONE
```

Figure 3.14: The Clean function

Vmon stands for *virtual memory on*. This expression can be included in your ACAD.LSP file. Once it is initialized, Vmon cannot be turned off.

When AutoLISP runs out of node space, Vmon causes AutoCAD to automatically store seldom-used functions in a temporary file, reclaiming node space for other functions. This temporary file is placed on your hard disk or in expanded or extended memory. Functions stored in this way are automatically retrieved from the temporary file when they are called back into use.

Though Vmon is useful when your program becomes large, you may notice a time lag when executing some functions. This can be somewhat annoying, especially when you are switching between functions frequently. You can avoid this problem by using the Clean function described earlier instead of Vmon. You cannot, however, use Vmon and Clean at the same time. This has to do with the way Auto-LISP manages memory.

*U*sing Extended Memory for AutoLISP

If you use MS-DOS on a computer equipped with an 80286 or 80386 processor and you have version 10 of AutoCAD, you can use extended memory for larger and more complex AutoLISP programs. *Extended* memory should not be confused with *expanded* memory, otherwise known as Lotus/Intel/Microsoft expanded memory. You must have version 2.0 or greater of MS- or PC-DOS and, at least 640K RAM for DOS and at least 512K RAM of unused extended memory before it can be used with Extended AutoLISP.

To use Extended AutoLISP, you must first have the following files in your AutoCAD directory:

ACADLX.OVL
EXTLISP.EXE
REMLISP.EXE

ACADLX.OVL is a special overlay file AutoCAD uses for Extended AutoLISP. EXTLISP.EXE is a resident program that you must load before you start AutoCAD. REMLISP.EXE is a program that allows you to "unload" EXTLISP.EXE to free up DOS memory for other applications. Once these files are on your hard disk and you are in the AutoCAD directory, enter **extlisp** at the DOS prompt and then start

AutoCAD. Go to the Configuration menu by selecting option 5 from the Main menu. You will get a listing of your current AutoCAD configuration. Press ↵ and go to the Configure Operating Parameters menu by entering **8**. Enter **7** to select the AutoLISP features option. You are first asked if you want AutoLISP enabled; answer yes. Next, you are asked if you want to use Extended AutoLISP; answer yes and then exit to the Main menu. AutoCAD is now set to use extended memory for AutoLISP. From now on, you must remember to load EXTLISP.EXE before you start AutoCAD.

*A*djusting Extended Memory Use

You can control the amount and location of extended memory used by EXTLISP.EXE by setting the DOS environment. You may want to control the amount and location of the extended memory that Auto-LISP uses. This is of special concern when you are using other programs that also use expanded or extended memory.

To set the amount of extended memory used by AutoLISP, use the DOS SET command and enter the following at the DOS prompt before starting AutoCAD:

SET LISPXMEM = *start_location,size*

The *start location* value can be anything between 1024K to 16384K, 1024K being the beginning of extended memory. Be sure you include the K following the memory location. The *size* can be any number, but it must also be followed by the K. The following example shows what to enter if you have 512K of extended memory and you wish to allocate the upper 256K of it to AutoCAD:

SET LISPXMEM = 1280K,256K

The value for the start location, 1280, is derived from subtracting the desired allocation amount, 256, from the total amount of extended memory, 512, and adding the result to the beginning of the extended memory, 1024. Note that there can be no spaces in the LISPXMEM specification. You can omit the size value if you want to allocate all of the remaining extended memory to AutoCAD. Likewise, you can omit the start location value if you want AutoCAD to select its own starting location. If you use only the size value, you must still precede the value with a comma. Finally, you can force AutoLISP to ignore extended memory by entering **none** in place of the start location and size value. You might want to do this when other programs use extended memory without regard for AutoCAD's use of it. Just as with LISPHEAP and LISP-STACK, you can include the LISPXMEM settings in your AUTOEX-EC.BAT file.

*S*ummary

In this chapter you examined methods for designing your programs in an organized fashion. The box example, though simple enough to leave as a single program, allowed you to explore the concept of modular programming. It also showed how a program might be structured to give a clear presentation to both the creator of the program and those who might have to modify it later.

You also examined issues concerning memory management, both from within AutoLISP and with DOS. Though most of the programs in this book won't require you to do anything special to your computer system, you should be aware of these issues when you begin to expand your program library.

4

Prompting the User for Information

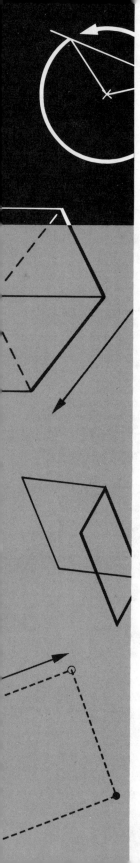

4

In the first three chapters of the book, you learned the basics of AutoLISP. You now have a framework within which you can begin to build your programs. I can now discuss each built-in AutoLISP function without losing you in AutoLISP nomenclature.

In previous chapters you learned that a key element in a user-defined function is how it obtains information from the user. In this chapter, you will look at some built-in functions that expedite your program's information gathering. You have already seen the use of two of these functions, Getpoint and Getcorner, in Chapters 2 and 3.

Table 4.1 shows all the functions that allow you to prompt the user for input. Keep in mind that all of these functions return values based on the user coordinate system (UCS) active at the time the function is called. Since the AutoLISP interpreter can be used interactively, you can enter the sample expressions shown in this chapter at the Auto-CAD command prompt to see first-hand how they work.

Table 4.1: *Functions for Obtaining User Input*

FUNCTION	DESCRIPTION
Getint	Allows input of integer. Returns integer.
Getreal	Allows input of reals. Returns reals.
Getstring	Allows input of strings. Returns strings.
Getkword	Allows filtering of string entries through a list of keywords. These keywords are defined by using the Initget function. Returns strings.
Getangle	Allows keyboard or cursor entry of angles based on the Units command setting for compass-orientation of angles. Returns real values in radians. A reference point can be used as an optional first argument.

Table 4.1: *Functions for Obtaining User Input (Continued)*

FUNCTION	DESCRIPTION
Getorient	Allows keyboard or cursor entry of angles based on the standard AutoCAD compass-orientation of angles. Returns real values in radians. A reference point can be used as an optional first argument.
Getdist	Allows keyboard or cursor entry of distances. This always returns values as real numbers regardless of the unit format used. A reference point can be used as an optional first argument. If the Flatland system variable is set to 0 or Initget is used with a bit code argument of 16 in conjunction with Getdist then Getdist returns a distance based on three-dimensional coordinates.
Getpoint	Allows the input of coordinates from either keyboard or cursor. A reference point can be used as an optional first argument. Returns a list of coordinates. If the Flatland system variable is set to 0 or Initget is used with a bit code argument of 16 in conjunction with Getpoint, then Getpoint returns a three-dimensional coordinate.
Getcorner	Allows selection of a point by using a window. This function requires a base-point value defining the first corner of the window. A window appears, allowing you to select the opposite corner. Returns a list of coordinates. If the Flatland system variable is set to 0 or Initget is used with a bit code argument of 16 in conjunction with Getcorner, then Getcorner returns a three-dimensional coordinate.

Prompting the User for Distances

You will often need to prompt the user to obtain a distance value. At times, it is easier for the user to select distances directly from the graphic screen by using the cursor. AutoLISP provides the Getdist function for this purpose.

How to Use Getdist

The syntax for Getdist is

(getdist *optional_point value optional_prompt_string*)

You may supply one or two optional arguments to Getdist, a point value indicating a position from which to measure the distance, or a string value to be used as a prompt when the program runs. Most likely, you will always include the prompt string argument. Without it, the prompt line will blank and the user will not know what action to take. Getdist will accept cursor input or keyboard input, and it always returns values in real numbers regardless of what unit style is current. This means, for example, that if your drawing is set up using an architectural unit style, Getdist will still return a value in decimal units. Version 10 users should note that Getdist will return a three-dimensional distance depending on the Flatland system variable setting and the use of the Initget function. (Initget is discussed later in this chapter.)

There are three ways to use Getdist. With it, you can input a distance by picking two points with the cursor, by entering a distance value at the keyboard, or by supplying a point value as an argument and picking the second point with the cursor. The exercises in this section will demonstrate these uses.

Let's look at the first use.

1. Open a file by entering **chapt4=** . Turn on Snap mode and the dynamic coordinate readout.

2. Enter the following:

    (setq dist1 (getdist "Pick point or enter distance: "))

    The prompt line will display

    Pick point or enter distance:

This is the optional prompt value used as the argument to Getdist. At this prompt, you can enter a numeric value from the keyboard in the current unit style or in decimal units, or you can pick a beginning point on the display screen using the cursor.

3. Pick a point at 3, 3 with your cursor. You will get the prompt

   Second point:

   and a rubber-banding line will appear from the first point selected. When Getdist is used with only a string prompt argument, and you pick a point with your cursor, it automatically prompts you for a second point.

4. Pick a second point at 8, 3. You can use the F6 key to toggle the dynamic coordinate readout on. You may have to press F6 several times to get the absolute coordinate readout as opposed to the polar readout. Once you pick a point, the distance between the two points selected is assigned to the variable Dist1 and the value of the entire expression is displayed at the prompt.

5. To ascertain that the variable Dist1 does indeed hold the distance value, enter the following:

   !dist1

   The distance value stored by Dist1 is displayed:

   5.0

Using the same expression, you can also enter a distance value at the keyboard.

1. Enter the following again:

   (setq dist1 (getdist "Pick point or enter distance: "))

   The prompt line will display

   Pick point or enter distance:

2. In the previous exercise, you picked a point at this prompt and Getdist responded by asking for a second point. This time, instead of picking a point, enter the value 6.5; it will be assigned to the variable Dist1 and again, the value of the entire expression is displayed in the prompt.

3. Enter the following to ascertain Dist1's new value:

   !dist1

   The distance value stored by Dist1 is displayed:

   6.5

You may recall that AutoLISP always goes through the cycle of reading the command line, evaluating the input and, if it is an Auto-LISP expression, printing the value of the expression at the prompt. AutoLISP returns the value of every expression it evaluates from the smallest math equation to the largest program. This means that no matter what size the expression is, the last value it returns is shown at the AutoCAD prompt. In the preceding examples, the value of the Setq function is printed at the prompt since it is the last expression evaluated by AutoLISP.

A third way to use Getpoint is to supply a point variable as an argument.

1. Enter the following at the command prompt:

   (setq pt1 (getpoint "Enter a point: "))

   When the "Enter a point" prompt appears, pick a point at 3, 3. The coordinate pair 3, 3 is assigned to the variable Pt1.

2. Now, enter the following expression:

   (setq dist1 (getdist pt1 "Enter a second point: "))

   Notice that the variable Pt1 is used as an argument to Getdist. A rubber-banding line appears from Pt1, and the prompt displays the string prompt argument you entered with the expression.

3. Pick a point at 9, 6. The distance from Pt1 to the point 9, 6 is assigned to the variable Dist1.

As you can see, Getdist is quite flexible in the way it will accept input. This flexibility makes it ideal when you need to get an object's size from the user. (Several AutoCAD commands act in a similar manner. For example, the Text command allows you to select a text size either by entering a height or by indicating a height with the cursor.) Figure 4.1 summarizes the three ways you can use Getdist.

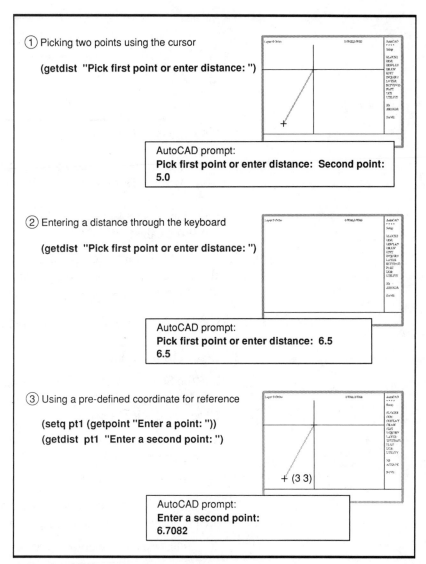

Figure 4.1: Three methods that Getdist accepts for input

A Sample Program Using Getdist

At times, you may need to find the distance between two points in an unusual format. Figure 4.2 lists a user-defined function that

```
;Function to get distance in decimal feet -- Decft.lsp----------------------
(defun decft (/ dst1 dst1s)
(setq dst1 (getdist "Pick first point or enter distance: "))   ;get distance
(setq dst1s (rtos (/ dst1 12.0) 2 4))                ;convert real value to string
(terpri)                                             ;advance prompt one line
(strcat dst1s " ft.")                                ;return string plus "ft."
)
```

Figure 4.2: *A program to display decimal feet*

displays distances in decimal feet, a common engineering system of measure that AutoCAD does not directly support in release 10.

1. Exit AutoCAD with the End command and open an Auto-LISP file called DECFT.LSP.

2. Copy the program listed in Figure 4.2 into the DECFT.LSP file. When you are done, and you are certain you have corrected any transcription errors you may have made, close the file.

Now let's see how the DECFT.LSP file works.

3. Return to the Chapt4 file.

4. Use the Setup option on the Main menu to set up your drawing. Use the architectural unit style at a scale of ¹/₈ inch to 1 foot, and select a sheet size of 11 by 17.

5. Set the snap distance to 12 by 12 and turn on the dynamic coordinate readout.

6. Load the DECFT.LSP file.

7. Enter **(decft)** at the command prompt (remember to include the parentheses). The following prompt appears:

   Pick first point or enter distance:

8. Pick a point at the coordinate 17'-0'', 9'-0''. The "Second point" prompt appears.

9. Pick a point at the coordinate 100'-0'', 70'-0''. The prompt displays the distance 103.0049 ft.

The first line of the Decft program defines the function. The second line obtains the distance using Getdist:

(setq dst1 (getdist "Pick first point: "))

The third line divides the distance value by 12 and then uses the Rtos function to convert the distance value from a real to a string (see Chapter 7):

(setq dst1s (rtos (/ dst1 12.0) 2 4))

This conversion is necessary because we want to append the string "ft." to the numeric distance value obtained from Getdist. The fourth line enters a carriage return to the prompt line, and the last line combines the string distance value with the "ft." string:

(terpri)
(strcat dst1s " ft.")

The function Terpri simply causes the prompt to move to the next line. AutoLISP always returns the value of the last expression evaluated, so the result of using Strcat to combine the distance value with "ft." is displayed on the command prompt. You could assign the result value to a variable for further processing, as in the following line:

(setq dist2s (decft))

In this simple expression, the final value returned by Decft is assigned to the variable Dist2s.

*H*ow to Get Angle Values

When you are manipulating drawings with AutoLISP, you will sometimes need to obtain angle values. AutoLISP provides the Getangle and Getorient functions for this purpose. These functions determine angles based on point input. This means that two point values are required before these functions will compute an angle.

Getangle and Getorient will accept keyboard input of relative or absolute coordinates, or accept cursor input to allow angle selection from the graphic screen. Getangle and Getorient always return angles in radians, regardless of the current AutoCAD Units settings. I will discuss radians in the next section.

*U*sing *Getangle and Getorient*

The difference between Getangle and Getorient is that Getangle will return an angle value relative to the current Units setting for the 0 angle while Getorient will return an angle based on the default 0 angle setting. For example, the default orientation for 0 degrees is a right horizontal, but you can use the Units command or the Angbase or Angdir system variables to make 0 degrees an upward vertical. In this case, Getangle will return values relative to this orientation while Getorient will continue to return values based on the default right horizontal orientation regardless of the Units, Angbase, or Angdir settings. Figure 4.3 illustrates these differences.

Note that Getangle and Getorient ignore the angle-direction setting. Even though the hypothetical setting in the figure uses a clockwise direction for the positive angle direction, Getangle and Getorient still return angles using the counterclockwise direction for a positive angle.

The syntax is the same for Getangle and Getorient:

(getangle *optional_point_value optional_prompt_string***)**
(getorient *optional_point_value optional_prompt_string***)**

You may supply one or two optional arguments to these functions, a point value indicating a position from which to measure the angle, or a string value to be used as a prompt. The point value can be a variable representing a coordinate list or a quoted coordinate list.

Getangle and Getorient accept three methods of input. These methods are similar to those offered by Getdist. With the first method, you can enter two points by picking them on the screen.

1. Enter the following:

   (setq ang1 (getangle "Pick a point using cursor: "))

2. Pick a point at 3, 3. A rubber-banding line appears from the picked point, and you see the prompt

   Second point:

3. Pick another point at 6, 6. The angle obtained from Getangle is then assigned to the variable Ang1 and displayed at the prompt.

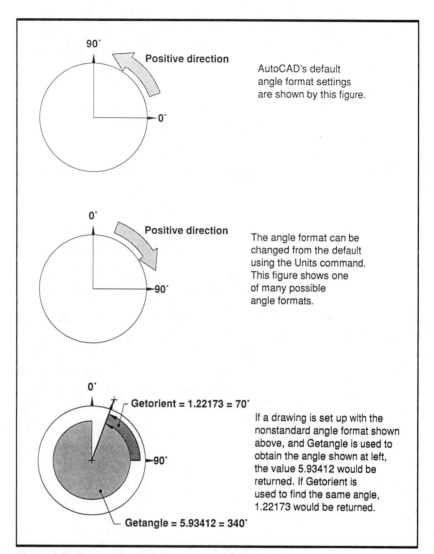

Figure 4.3: Comparing Getorient and Getangle

If the value returned looks unfamiliar, it is because it is in radians. *Radians* are a way of describing angles based on a circle whose radius is one unit. Such a circle will have a circumferance of 2 pi. For example, an angle of 90 degrees would describe a distance along the circle equivalent to one quarter of the circle's circumference, or pi/2, or 1.5708 (see Figure 4.4). This distance is the radian equivalent of

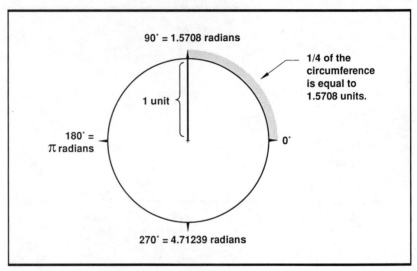

Figure 4.4: A 90-degree angle described in radians

90 degrees. I will discuss radians and their conversion to degrees in more detail in Chapter 6.

Just as with Getdist, if you select a point with the cursor, you will be prompted for a second point, and a rubber-banding line will appear. This rubber-banding line allows you to see the angle you are displaying in the drawing area.

The second method is to enter an angle from the keyboard.

1. Enter the same expression you did previously:

   (setq ang1 (getangle "Enter angle from keyboard: "))

2. Enter the following:

   <45

   The angle of 45 degrees is applied to the variable Ang1 in radians and the value 0.785398 is returned. This is the radian equivalent of 45 degrees.

Just as with Getdist, you can supply a point variable as an argument to Getangle.

1. Enter the following expression:

   (setq pt1 '(3 3))

This assigns the coordinate pair 3, 3 to the variable Pt1.

2. Enter the expression

   (setq ang1 (getangle pt1 "Indicate angle: "))

   A rubber-banding line appears from the point 3, 3.

3. Indicate an angle by picking a point at 7, 6. The angle from Pt1 to 7, 6 is assigned to Ang1 and the value 0.6463501 is returned. This is the radian equivalent of approximately 37 degrees.

By accepting both keyboard and cursor input, these two functions offer flexibility to the user—angles can be specified as exact numeric values or indicated on screen. Figure 4.5 summarizes the three ways you can use Getangle.

*H*ow to Get Text Input

You can prompt the user for text input using the Getstring and Getkword functions. These two functions always return string variables even if a number has been entered as a response. Getstring will accept almost anything as input, so it can be used to input words or sentences of up to 132 characters long with no particular restriction to content. Getkword, however, is designed to work in conjunction with the Initget function (described in detail later in this chapter) to accept only specific strings, or keywords, as input. If the user tries to enter a string to Getkword that is not a predetermined keyword, the user will be asked to try again.

*U*sing Getstring

The syntax for Getstring is

(getstring *optional_variable_or_number optional_prompt_string*)

You may supply one or two optional arguments to Getstring, a string value to be used as a prompt, or a *non-nil* expression or symbol to signify that

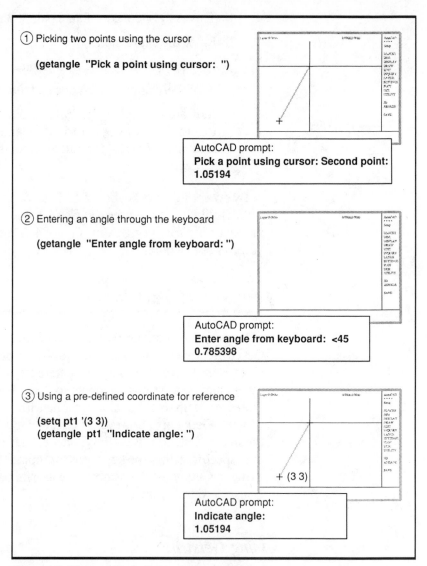

Figure 4.5: Three methods Getangle accepts for input

Getstring should accept spaces in the user input. (Non-nil means any value that is not nil.) With Getstring, as with many AutoCAD commands, pressing the spacebar on your keyboard has the same effect as pressing ←┘. Normally, this will prevent more than a single word from being input to the Getstring function. To illustrate this problem, try this:

1. Enter the following expression:

   (setq str1 (getstring "Enter a word: "))

   the following prompt appears:

   Enter a word:

2. Try entering your first and last name. As soon as you press the spacebar, your first name is read by the Getstring function and the command prompt returns.

3. Ascertain the value of Str1 by entering

   !str1

   Since the spacebar is read as a ←┘, once it is pressed, the string is entered and AutoLISP goes on to other business.

If you provide a non-nil value as an argument, however, Getstring will treat a spacebar input as a space in the text string. This will allow the user to enter whole sentences or phrases.

4. Enter the following:

   (setq str2 (getstring T "Enter a name: "))

   Here we use T as our non-nil value. T is a special AutoLISP symbol that means true. The following prompt appears:

   Enter a name:

5. Now try entering your first and last name again. This time you are able to complete your name.

The T argument in the above example could be replaced by an integer, a real value, or any expression that will not evaluate to nil.

Remember, you can enter numbers in response to Getstring, but they will be treated as strings and you won't be able to apply math functions to them. You can, however, convert a number that is a string variable into a real or integer, using the Atof, Atoi, and Ascii functions (see Chapter 7 for details).

Using Getkword

The syntax for Getkword is

(getkword *optional_prompt_string***)**

Getkword offers only one argument option, the prompt string. Get-kword must be used in conjunction with the Initget function. Initget is used to allow only certain values for input. If the user enters a disallowed value, he or she will be prompted to try again.

In the case of Getkword, Initget allows you to specify special words that you expect as input. The most common use of these functions is a Yes/No prompt. Try this example to see how Initget and Getkword work together:

1. Enter the following:

    (initget "Yes No")
    (setq str1 (getkword "Are you sure? <Yes/No>: "))

    The following prompt appears:

    Are you sure? <Yes/No>:

2. If the user does not enter a Yes, Y, No, or N, Getkword will con-tinue to prompt the user until one of the keywords is entered. Initget does allow the user to enter a lowercase response. Also, the user is allowed to supply just the capitalized portion of the string argument. Try entering **MAYBE**. You get the message:

    Invalid option keyword.
    Are you sure? <Yes/No>:

3. Now try entering **Y**. Getkword accepts it and the whole keyword Yes is assigned to the variable Str1. If you had entered n or N, then the entire keyword No would have been assigned to Str1.

The Initget function establishes the keywords, in this case, Yes and No. Getkword then issues the prompt and waits for the proper keyword to be entered. If you use capital letters in the Initget function's string argument, the capitalized letters by themselves will be acceptable entries. This is why Y was allowed as input in the above example (see "How to Use Initget to Control User Input" later in this chapter for more details). It doesn't matter if you enter an uppercase or lowercase Y. It only matters that you enter the letter that is capitalized in the Initget string argument.

How to Get Numeric Values

At times, you may want to prompt the user for a numeric value, such as a size in decimal units or the number of times a function is to be performed. You use the Getreal and Getint functions to obtain numeric input.

Getreal always returns real number values, and Getint always returns integer values. The syntax for Getint is

(getint *optional_prompt_string*)

And the syntax for Getreal is

(getreal *optional_prompt_string*)

Getreal and Getint can be supplied an optional prompt string argument. Just as with all the previous Get functions, this string is displayed as a prompt when an expression using Getreal or Getint is evaluated.

If you attempt to enter a real value in response to a Getint prompt, you get an error message.

1. Enter the following expression:

    (getint "Enter number: ")

2. Now enter the number **1.2**. The error message

    Requires an integer value.
    Try again:

    appears.

3. Enter the number **1**. AutoLISP returns 1 as the value of the expression.

If you attempt to enter an integer in response to a Getreal function, the integer will be converted to a real.

1. Enter the following expression:

    (getreal "Enter number: ")

2. Enter the number **6**. AutoLISP returns the value 6.0 as the value of the expression. Note that 6 and 6.0 are the same value. 6.0 is the real representation of the value 6.

How to Use Initget to Control User Input

You can add some additional control to the Get functions described in this chapter with the Initget function. In version 2.6 of AutoCAD, Initget was only used to provide keywords for the Getkword function. With version 9, other functions have been added to give more control over input to the other Get functions. With Initget, you can prevent a Get function from accepting zero or negative values.

The syntax for Initget is

(initget *optional_bit_code optional_string_input_list*)

You must supply at least one argument to Initget. The bit code option controls the restriction on the type of input, or, in some cases, how rubber-banding lines or windows are displayed. Table 4.2 lists the bit codes and their meaning.

Table 4.2: The Initget Bit Codes and What They Mean

CODE	MEANING
1	Null input not allowed
2	Zero values not allowed
4	Negative values not allowed
8	Do not check limits for point values
16	Return 3-D point rather than 2-D point
32	Use dashed lines for rubber-banding lines and windows

Bit codes can be used singly or added together to exclude several types of input at once. For example, if you do not want a Get function to accept null, zero, or negative values, you could enter the following expressions:

```
(initget 7)
(setq int1 (getint "Enter an integer: "))
```

A null response is the same as pressing ◄─┘ without entering anything. In this example, though there is no formal bit-code value of 7 for Initget, because 7 is 1+2+4, the restrictions associated with bit codes 1, 2, and 4 are applied to the Getint that follows. You can also write the Initget expression above as:

(initget (+ 1 2 4))

for better readibility. Not all Initget bit codes are applicable to all Get functions. Table 4.3 shows which codes work with which Get functions.

Table 4.3: The Get Functions and Bit Codes They Honor

FUNCTION	INITGET BIT CODES HONORED
Getint	1, 2, 4
Getreal	1, 2, 4
Getdist	1, 2, 4, 16, 32
Getangle	1, 2, 32
Getorient	1, 2, 32
Getpoint	1, 8, 16, 32
Getcorner	1, 8, 16, 32
Getkword	1
Getstring	None

Prompting for Dissimilar Variable Types

The Initget function can allow Get functions to accept string input even when they expect data in another format. For example, you may want your function to accept either a point or string value from a prompt. To show how this is done, enter the following expressions:

(initget 1 "Next")
(setq pt1 (getpoint "Next/<pick a point>: "))

You get the prompt

Next/<pick a point>:

Now enter **n**. The variable Pt1 is assigned the string "Next". Initget sets up the word Next as a keyword. Once this is done, The Getpoint function in the following expression is allowed to accept either a point value or the string "next" or "n". (Note that the user can enter a response in either upper- or lowercase letters.)

Specifying Multiple Keywords

You can include more than one keyword in order to offer multiple choices. For example, you might want the user to choose from several fonts, as in the following expressions:

```
(initget "Roman Gothicg Scripts")
(setq str1 (getkword "Font style = Roman/Gothicg/Scripts: "))
```

Capitalization is important in specifying keywords, as Initget will allow the whole word or the capitalized portion of the word as input. In the above example, the user can enter one of the three keywords listed in the prompt or the capital letters they begin with.

In the following example, the user can enter S for style, ST for steak, or STROKE for stroke.

```
(initget "Style STeak STROKE")
(setq kword (getkword "Style/STteak/STROKE: "))
```

Another way to specify keywords is to capitalize all the characters of the word, and follow it with a comma and the abbreviation, as in the following:

```
(initget "STYLE,S STEAK,ST STROKE")
```

This expression has the same effect as the previous example. This optional way of specifying keywords allows you to handle situations where case conversion would be difficult.

How to Select Groups of Objects

AutoCAD uses the "Select objects" prompt to allow you to select a group of objects that you wish to edit in some way. For example, when you issue the Move command, you are prompted to select objects. You can then use any number of options to select groups of objects to move. These options range from the use of windows to single object selection or de-selection with the cursor. The group of objects you select is called a *selection set*.

AutoLISP offers a similar facility in the Ssget function. Ssget is an abbreviation for *selection set get*. When this function is used without any arguments as part of an expression, the "Select objects" prompt appears and the user can then select a single object or groups of objects to be processed by your program.

Ssget allows you to select entities to be processed by your program. It returns a set of entities as a value. That set of entities appears to you in the following form:

<Selection set: *n*>

where *n* is a number representing the selection set. Generally, you won't have to concern yourself with the number of the selection set as you will normally assign a selection set to a variable.

The syntax for Ssget varies depending on the arguments used. If no arguments are supplied, as in

(ssget)

then the "Select objects" prompt appears and the user is allowed to use any of the standard AutoCAD selection options normally available at this prompt. These options include the previous selection set, the last entity drawn, crossing or standard windows, or individual entity selection.

You can supply the "P" or "L" arguments to Ssget to specify the previous selection set or the last entity drawn, respectively:

(ssget "P")   Selects the last selection set

(ssget "L")   Selects the last entity drawn

The user is not prompted for anything if you use these arguments.

You can also supply the "W" or "C" arguments to Ssget to select entities based on a standard window or a crossing window respectively. If you use these arguments you must also provide two coordinates to indicate the location of the corners of the window or crossing window:

(ssget "W" '(1 1) '(4 4))	Selects entities in a window whose corners are located at the coordinates 1, 1 and 4, 4.
(ssget "C" '(3 3) '(8 8))	Selects entities in a crossing window whose corners are located at the coordinates 3,3 and 8,8.

The user is also not prompted for anything if you use these arguments.

Finally, you can select a single object by supplying a coordinate pair as an argument to Ssget:

(ssget '(3 4))	Selects an entity at the coordinates 3, 4.

This assumes that there is an entity at the coordinate 3, 4.

Variables representing coordinates can be used in place of the quoted lists shown in all the examples above. Suppose two points, Pt1 and Pt2, have been previously defined in your program. Later in the program you can use Pt1 and Pt2 to select objects with a window, as in this example:

(setq obj1 (ssget "W" pt1 pt2))

Most of these options should be familiar to you as standard Auto-CAD selection options. There is yet another selection mode, specified with the "X" argument. The "X" Ssget option allows you to specify an entity or group of entities based on certain properties such as layers or linetypes. I won't discuss this option until Chapter 11, as it is rather involved.

To see first-hand how Ssget works, try the following:

1. Draw eight vertical lines in the drawing area.

2. Enter the following expression at the command prompt:

   (setq grp (ssget))

   The following prompt appears:

   Select objects:

3. Pick the leftmost three lines. You can use a window or a crossing

window, or pick them individually. Once you have selected them, press ←┘. You will see a message similar to the following:

<Selection set: *n*>

This is how selection sets appear to the user. The value of *n* you see will depend on the number of selection sets previously used in the current editing session. This selection set representation is a way to describe an internal data structure. As AutoLISP users, we only need to know what selection sets do for us.

4. Now issue the Move command. At the "Select objects" prompt, pick the leftmost line and move it to the right of the eight lines.

5. Issue the Move command again, and at the "Select objects" prompt, enter the following:

   !grp

   The objects you picked using the Ssget function are highlighted just as if you had picked them manually. Notice that the line you moved to the right is also highlighted. Even though you moved it, it still belongs to the selection set Grp you created with the Ssget function.

The expression you just used simply obtains a selection set using Ssget and assigns that selection set to a global variable named Grp. You can recall the selection set stored by Grp at any time during the current editing session.

AutoLISP allows up to six selection sets to be available at once. If you try to create more than six at any given time, Ssget will return nil instead of a selection set. This means that if you have six different variables, each assigned a selection set with Ssget, then Ssget will no longer return a selection set when it is called from a program or user-defined function. If this situation occurs, you must take certain steps to recover the use of Ssget.

Suppose you have just assigned your sixth selection set to the variable Grp. The following expressions delete the Grp selection set and restore the use of Ssget.

   (set grp nil)
   (gc)

The first expression sets the global variable Grp to nil, thereby removing its reference to the selection set. However, this alone won't restore the use of Ssget. The Gc function must also be used before Ssget will work. Gc stands for "garbage collection." Garbage collection is a method AutoLISP uses to recover memory that is no longer used by a symbol or value. Normally, garbage collection occurs automatically whenever AutoLISP needs more memory for a new symbol or value. However, if you find yourself in the situation where Ssget does not function, you will want to force a garbage collection. Garbage collection can be a time-consuming operation so it is not recommended for frequent use.

This limitation on the number of selection sets is not a problem as long as you keep your selection set variables local to your program and you reuse variables to store your selection sets. Remember that a variable is made local by including it in the program or functions argument list. If you must have a global selection-set variable, then reuse the variable name whenever you can rather than creating more global selection-set variables with different names.

*S*ummary

This chapter has introduced the many ways AutoLISP allows you to interact with the user to gather information. The following points were discussed:

- Several functions allow you to pause your program to allow the user to input data.

- Many of these functions accept data either from the keyboard or from the cursor

- You can place controls on the type of data being input through the Initget function.

In addition, you saw how objects can be selected using the Ssget function. Though there are only a handful of functions that give AutoLISP its interactive capabililties, the flexibility of these functions allows a wide range of possibilities for gathering data from the user.

In the next chapter, you will explore how you can make your program do more of your work for you by making decisions and performing repetitive tasks.

5

Making Decisions with AutoLISP

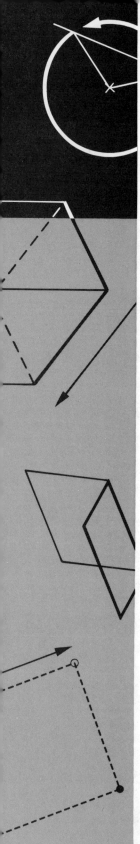

5

As I mentioned in Chapter 3, AutoLISP is designed to help solve problems. One of the key elements of problem solving is the ability to decide between one task and another based on some existing condition. You might think of this ability as a way for a program to make decisions by testing whether certain conditions are true or false. Another element of problem solving is repetitive computation. Some tasks that would be repetitive, tedious, and time consuming for the user can be done quickly using AutoLISP. In this chapter, we will look at these two facilities in AutoLISP.

You can use AutoLISP to create macros that comprise a predetermined sequence of commands and responses. A macro-building facility alone would be quite useful but still limited. AutoLISP additionally offers two *conditional* functions that allow you to build some decision-making capabilities into your programs. These are the If and Cond functions. They work in similar ways but there are some important differences.

*H*ow to Test for Conditions

The If function first tests to see whether a condition is met and then performs one option or another depending on the outcome of the test. This sequence of operations is often referred to as an *if-then-else* conditional statement: *if* a condition is met, *then* perform computation A, *else* perform computation B. The following shows the general syntax of the if function:

```
(if (test_expression)
    (expression) (optional_expression)
)
```

As usual in AutoLISP, the If function is used as the first element of an expression. It is followed by an expression that provides the test. A second argument and an optional third argument follow the test expression. The second argument is an expression to be evaluated if the test condition is true. If the test returns false or nil, If either evaluates the third argument or returns nil if there is no third argument.

*T*esting with Predicates and Logical Operators

The test expression can use any function, but most often will use either a predicate or a logical operator. *Predicates* and *logical operators* are functions that return either true or false. They don't return values the way most functions do; instead they return the atom T (to represent a non-nil, or true, value) or nil. Functions that return either T or nil when evaluated are shown in Table 5.1.

Table 5.1: A List of AutoLISP Predicates and Logical Operators

FUNCTION	RETURNS T (TRUE) IF
Predicates	
<	a numeric value is less than another
>	a numeric value is greater than another
< =	a numeric value is less than or equal to another
> =	a numeric value greater than or equal to another
=	two numeric or string values are equal
/ =	two numeric or string values are not equal
eq	two values are exactly the same
equal	two values are the same
atom	an object is an atom (as opposed to a list)
boundp	symbol has a value bound to it
listp	an object is a list
minusp	a numeric value is negative
numberp	an object is a number, real or integer
zerop	an object evaluates to zero

Table 5.1: A List of AutoLISP Predicates and Logical Operators (Continued)

FUNCTION	RETURNS T (TRUE) IF
Logical Operators	
and	all of several expressions or atoms return non-nil
not	a symbol is nil
nul	a list is nil
or	one of several expressions or atoms returns non-nil

You may notice that several of the predicates end with a *p*. The *p* denotes *predicate*. Also note the use of the term *object* in the table. Object means any list or atom that includes symbols and numbers. Numeric values can be numbers or symbols that are bound to numbers.

All predicates and logical operators follow the standard format for AutoLISP expressions. They appear as the first element in an expression followed by arguments, as in the following example:

(> 2 4)

The greater-than predicate compares two numbers to see if the one on the left is greater than the one on the right. The value of this expression is nil since 2 is not greater than 4.

The predicates >, <, >=, and <= allow more than two arguments as in the following:

(> 2 1 5 8)

With more than two arguments, > will return T only if each value is greater than the one to its right. The above expression returns nil since 1 is not greater than 5.

The functions And, Not, Nul, and Or are similar to predicates in that they too return T or nil. But these functions, which are logical operators, are most often used to test predicates. For example, you could use a predicate to see if one value is greater than another:

```
(setq val1 1)
(zerop val1)
nil
```

If you set the value of the variable Val1 to 1 and then test to see if Val1 is equal to zero, the Zerop predicate returns nil. But suppose you wanted to get a true response whenever Val1 does not equal zero. You could use the Not logical operator to "reverse" the result of Zerop, as follows:

```
(setq val1 1)
(not (zerop val1))
T
```

Since Not returns T when its argument returns nil, the end result of the test is T. Not and Nul can also be used as predicates to test atoms and lists.

Using the If Function

In Chapter 2, you saw briefly how the If function worked with the Not logical operator to determine whether to load a program or not. If you look at that expression again (Figure 5.1), you'll see a typical use of the If function.

This expression loads the c:Box function if it is not already loaded. The test function in this case is Not. Let's look at how you might apply If to another situation. In the following exercise, you will add an expression to the Box1 program that decides between drawing a two- or three-dimensional box.

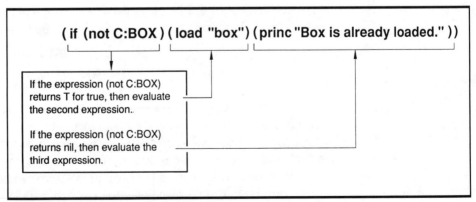

Figure 5.1: An expression showing the syntax of the If function

1. Open the BOX1.LSP file.

2. Change the first line of the Box1 program so it reads as follows:

(defun BOX1 (/ pt1 pt2 pt3 pt4)

By removing the c: from the function name, you allow Box1 to be called from other functions.

3. Change the first line of the 3dbox program so it reads as follows:

(defun 3DBOX (/ pt1 pt2 pt3 pt4h)

4. Add the program shown in boldface print in Figure 5.2 to the end of the BOX1.LSP file. Your BOX1.LSP file should now look like Figure 5.2.

You may have noticed the \n at the beginning of the Getstring prompt string. This is a code used in string values that tells AutoLISP to start a new line. The effect of adding this code to the prompt string is the prompt's appearance on a new line rather that its being appended to the current line.

Now print out BOX1.LSP and check it against Figure 5.2.

5. Save and exit BOX1.LSP.

6. Open an AutoCAD file called Chapt5. Be sure to use the = suffix with the drawing name.

7. Load the BOX1.LSP file along with the RXY.LSP file.

8. Run the Mainbox program by entering **mainbox** at the command prompt. You will see the following prompt:

Do you want a 3D box <Y = yes/Return = no>?

9. Enter y. The 3dbox function executes.

In this example, you first turned the programs c:Box1 and c:3dbox into functions by removing the c: from their names. Next, you created a control program called c:Mainbox that prompts the user to choose whether to make a three-dimensional box. The first line in the c:Mainbox program, as usual, gives the program its name and determines the local variables. The next line uses the Getstring function to obtain a

```
(defun getinfo ()
 (setq pt1 (getpoint "Pick first corner: "))
 (princ "Pick opposite corner: ")
 (setq pt3 (rxy))
)

(defun procinfo ()
 (setq pt2 (list (car pt3) (cadr pt1)))
 (setq pt4 (list (car pt1) (cadr pt3)))
)

(defun output ()
 (command "line" pt1 pt2 pt3 pt4 "c" )
)

(defun BOX1 (/ pt1 pt2 pt3 pt4)
 (getinfo)
 (procinfo)
 (output)
)

(defun 3DBOX (/ pt1 pt2 pt3 pt4 h)
  (getinfo)
  (setq h (getreal "Enter height of box: "))
  (procinfo)
  (output)
    (command "change" "Last" "" "Properties" "thickness" h ""
             "3dface" pt1 pt2 pt3 pt4 ""
             "3dface" ".xy" pt1 h ".xy" pt2 h
                      ".xy" pt3 h ".xy" pt4 h ""
    )
)

(defun C:3DWEDGE (/ pt1 pt2 pt3 pt4 h)
  (getinfo)
  (setq h (getreal "Enter height of wedge: "))
  (procinfo)
  (output)
    (command "3dface" pt1 pt4 ".xy" pt4 h ".xy" pt1 h pt2 pt3 ""
             "3dface" pt1 pt2 ".xy" pt1 h pt1 ""
             "copy" "L" "" pt1 pt4
    )
)

(defun C:MAINBOX (/ choose)
 (setq choose (getstring "\nDo you want a 3D box Y=yes/Return=no? "))
 (if (or (equal choose "y")(equal choose "Y"))(3dbox)(box1))
)
```

Figure 5.2: The BOX1.LSP file with c:Mainbox added

string value in response to a prompt:

(setq choose
      (getstring "\nDo you want a 3D box <Y = yes/Return = no>? "))

The third line uses the If function to determine whether to run Box1 or 3dbox. Notice how the Or and the Equal predicates are used together:

(if (or (equal choose "y")(equal choose "Y"))(3dbox)(box1))

The Or function returns T if any of its arguments returns anything other than nil. Two arguments are provided to Or. One tests to see if the variable Choose is equal to lowercase y, while the other checks to see if it's equal to uppercase Y. If the value of either expression is T, then Or returns T. So if the user responds with an upper- or lowercase y at the prompt in the second line, then Or returns T. Any other value for Choose will result in a nil value from Or (see Figure 5.3).

When Or returns T, If evaluates the second argument, executing the 3dbox function. When Or returns nil, If evaluates the third argument, executing the Box1 function.

The And function works in a similar way except it returns T only when *all* its arguments return non-nil values. Both Or and And will accept more than two arguments.

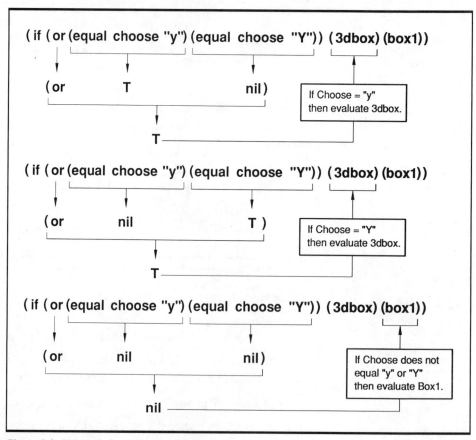

Figure 5.3: *Using the logical operator Or*

How To Make Several Expressions Act Like One

There will be times when you will want several expressions to be evaluated depending on the results of a predicate. As an example, let's assume that you have decided to make the two-dimensional and three-dimensional box functions part of the c:Mainbox program in order to save memory. You could place the code for these functions directly in the c:Mainbox program and create a file that looks like Figure 5.4. This program runs exactly like the previous one. But in Figure 5.4, the Box1 and 3dbox functions are incorporated into the If expression as arguments.

```
(defun C:MAINBOX (/ pt1 pt2 pt3 pt4 h choose)
(setq choose (getstring "\nDo you want a 3D box <Y=yes/Return=no>? "))
   (if (or (equal choose "y") (equal choose "Y"))
       (progn              ;if choose = Y or y then draw a 3D box
             (getinfo)
             (setq h (getreal "Enter height of box: "))
             (procinfo)
             (output)
             (command "change" "Last" "" "Properties" "thickness" h ""
                      "3dface" pt1 pt2 pt3 pt4 ""
                      "3dface" ".xy" pt1 h ".xy" pt2 h
                               ".xy" pt3 h ".xy" pt4 h ""
          );end command
      );end progn
       (progn              ;if choose /= Y or y then draw a 2D box
             (getinfo)
             (procinfo)
             (output)
       );end progn
    );end if
);end MAINBOX
```

Figure 5.4: The c:Mainbox program incorporating the code from Box1 and 3dbox

You can do this with the Progn function. Progn allows you to include several expressions where only one is expected. Its syntax is as follows:

(progn
> **(expression1) (expression2) (expression3)** . . .
)

Figure 5.5 shows how the program in Figure 5.4 was constructed. As you can see, the calls to Box1 and 3dbox were replaced by the actual expressions used in those functions.

```
(defun BOX1 (/ pt1 pt2 pt3 pt4)
(getinfo)
(procinfo)
(output)
)



(defun 3DBOX (/ pt1 pt2 pt3 pt4 h)
  (getinfo)
  (setq h (getreal "Enter height of box: "))
  (procinfo)
  (output)
    (command "change" "Last" "" "Properties" "thickness" h ""
         "3dface" pt1 pt2 pt3 pt4 ""
         "3dface" ".xy" pt1 h ".xy" pt2 h
              ".xy" pt3 h ".xy" pt4 h ""
    )
)



(defun C:MAINBOX (/ pt1 pt2 pt3 pt4 h choose)
(setq choose (getstring "\nDo you want a 3D box <Y=yes/Return=no>? "))
  (if (or (equal choose "y")(equal choose "Y"))
      (progn
        (getinfo)
        (setq h (getreal "Enter height of box: "))
        (procinfo)
        (output)
          (command "change" "Last" "" "Properties" "thickness" h ""
              "3dface" pt1 pt2 pt3 pt4 ""
              "3dface" ".xy" pt1 h ".xy" pt2 h
                  ".xy" pt3 h ".xy" pt4 h ""
          );end command
      );end progn
      (progn
            (getinfo)
            (procinfo)
            (output)
      );end progn
  );end if
)
```

Figure 5.5: How the Progn function is used

How to Test Multiple Conditions with Cond

Another function that acts very much like If is the Cond function. Arguments to Cond consist of one or more expressions that each include a test expression followed by an object to be evaluated if the test returns T. Cond performs each test until it comes to one that returns T. It then evaluates the expression or atom associated with that test and ignores any other test expressions that may follow.

The syntax for Cond is as follows:

(cond

      ((*test_expression*) *expression/atom expression/atom...*)

      ((*test_expression*) *expression/atom expression/atom...*)

        .

        .

        .

)

Figure 5.6 shows how the Cond function can be used in place of If. As Cond's syntax allows for more than one argument for each test expression, you don't have to use the Progn function with Cond if you want several expressions evaluated as a result of a test.

Figure 5.7 shows another program called Chaos that uses the Cond function. Chaos is an AutoLISP version of a mathemetical game used to demonstrate the creation of fractals through an iterated function. The game works by following the steps shown in Figure 5.8.

The Chaos program automates this process, thereby allowing you to see the result of this seemingly random placement of points.

The program first defines three points and then prompts the user to pick a point. Any point will do. Another function, Rand, is used to derive a random number. This Rand function acts like a single die.

```
(defun C:MAINBOX (/ choose)
 (setq choose (getstring "\nDo you want a 3D box <Y=yes/Return=no>? "))
   (cond
       ( (or (equal choose "y") (equal choose "Y")) (3dbox))
       ( (or (/= choose "y") (/= choose "Y"))  (box1))
   )
 )
```

Figure 5.6: *Using Cond in place of If*

```
;function to find the midpoint between two points
(defun mid (a b)
 (list (/ (+ (car a)(car b)) 2)
       (/ (+ (cadr a)(cadr b)) 2)
 )
)

;function to generate random number
(defun rand (pt / rns rleng lastrn)
 (setq rns (rtos (* (car pt)(cadr pt)(getvar "tdusrtimer"))))
 (setq rnleng (strlen rns))
 (setq lastrn (substr rns rnleng 1))
 (setq rn (* 0.6 (atof lastrn)))
 (fix rn)
)

;The Chaos game
(defun C:CHAOS (/ pta ptb ptc rn count lastpt randn key)
 (setq pta '( 2.0000 1 ))                      ;define point a
 (setq ptb '( 7.1962 10))                      ;define point b
 (setq ptc '(12.3923 1 ))                      ;define point c
 (setq lastpt (getpoint "Pick a start point:")) ;pick a point to start
 (while (/= key 3)                             ;while pick button not pushed
  (setq randn (rand lastpt))                   ;get random number
  (cond                                        ;find midpoint to a b or c
   ( (= randn 0)(setq lastpt (mid lastpt pta)) ) ;use corner a if 0
   ( (= randn 1)(setq lastpt (mid lastpt pta)) ) ;use corner a if 1
   ( (= randn 2)(setq lastpt (mid lastpt ptb)) ) ;use corner b if 2
   ( (= randn 3)(setq lastpt (mid lastpt ptb)) ) ;use corner b if 3
   ( (= randn 4)(setq lastpt (mid lastpt ptc)) ) ;use corner c if 4
   ( (= randn 5)(setq lastpt (mid lastpt ptc)) ) ;use corner c if 5
  );end cond
  (grdraw lastpt lastpt 5)                     ;draw midpoint
  (setq key (car (grread T)))                  ;test for pick
 );end while
);end Chaos
```

Figure 5.7: The Chaos game program

Once a random number is derived, the Cond function is used to compare the numbers value against integers from 0 to 5. When a match is found, the appropriate midpoint is located and a point is placed there. Then the whole process is repeated using the newly found point as the reference for the next point. The Grread function allows the user to stop the game by picking a point on the screen with a mouse or digitizer.

Cond can be used anywhere you would use If. For example,

(if (not C:BOX) (load "box") (princ "Box is already loaded. "))

can be written

(cond
        ((not C:BOX) (load "box"))
        (C:BOX (princ "Box is already loaded. "))
)

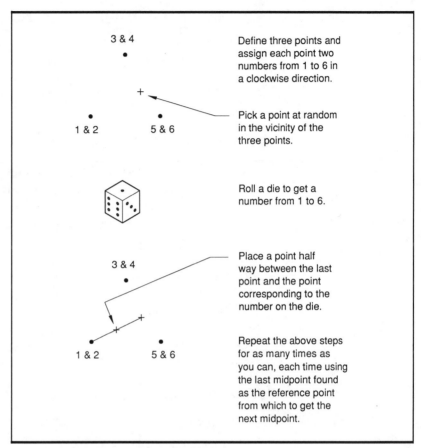

3 & 4

Define three points and
assign each point two
numbers from 1 to 6 in
a clockwise direction.

Pick a point at random
in the vicinity of the
three points.

1 & 2   5 & 6

Roll a die to get a
number from 1 to 6.

3 & 4

Place a point half
way between the last
point and the point
corresponding to the
number on the die.

Repeat the above steps
for as many times as
you can, each time using
the last midpoint found
as the reference point
from which to get the
next midpoint.

1 & 2   5 & 6

Figure 5.8: *How to play the Chaos game*

Cond is actually the primary conditional function of AutoLISP.
The If function is offered as an alternative to Cond since it is similar to
conditional functions used in other programming languages. Since the
If function syntax is simpler and often more readable, you may want
to use it where the special features of Cond are not required.

How to Repeat Parts of a Program

Another useful aspect of a language such as AutoLISP is its ability
to perform repetitive tasks. For example, suppose you want to record

a series of keyboard entries as a macro. One way to do this would be to use a series of Getstring functions:

```
(Setq str1 (getstring "\nEnter macro: "))
(Setq str2 (getstring "\nEnter macro: "))
(Setq str3 (getstring "\nEnter macro: "))
(Setq str4 (getstring "\nEnter macro: "))
    .
    .
    .
```

All of the Str variables could then be combined to form one variable storing the keystrokes. Unfortunately, this method is inflexible. It requires that the user input a fixed number of entries, no more and no less. Also, this method would use a lot of memory storing each keyboard entry as a single variable.

You need a way to read keyboard input continually. The While function can be used to repeat a prompt and obtain data from the user until some test condition is met.

Another function, Repeat, acts in a similar way to While. Repeat will evaluate a set of expressions repeatedly for a specific number of times. This repetitive evaluation of a set of functions is called *iteration*.

*U*sing the While Function

The syntax for While is

```
(while (test_expression)
    (expression1)(expression2)(expression3) ...
)
```

The first argument to While is a test expression. Any number of expressions can follow. These following expressions are evaluated repeatedly as long as the test returns a non-nil value.

The program in Figure 5.9 is a keyboard macro program that uses the While function. In the following exercise you'll use this program to create a keyboard macro that changes the last object drawn in the Chapt5 file, which you created earlier in this chapter.

1. Open an AutoLISP file called MACRO.LSP and copy the contents of Figure 5.9 into this file. Since this is a larger program file than you have worked with previously, you should

```
;Program to create keyboard macros -- Macro.lsp

(defun C:MACRO (/ str1 def macro macname)
(setq macro '(command))                               ;start list with command
(setq macname (getstring "\nEnter name of macro: "))  ;get name of macro
   (while (/= str1 "/")                               ;do while str1 not eq. /
      (setq str1 (getstring "\nEnter macro or / to exit: " ))  ;get keystrokes
      (if (= str1 "/")
         (princ "\nEnd of macro ")                    ;if / then print message
         (Setq macro (append macro (list str1)))      ;else append keystrokes to
      );end if                                         macro list
   );end while
(eval (list 'defun (read macname) '() macro))         ;create function
);end macro
```

Figure 5.9: A program to create keyboard macros

print it out and check your printout against the figure to make sure you haven't made any transcription errors.

2. Go back to the Chapt5 drawing.

3. Draw a diagonal line from the lower-left corner of the drawing area to the upper-right corner.

4. Load the MACRO.LSP file.

5. Enter **macro** at the command prompt.

6. At the prompt

   Enter name of macro:

   enter **chlt**.

7. Then at the prompt

   Enter macro or / to exit:

   enter the word **change**.

8. The "Enter macro" prompt appears again. Enter the following series of words at the series of prompts that appears:

   l
   ↵

   p
   lt
   hidden
   ↵
   /

Here you see the While function in action. As you enter each response at the prompt, While tests to see if you entered a slash. If not, it evaluates the expressions included as its arguments. When you enter the slash, While ends the repetition and you get the prompt

End of macro CHLT

The commands you entered at the prompt are exactly what you would have entered to use the Change command normally.

9. Now run your macro by entering

(chlt)

The line you drew changes to the hidden linetype.

When Macro starts, it first defines a variable named Macro:

(setq macro '(command))

Macro is a list variable that is used to store the keystrokes of the macro. Its first element is the Command function. Your keystrokes will be appended to this list and it will eventually become a command expression.

The next line prompts the user to enter a name for the macro:

(setq macname (getstring "\nEnter name of macro: "))

The entered name is then stored with the variable Macname.

Finally, there is the While function:

(while (/ = str1 "/")

The While expression is broken into several lines. The first line contains the While function itself along with the test expression. In this case, the test compares the variable Str1 with the string "/" to see if they are not equal. So long as Str1 is not equal to "/" While will repeatedly execute the arguments that follow the test.

The next four lines are the expressions to be evaluated. The first of these lines prompts the user to enter text that is an element of the macro:

(setq str1 (getstring "\nEnter macro or / to exit: "))

When the user enters a value at this prompt, it is assigned to the variable Str1. The next line uses an If function to test whether Str1 is equal to "/":

(if (= str1 "/")

If the test results in T, the next line prints the string "End of macro".

(princ "\nEnd of macro ")

If the test results in nil, the following line appends the value of Str1 to the variable Macro:

(Setq macro (append macro (list str1)))

The Append function takes one list and appends its contents to the end of another list. In this case whatever is entered at the "Enter macro" prompt is appended to the variable Macro, creating a list of keyboard entries to be saved (see Figure 5.10).

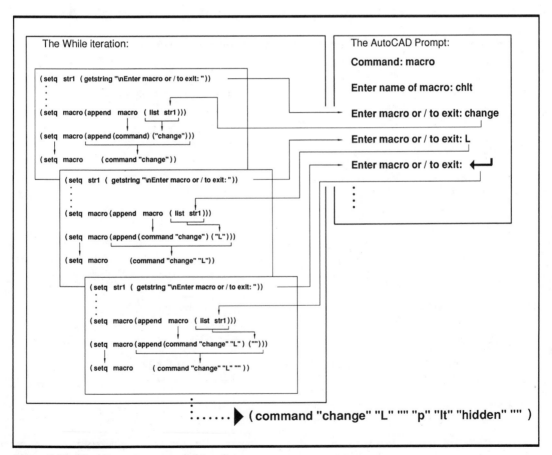

Figure 5.10: *How items are appended to a list*

The next two lines close the If and While expressions. Note that the comments help make the program easier to understand:

```
);end if
);end while
```

The last line combines all the elements of the program into an expression that, when evaluated, creates a new macro program:

```
(eval (list 'defun (read macname) '() macro))
)
```

Figure 5.11 shows how this last line works.

The Read function used in this expression converts a string value into a symbol. If the string argument to be read contains any spaces,

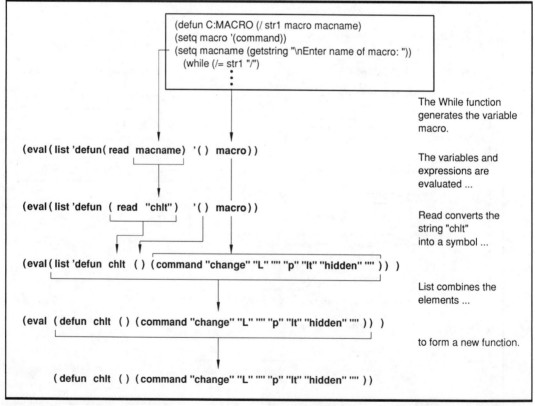

Figure 5.11: *How the macro is defined*

Read will convert the first part of the string and ignore everything after the first space.

The While expression does not need to include prompts for user input. Figure 5.12 shows a simple program that produces an increasing sequence of numbers in the drawing area. Each number is 1 greater than the last and they are spaced 0.5 units apart. The user is prompted for a starting point and a first and last number. Once the user enters this information, the program calculates the first number to be inserted, inserts it using the Text command, then calculates the next number, and so on until the last number is reached. (This program expects the current text style to have a height of 0.)

```
;Program to draw sequential numbers -- Seq.lsp
(defun C:SEQ (/ pt1 currnt last)
(setq pt1   (getpoint "\nPick start point: "))
(setq currnt (getint "\nEnter first number: "))
(setq last   (getint "\nEnter last number: "))
(command "text" pt1 "" "" currnt)            ;write first number
  (while (< currnt last)                      ;while not last number
    (setq currnt (1+ currnt))                 ;get next number
    (command "text" "@.5<0" "" "" currnt)     ;write value of currnt
  );end while
);end seq
```

Figure 5.12: A sequential number program using While

Using the Repeat Function

Another function that performs iterations is the Repeat function. Repeat works in a similar way to While but instead of using a predicate to determine whether to evaluate its arguments, Repeat uses an integer value to determine the number of times to perform an evaluation. The syntax for repeat is

(repeat *n*

    (expression1) (expression2) (expression3) ...

)

The *n* above can be an integer or a symbol representing an integer.

The program in Figure 5.13 shows a version of the sequential number program in Figure 5.12 that uses Repeat instead of While. This program appears to the user to act in the same way as the program that uses While.

```
;Program to write sequential numbers using Repeat
(defun C:SEQ (/ pt1 currnt last)
(setq pt1 (getpoint "\nPick start point: "))
(setq currnt (getint "\nEnter first number: "))
(setq last   (getint "\nEnter last number: "))
(command "text" pt1 "" "" currnt)                  ;write first number
  (repeat (- last currnt)                          ;repeat last - currnt times
    (setq currnt (1+ currnt))                      ;add 1 to currnt
    (command "text" "@.5<0" "" "" currnt)          ;write value of currnt
  );end repeat
);end seq
```

Figure 5.13: A sequential number program using Repeat

Using Test Expressions

So far, I have shown you functions that perform evaluations based on the result of some test. In all the examples, I used predicates and logical operators to test values. While predicates and logical operators are most commonly used for tests, you are not strictly limited to these functions. Any expression that can evaluate to nil can also be used as a test expression. Since virtually all expressions are capable of returning nil, this means you can use almost any expression as a test expression. The function in Figure 5.14 demonstrates this point.

This function gives the user a running tally of distances. The user is prompted to pick a distance or press ◄— to exit. If a point is picked, the user is prompted for a second point. The distance between these two points is then displayed at the prompt. The "Pick distance" prompt appears again and, if the user picks another pair of points, the second distance is added to the first and the total distance is displayed. This continues until the user presses ◄—.

```
;Program to measure non-sequential distances -- Mdist.lsp
(Defun C:MDIST (/ dstlst dst)
(setq dstlst '(+ ))                                ;create list with plus
  ;while a return is not entered ...
  (while (setq dst (getdist "\nPick point or Return to exit: "))
       (Setq dstlst (append dstlst (list dst)))   ;append distance value
       (princ (Eval dstlst))                      ;print value of list
  );end while
);end mdist
```

Figure 5.14: The Mdist function

As usual, the first line defines the function. The second line creates a variable called Dstlst and gives it the list value (+ 0):

```
(defun MDIST (/ dstlst dst)
(setq dstlst '(+ 0))
```

The next line begins the While portion of the program. Instead of a predicate test, however, this expression uses a Setq expression:

```
(while (setq dst (getdist "\nPick point or Return to exit: "))
```

As long as points are being picked, Getdist returns a non-nil value to Setq and While repeats the evaluation of its arguments. When the user presses ←⏎, Getdist returns nil and While quits evaluating its arguments. Although the test expression in this example returns values other than T, While is really only concerned with whether a value is nil.

The next few lines append the current distance to the list Dstlst and then evaluate the list to obtain a total:

```
(Setq dstlst (append dstlst (list dst)))
(princ (eval dstlst))
```

The function Princ prints the value obtained from the (eval dstlst) expression at the prompt.

*S*ummary

You have now been introduced to several of the most useful functions available in AutoLISP. You can begin to create functions and programs that will perform time-consuming, repetitive tasks quickly and easily. You can also build some intelligence into your programs by using decision-making functions. You may want to try your hand at modifying the programs in this chapter. For example, you could try to modify the Mdist function to save the total distance as a global variable you can later recall.

In the next chapter, you will get a brief refresher course in geometry.

6

Solving Graphics Problems with Trigonometric Programs

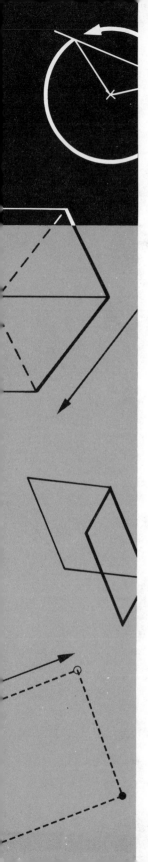

6

Your work with AutoLISP will inevitably involve some geometric manipulations. With the Box program in Chapter 2, you have already created a function that derives new point locations based on user input. You learned how to take coordinate lists apart and then reassemble them to produce new coordinates. In this chapter, I will introduce other AutoLISP functions that will help you determine locations in your drawings' coordinate systems. In the process you will review some basic geometry and trigonometry.

How to Find Angles and Distances

In Chapter 4, you learned how to prompt the user for angles and distances. At times, however, you will want to find angles and distances based on the location of existing point variables rather than user input.

Suppose you want to devise a function that breaks two parallel lines between two points in a manner similar to the standard AutoCAD Break command. In addition, you would like this function to draw lines that would join the ends of the two broken lines to form an opening. A function similar to this is commonly used with architectural drawings to place an opening in a wall. Figure 6.1 shows a drawing of the process along with a description of what must occur. This description can be developed into pseudocode for your program.

In the following exercise you'll create and use this parallel-line break program. In Chapter 3, I discussed the importance of designing your programs so that they are simple to use. This program is designed to obtain the information needed to perform its task with a minimum of user input. Since it is similar to the Break command, it also tries to mimic the Break program to some degree so the user feels comfortable with it. As you work through this exercise, pay special attention to the way information is gathered and used to accomplish the final result.

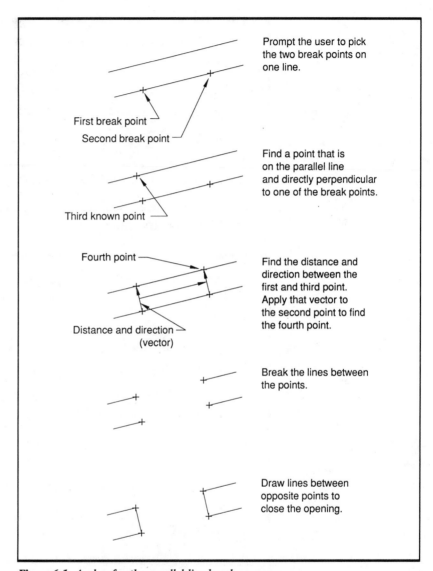

Figure 6.1: A plan for the parallel-line break program

1. Open an AutoLISP file called BREAK2.LSP and copy the program listed in Figure 6.2.

2. Open a new AutoCAD file called Chapt6. Draw a line from point 2, 4 to point 12, 4 and then offset that line 0.25 units. Your screen should look like Figure 6.3.

```
(defun c:break2 (/ pt1 pt2 pt3 pt4 pt0 ang1 dst1)
   (setvar "osmode" 512)                             ;near osnap mode
   (setq pt1 (getpoint "\nSelect object: "))         ;get first break point
   (setq pt2 (getpoint pt1 "\nEnter second point: ")) ;get second break point
   (setvar "osmode" 128)                             ;perpend osnap mode
   (Setq pt3 (getpoint pt1 "\nSelect parallel line: ")) ;get 2nd line
   (Setvar "osmode" 0)                               ;no osnap mode
   (setq ang1 (angle pt1 pt3))                       ;find angle btwn lines
   (setq dst1 (distance pt1 pt3))                    ;find dist. btwn lines
   (setq pt4 (polar pt2 ang1 dst1))                  ;derive pt4 on 2nd line
      (command
            "break" pt1 pt2                           ;break 1st line
            "break" pt3 pt4                           ;break 2nd line
            "line" pt1 pt3 ""                         ;close ends of lines
            "line" pt2 pt4 ""
      )
)
```

Figure 6.2: The parallel-line break program

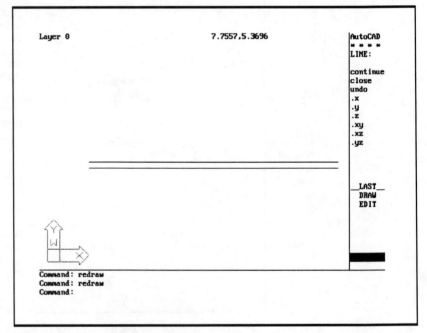

Figure 6.3: Two parallel lines drawn

3. Load the BREAK2.LSP file and enter **break2** at the command prompt.

4. At the "Select object" prompt the Osnap cursor appears. Pick the lowermost line near coordinates 5, 4.

5. At the "Enter second point" prompt pick the lowermost line near coordinates 10, 4.

6. Finally, at the "Select parallel line" prompt pick the upper line near its midpoint. The two lines break and are joined at their break points to form an opening (see Figure 6.4).

Now draw several parallel lines at different orientations and try the Break2 program on each pair of lines. Break2 places an opening in a pair of parallel lines regardless of their orientation. Let's look at how Break2 accomplishes this.

*U*sing the Angle Function

The first line after the Defun line uses the Setvar function to set Osnap to the Nearest mode:

(setvar "osmode" 512)

Osmode is the system variable that controls the Osnap mode. This

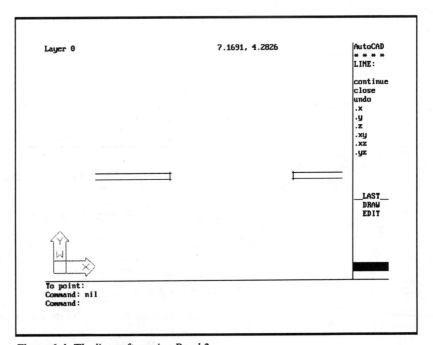

Figure 6.4: The lines after using Break2

expression ensures that the point the user picks at the next prompt is exactly on the line. It also gives the user a visual cue to pick something, since the Osnap cursor appears.

When Setvar is used with the Osmode system variable, a numeric code (512 in this case) must also be supplied. This code determines the Osnap mode to be used. Table 6.1 shows a list of the codes and their meaning.

Table 6.1: *Numeric Codes to Set the Osnap Mode*

CODE	EQUIVALENT OSNAP MODE
0	None
1	Endpoint
2	Midpoint
4	Center
8	Node
16	Quadrant
32	Intersection
64	Insertion
128	Perpendicular
256	Tangent
512	Nearest
1024	Quick

The next line prompts the user to select an object using the Getpoint function:

```
(setq pt1 (getpoint "\nSelect object: "))
```

Here, the variable Pt1 is used to store the first point location for the break. Since the Nearest Osnap mode is used, the point picked falls exactly on the line (see Figure 6.5).

Next, the user is prompted to pick another point:

```
(setq pt2 (getpoint pt1 "\nEnter second point: "))
```

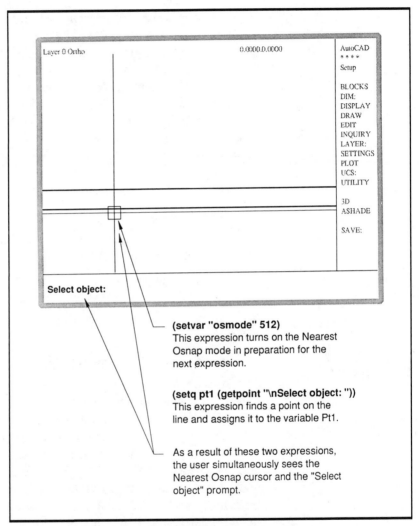

Figure 6.5: *Getting a point using the Nearest Osnap mode*

The variable Pt2 is assigned a point location for the other end of the break. The next line

(setvar "osmode" 128)

sets the Osnap mode to Perpendicular in preparation for the next prompt:

(Setq pt3 (getpoint pt1 "\nSelect parallel line: "))

Here, the user is asked to select a line parallel to the first line. The user can pick any point along the parallel line. The Perpendicular Osnap mode ensures that the point picked on the parallel line, Pt3, defines a perpendicular direction from the point stored by the variable Pt1. The Perpendicular Osnap mode requires that a point argument be supplied to the Getpoint function. In this case, the point Pt1 is supplied as a reference from which the perpendicular location on the parallel line is to be found (see Figure 6.6). This new point variable, Pt3, will be important in calculating the location of the two break points on the parallel line.

The next line sets the Osnap mode back to None:

(Setvar "osmode" 0)

The next two lines find the angle and distance described by the two point variables Pt1 and Pt3.

(setq ang1 (angle pt1 pt3))
(setq dst1 (distance pt1 pt3))

You can obtain the angle described by two points using the Angle function. Angle's syntax is

(angle *coordinate_list coordinate_list*)

The arguments to Angle are always coordinate lists. The lists can either be variables or quoted lists.

Angle returns a value in radians. You worked with radians briefly in Chapter 4. A *radian* is the unit of angle measure in a system based on a circle with a 1-unit radius. In such a circle, an angle can be described as a distance along the circle's circumference. You may recall from high school geometry that a circle's circumference is equal to 2 times pi times its radius (since the hypothetical circle has a radius of 1, we drop the radius from the equation):

circumference = 2pi

90 degrees is equal to one quarter the circumference of the circle, or pi/2 radians, or 1.5708 (see Figure 6.7). 180 degrees is equal to half the circumference of a circle, or pi radians, or 3.14159. 360 degrees is equal to the full circumference of the circle, or 2 pi radians, or 6.28319. A simple formula to convert radians to degrees is

radians * 57.2958

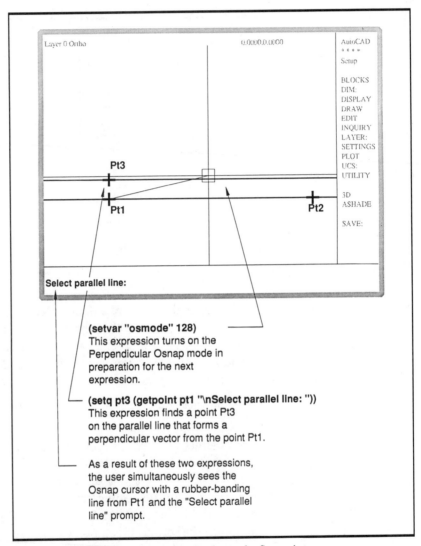

Figure 6.6: Picking the point perpendicular to the first point

To convert degrees to radians, the formula is

degrees * 0.0174533

Angle uses the current UCS orientation as its basis for determining angles. Though you can supply three-dimensional point values to

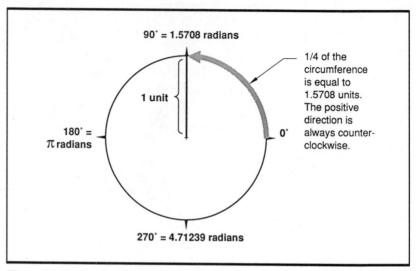

Figure 6.7: Comparing degrees and radians

Angle, the angle it returns will be based on a two-dimensional projection of those points on the current UCS. Finally, radians are always measured with a counterclockwise direction being positive.

The Distance function is similar to Angle in that it requires two point lists for arguments:

(distance *coordinate_list coordinate_list*)

The value returned by distance is in drawing units regardless of the current Units style setting. This means that if you have the units set to architectural, Distance will still return distances in 1-inch units.

By storing the angle and distance values based on Pt1 and Pt3, the program can now determine the location of the second break point on the parallel line. This is done by applying this angle and distance information to the second break point of the first line using the following expression:

(setq pt4 (polar pt2 ang1 dst1))

Here the angle variable Ang1 and the distance variable Dst1 are used as arguments to the Polar function to find a point Pt4. Polar returns a point value (see Figure 6.8).

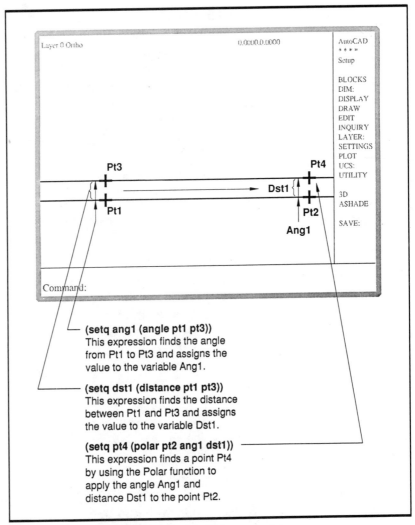

Figure 6.8: Using the Polar function to find a new point

*F*inding Relative Point Locations with the Polar Function

The syntax for Polar is

(polar *point_value angle_in_radians distance*)

Polar is used to find relative point locations. It requires a point value as its first argument followed by angle and distance values. The new point value is calculated by applying the angle and distance to the point value supplied. This is similar to describing a relative location in AutoCAD using @. For example, to describe a relative location of .25 units at 90 degrees from the last point entered, you would type the following in AutoCAD:

```
@.25<90
```

The same relative location can be described using the Polar function as follows:

```
(setq pt1 (getvar "lastpoint"))
(polar pt1 1.5708 .25)
```

The first expression in this example uses the Getvar function to obtain the last point selected. Setq then assigns that point to the variable Pt1. Polar is used in the next line to find a point that is 1.5708 radians (90 degrees) and .25 units away from Pt1.

The last several lines of the Break2 program use all the point variables to first break the two lines and then draw the joining lines between them:

```
(command
    "break" pt1 pt2
    "break" pt3 pt4
    "line" pt1 pt3 ""
    "line" pt2 pt4 ""
)
```

You could have used the Getdist and Getangle functions in the Break2 program, but to do so would have meant including an additional prompt. By using the combination of the Perpendicular Osnap mode along with the Getpoint function, you establish a point value from which both the angle and distance value is derived. In general, if you know that you will need to gather both distance and angle information, it is better to establish coordinate variables first and then derive angles and distances from those coordinates using the Angle and Distance functions.

Using Trigonometry to Solve a Problem

The Break2 function is relatively simple as far as its manipulation of data is concerned. At times you will need to enlist the aid of some basic trigonometric functions to solve problems. Suppose you want a function that will cut a circle along an axis defined by the user. Figure 6.9 shows a sketch along with a written description of a program that does this.

This program makes use of the Pythagorean theorem as well as the sine trigonometric function, as you will see in the next section.

In this section you use some basic trigonometric functions, but first you'll learn how to gather information that you'll need in order to use these functions.

Gathering Information

Before a problem can be solved, you must first gather all the known factors affecting the problem. The program you will explore next, the circle-cutting program described above, will give an example of how you might go about your information gathering.

1. Exit from AutoCAD and open an AutoLISP file called CUTCR.LSP. Carefully copy the program in Figure 6.10 into this file.

2. Save and exit the CUTCR.LSP file and then start AutoCAD and open the Chapt6 drawing again.

3. Load the CUTCR.LSP file.

4. Erase everything on the screen and draw a circle with a radius of 3 units and its center at 8, 6 (see Figure 6.11).

5. Enter **cutcr** at the command prompt to start the Cutcr program.

6. At the prompt

   Pick circle to cut:

   pick the circle you just drew.

7. At the next prompt

   Pick first point of cut line:

   pick a point at coordinates 5, 9.

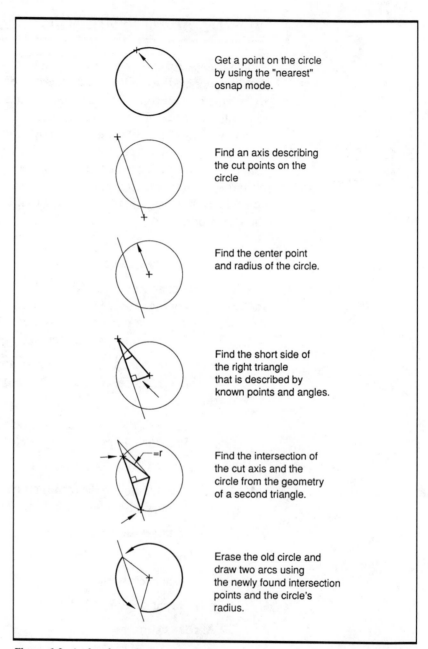

Figure 6.9: *A plan for a circle-cutting program*

```
;Program to cut a circle into two arcs -- Cutcr.lsp
(defun C:CUTCR (/ cpt1 lpt1 lpt2 cent rad1 ang1
                  dst1 dst2 cord ang2 wkpt cpt2 cpt3)
  (setvar "osmode" 512)                               ;osnap to nearest
  (setq cpt1 (getpoint "\nPick circle to cut: "))     ;find point on circle
  (setvar "osmode" 0)                                 ;osnap to none
  (setq lpt1 (getpoint "\nPick first point of cut line: ")) ;1st point of cut
  (setq lpt2 (getpoint lpt1 "\nPick second point: "))      ;2nd point of cut
  (setq cent (osnap cpt1 "center"))                   ;find center pt
  (setq rad1 (distance cpt1 cent))                    ;find radius of circle
  (setq ang1 (- (angle lpt1 cent)(angle lpt1 lpt2)))  ;find difference of angles
  (setq dst1 (distance lpt1 cent))                    ;find dist.lpt1 to cent
  (setq dst2 (* dst1 (sin ang1)))                     ;find side of triangle
  (setq cord (sqrt(-(* rad1 rad1)(* dst2 dst2))))     ;find half cord
  (setq ang2 (- (angle lpt1 lpt2) 1.57))              ;find perpend angle
  (setq wkpt (polar cent ang2 dst2))                  ;find workpoint
  (setq cpt2 (polar wkpt (angle lpt1 lpt2) cord))     ;find first intersect
  (setq cpt3 (polar wkpt (angle lpt2 lpt1) cord))     ;find second intersect
  (command "erase" cpt1 ""                            ;erase circle
           "arc" "c" cent cpt2 cpt3                   ;draw first circle seg.
           "arc" "c" cent cpt3 cpt2                   ;draw second circle seg.
  )                                                   ;close command funct.
)                                                     ;close defun
```

Figure 6.10: *The circle-cutting program*

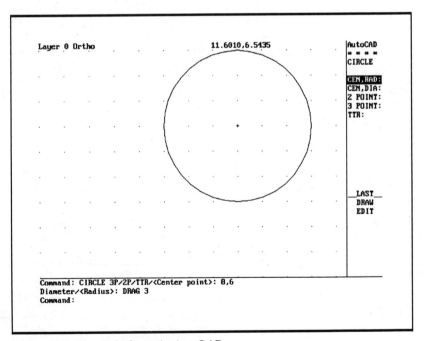

Figure 6.11: *The circle drawn in AutoCAD*

8. Then at the prompt

    Pick second point:

    pick a point at coordinates 8, 2 (see Figure 6.12). The circle is cut into two arcs along the axis represented by the two points you picked.

9. Use the Erase command to erase the left half of the circle. You can now see that the circle has been cut (see Figure 6.13).

Let's take a closer look at how the circle-cutting program works. The first three expressions in the program after the Defun function and its arguments obtain a point on the circle:

```
(setvar "osmode" 512)
(setq cpt1 (getpoint "\nPick circle to cut: "))
(setvar "osmode" 0)
```

The Setvar function sets the Osnap to the Nearest mode. Then the user is prompted to pick the circle to cut and this point is stored as Cpt1.

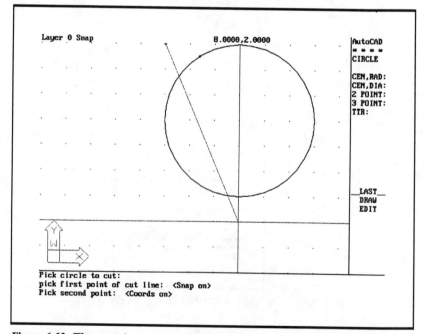

Figure 6.12: The cut axis

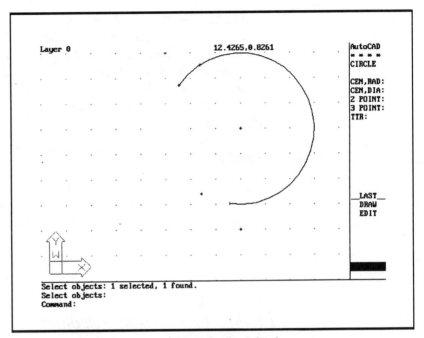

Figure 6.13: Erasing one part of the circle after it has been cut

The Osnap mode ensures that the point picked is exactly on the circle. Later, this point will be used to both erase the circle and to find the circle's center. The next function sets the Osnap back to None.

The next two lines prompt the user to select the points that define the axis along which the circle is to be cut:

```
(setq lpt1 (getpoint "\nPick first point of cut line: "))
(setq lpt2 (getpoint lpt1 "\nPick second point: "))
```

The Getpoint function is used in both these expressions to obtain the endpoints of the cut axis. These endpoints are stored as Lpt1 and Lpt2.

The next expression uses a new function called Osnap:

```
(setq cent (osnap cpt1 "center"))
```

Here the point on the circle picked previously, Cpt1, is used in conjunction with the Osnap function to obtain the center point of the circle. The syntax for Osnap is

```
(osnap point_value osnap_mode)
```

The Osnap function acts in the same way as the Osnap overrides in AutoCAD. If you use the Center Osnap override and pick a point on the circle, you'll get the center of the circle. Likewise, the Osnap function takes a point value and applies an Osnap mode to it to obtain another point. In this case, Osnap applies the Center override to the point Cpt1, which is located on the circle, returns the center of the circle, and assigns it to the symbol Cent.

The next expression obtains the circle's radius with the Distance function:

(setq rad1 (distance cpt1 cent))

The Distance function gets the distance between Cpt1, the point located on the circle, and Cent, the center of the circle. This value is assigned to the symbol Rad1.

Finding Points Using Trigonometry

At this point, you have all the known points you can obtain without using some math. Ultimately, you want to find the intersection point between the circle and the cut axis. With some basic trigonometric functions you can derive the relationship between the sides of a triangle. In particular, you want to look for triangles that contain right angles. If you analyze the known elements of this problem, you can see that two triangles can be used to find one intersection on the circle (see Figure 6.14).

In this analysis, you see that you can find a point along the cut axis that describes the corner of a right triangle. To find this point, you only need an angle and the length of the hypotenuse of the triangle. Figure 6.15 shows some basic trigonometric functions and the information that is required to use them.

The sine function will be most useful with the information you have:

sine(angle) = opposite side / hypotenuse

However, this formula has to be modified using some basic algebra to suit our needs:

opposite side = hypotenuse * sine(angle)

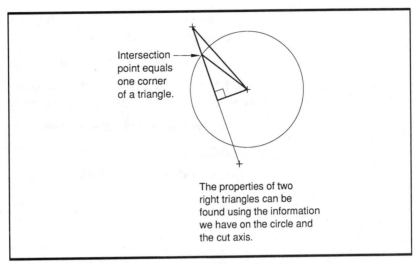

Figure 6.14: Triangles used to find the intersection

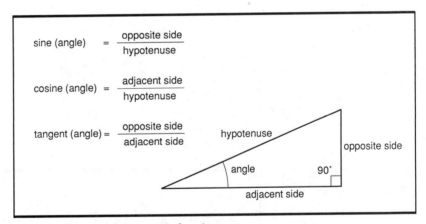

Figure 6.15: Basic trigonometric functions

Before you can use the sine function, you need to find the angle formed by points Lpt2, Lpt1, and Cent (see Figure 6.16). The following function does this for us:

(setq ang1 (- (angle lpt1 cent) (angle lpt1 lpt2)))

The first of these three functions finds the angle of the line between Lpt1 and Lpt2. The second expression finds the angle from Lpt1 to the center of the circle. The third line finds the difference between these two angles (see Figure 6.17).

You also need the length of the hypotenuse of the triangle. This is the distance between Lpt1 and the center of the triangle:

(setq dst1 (distance lpt1 cent))

The length of the hypotenuse is saved as the variable Dst1. You can now apply the angle and hypotenuse to the formula:

opposite side = hypotenuse * sine (angle)

becomes

(setq dst2 (* dst1 (sin ang1)))

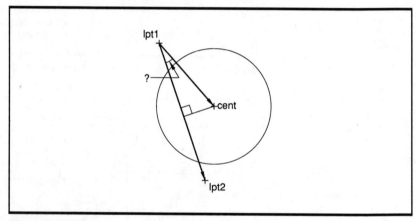

Figure 6.16: The angle needed for the sine function

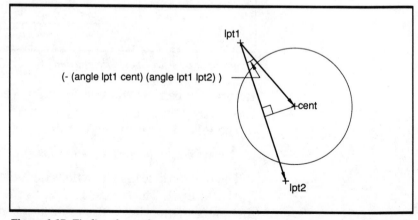

Figure 6.17: Finding the angle

Now you have the length of the side of the triangle, but we need to know the direction of that side in order to find the corner point of the triangle. You already know that the direction is at a right angle to the cut axis. Therefore, you can determine the right angle to the cut axis by subtracting 1.5708 radians, which is 90 degrees, from the cut-axis angle (see Figure 6.18). The following expression does this:

(setq ang2 (- (angle lpt1 lpt2) 1.5708))

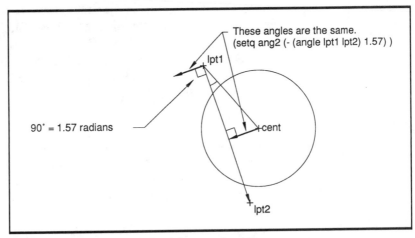

Figure 6.18: Finding the angle of the opposite side

You are now able to place the missing corner of the triangle using the Polar function (see Figure 6.19):

(setq wkpt (polar cent ang2 dst2))

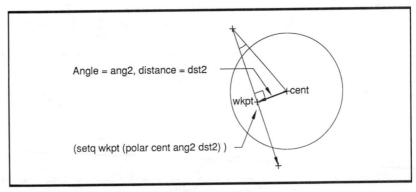

Figure 6.19: Finding the missing corner

This expression assigns the corner-point location to the variable Wkpt.

The math exercise is not finished, however. You still need to find the intersection of the cut axis and the circle. Looking at the problem-solving sketch, you can see that the problem can be solved with yet another triangle. You know that the intersection lies along the cut axis, so you can describe a triangle whose corner is defined by the intersection of the circle and the cut axis (see Figure 6.20).

You already know the lengths of two of the sides of this new triangle. One is the radius of the circle, stored as Rad1. The other is the side of the triangle used earlier, stored as Dst2. The most direct way to locate the intersection is to find the length of the third side with the Pythagorean theorem, which is illustrated in Figure 6.21.

Again you must apply algebra to derive a formula to suit your needs. The formula

$$a^2 = b^2 + c^2$$

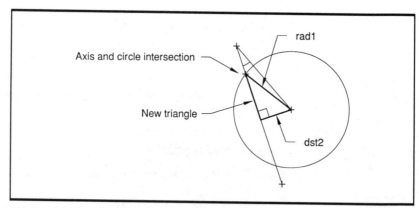

Figure 6.20: The triangle describing one intersection point

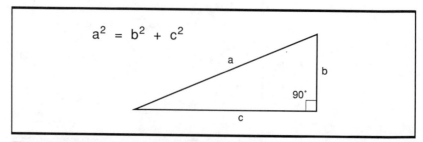

Figure 6.21: The Pythagorean theorem

becomes the expression

(setq cord (sqrt(-(* rad1 rad1)(* dst2 dst2)))))

This assigns the distance value from the Pythagorean theorem to the variable Cord. Using the Polar function, you can now find one intersection point between the circle and the cut axis:

(setq cpt2 (polar wkpt (angle lpt2 lpt1) cord))

This expression derives one intersection by applying the angle described by Lpt1 and Lpt2 and the distance stored as Cord to the Polar functions (see Figure 6.22).

A basic theorem in geometry states that a diameter that is perpendicular to a chord bisects the chord and its arc. The line segment described by the center of the circle and the point Wkpt is on a diameter of the circle. This diameter is perpendicular to the chord

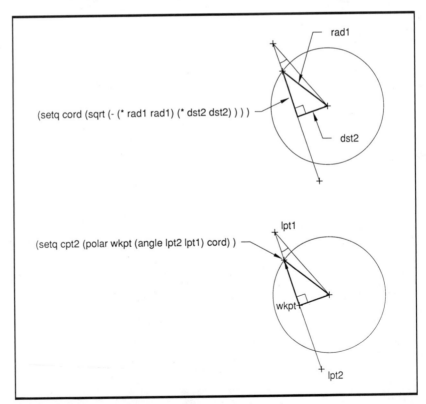

Figure 6.22: Finding the location of an intersection point

described by Lpt1 and Lpt2. Applying this theorem to the problem, you know that Wkpt bisects the chord described by Lpt1 and Lpt2. Therefore, you can find the second intersection point by reversing the direction of the angle in the previous expression:

(setq cpt3 (polar wkpt (angle lpt1 lpt2) cord))

Finally, you can get AutoCAD to do the actual work of cutting the circle:

```
(command "erase" cpt1 ""
            "arc" "c" cent cpt2 cpt3
            "arc" "c" cent cpt3 cpt2
)
```

Actually, you don't really cut the circle. Instead, the circle is erased entirely and replaced with two arcs (see Figure 6.23).

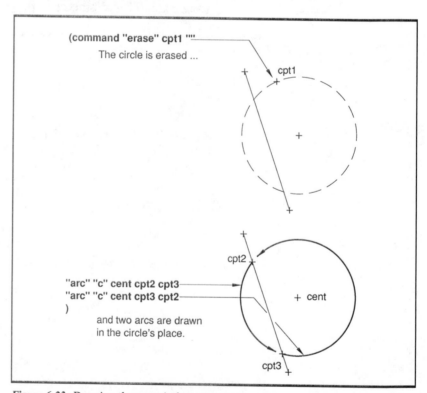

Figure 6.23: Drawing the new circle as two arcs

Finally, if you feel comfortable with algebra you may want to try rewriting the CUTR.LSP program using the formulas for lines, circles, and the quadratic formula. The formula for a line is

$$m = \frac{Y_2 - Y_1}{X_2 - X_1}$$

where *m* equals the slope of the line. The formula for a circle is

$$(x - a)^2 + (y - b)^2 = r^2$$

where *a* and *b* are the x and y coordinates for the center of the circle, and *r* is radius of the circle. The quadratic formula is

$$x = \frac{-b \pm \sqrt{b^2 - 4ac}}{2a}$$

Functions Useful in Geometric Transformations

The majority of your graphic problems can be solved with the basic trigonometric functions used in the Cutcr program. But AutoLISP provides the tools to solve even the most arcane trigonometric problems. This section shows the functions you are most likely to use in situations that require geometry.

Trans

Trans translates a coordinate or displacement from one user coordinate system to another. Its first argument is a point of reference. The second argument is a code indicating which coordinate system the point is expressed in. The third argument is a code indicating which coordinate system the point is to be translated to. An optional fourth True/nil argument can be included. If this fourth argument evaluates to T or non-nil, then the first argument will be treated as a displacement rather than a point value. The following are the codes for the second and third arguments.

Code	Coordinate System
0	World coordinate system
1	Current user coordinate sytem
2	Coordinate system of the current view plane

Trans returns a coordinate or displacement list.

The syntax for Trans is

(trans *coordinate_list UCS_code UCS_code optional_T/nil*)

*A*tan

Atan returns the arctangent in radians of its first argument. If the argument is negative, then the value returned will be negative. If two arguments are supplied, then Atan returns the arctangent of the first argument divided by the second argument.

The syntax for Atan is

(atan *number optional_2nd_number*)

Inters

Inters returns a coordinate list of the intersection of two vectors. The first two arguments to Inters are the endpoints of one vector, while the third and fourth arguments define the other vector. If an optional fifth argument is present and evaluates to nil, then Inters will attempt to locate an intersection point of the two vectors regardless of whether the intersection fails between the specified points or not.

The syntax for Inters is

(inters *point point point point optional_T/nil*)

Sin

Sin returns the sine of an angle as a real number. The angle must be expressed in radians.

The syntax for Sin is

(sin *angle*)

Cos

Cos returns the Cosine of an angle as a real number. The angle must be expressed in radians.

The syntax for Cos is

(cos *angle*)

Summary

In this chapter you've learned how to obtain angles and distances based on the locations of points. You have also learned how to derive a new point given an existing point and an angle and displacement.

In addition to this, you have seen how to use some of AutoLISP's trigonometric functions to manipulate geometric or spatial information. If you find you need to work with these trig functions, consider making liberal use of a sketch pad (or, for that matter, AutoCAD itself) to plan and document your program. You may want to reuse or modify a program such as the previous example and, without graphic documentation explaining how it works, you may have a difficult time understanding why you wrote your program as you did.

7

Working with Text

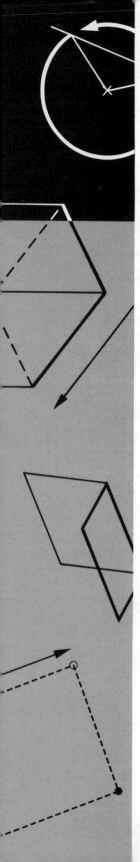

7

If you have ever had to edit large amounts of text in a drawing, then you have encountered one of AutoCAD's most frustrating limitations. While AutoCAD's text-handling capability is one of its strong points, it still leaves much to be desired where editing text is concerned. Fortunately AutoLISP can be used to supplement AutoCAD's text-editing tools. In this chapter, you will look at the many functions that AutoLISP offers for text, or string, manipulation. You will also look at how textual information can be stored and retrieved from a file on disk and how data can be converted to and from string data types.

Creating a Text-Editing Program

Without the aid of AutoLISP, editing text can be tedious. You have to use the Change command to select a text line, and then press ⏎ several times before you can actually make changes to the text. Even then, you must reenter the entire line of text just to change one word.

The program Chtxt shown in Figure 7.1 is a simple line editor. It uses AutoLISP's string-handling functions to locate a specific string, and then it replaces that string with another one specified by the user.

Open a file called CHTXT.LSP and copy the program shown in Figure 7.1 into the file. Save and close this file and then open a new AutoCAD drawing called Chapt7.

Now load the CHTXT.LSP file and try this exercise:

1. Issue the Dtext command and write the following line of text:

   For want of a battle, the kingdom was lost.

2. Enter **chtxt**.

3. At the prompt

   Pick text to edit:

```
;function to find text string from text entity------------------------------
(defun gettxt ()
(setvar "osmode" 64)                                   ;set osnap to insert
(setq pt1 (getpoint "\nPick text to edit: "))          ;get point on text
(Setvar "osmode" 0)                                    ;set osnap back to zero
(setq oldobj (entget (ssname (ssget pt1) 0) ))         ;get entity zero from prop.
(setq txtstr (assoc 1 oldobj))                         ;get list containing string
(cdr txtstr)                                           ;extract string from prop.
)

;function to update text string of text entity-----------------------------
(defun revtxt ()
(setq newtxt (cons 1 newtxt))                          ;create replacement propty.
(entmod (subst newtxt txtstr oldobj))                  ;update database
)

;program to edit single line of text----------------------------------------
(defun C:CHTXT (/ count oldstr newstr osleng otleng oldt old1
                   old2 newtxt pt1 oldobj txtstr oldtxt)
(setq count 0)                                         ;setup counter to zero
(setq oldtxt (gettxt))                                 ;get old string from text
(setq otleng (strlen oldtxt))                          ;find length of old string
(setq oldstr (getstring T "\nEnter old string "))      ;get string to change
(Setq newstr (getstring T "\nEnter new string "))      ;get replacement string
(setq osleng (strlen oldstr))                          ;find length of substring-
  ;while string to replace is not found, do...          to be replaced
  (while (and (/= oldstr oldt)(<= count otleng))
    (setq count (1+ count))                            ;add 1 to counter
    (setq oldt (substr oldtxt count osleng))           ;get substring to compare
  );end WHILE
  ;if counting stops before end of old string is reached...
  (if (<= count otleng)
      (progn
        (setq old1 (substr oldtxt 1 (1- count))) ;get 1st half of old string
        (setq old2 (substr oldtxt (+ count osleng) otleng));get 2nd half
        (setq newtxt (strcat old1 newstr old2))  ;combine to make new string
        (revtxt)                                 ;update drawing
      )
      (princ "\nNo matching string found.")          ;else print message
  );end if
(PRINC)
);END C:CHTXT
```

Figure 7.1: *The CHTXT.LSP file*

pick the text you just entered. Note that the Osnap cursor appears.

4. At the next prompt

   Enter old string:

   enter the word **battle** in lowercase letters.

5. At the next prompt

   Enter new string:

   enter the word **nail**. The text changes to read

   For want of a nail, the kingdom was lost.

In the Chtxt program, you are able to change a group of letters in a line of text without having to enter the entire line again. Also, you don't have to go through a series of unneeded prompts as you would with the Change command. The following describes how Chtxt accomplishes this.

*O*btaining the Old and New Text Strings

The Chtxt program starts out with a call to a user-defined function called Gettxt.

```
(defun C:EDTXT (/ count oldstr newstr osleng otleng oldt old1
                old2 newtxt pt1 oldobj txtstr oldtxt)
(setq count 0)
(setq oldtxt (gettxt))
```

Gettxt prompts you to select the text to be edited. It then extracts from the drawing database the text string associated with the text you selected. The extracted text is assigned to the symbol Oldtxt. I will discuss this extraction process in Chapter 9, but for now, think of Gettxt merely as a function for getting text.

The next line uses a new function, Strlen:

```
(setq otleng (strlen oldtxt))
```

Strlen finds the number of characters in a string. The syntax for Strlen is

```
(strlen string)
```

Strlen returns an integer value representing the number of characters found in its arguments. Blank spaces are counted as characters. In the above expression, the value found by Strlen is assigned to the variable Otleng.

The next two expressions obtain from the user the old portion of the text to be replaced and the replacement text:

```
(setq oldstr (getstring T "\nEnter old string: "))
(setq newstr (getstring T "\nEnter new string: "))
```

These two strings are saved as Oldstr and Newstr. Note that the T argument is used with Getstring to allow the user to use spaces in the string.

*R*eplacing the Old Text with the New

The next set of expressions does the work of the program. First, the number of characters in Olstr, the string to be replaced, is found with the Strlen function:

```
(setq osleng (strlen oldstr))
```

This value is stored with a variable called Osleng. Osleng will be used to find exactly where the old string occurs in the line of text being edited (see Figure 7.2).

The following While function uses Osleng to find the exact location of Oldstr within Oldtxt:

```
(while (and (/ = oldstr oldt)(< = count otleng))
    (setq count (1 + count))
    (setq oldt (substr oldtxt count osleng))
);end WHILE
```

The While expression tests for two conditions. The first test is to see if the current string being read matches the string entered at the prompt. The second test checks to see if the end of the text line has been reached. The And logical operator is used to make sure that both test conditions are met before it continues evaluating its other expressions.

There is a new function, Substr, in this group of expressions:

```
(setq oldt (substr oldtxt count osleng))
```

Substr extracts a sequence of characters from a string. Its syntax is

```
(substr
      string
      beginning_of_substring length_of_substring
)
```

The first argument to Substr is the string from which a substring is to be extracted. A substring is any contiguous sequence of characters within

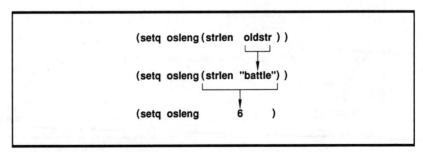

Figure 7.2: *Using the Strlen function*

the main string. It can even be the entire string. The second argument is the beginning location for the substring. This can be any integer between 1 and the total number of characters in the main string. The third argument is the length of the substring (see Figure 7.3).

The While expression extracts a group of characters from Oldtxt starting at the beginning. It stores this substring in the variable Oldt. Oldt is then compared with Oldstr to see if they match. If they don't match, While advances to the next group of characters in Oldtxt and compares this new group to Oldstr. This goes on until a match is found or the end of Oldtxt is reached (see Figure 7.4).

String data types are case sensitive. This means that if you had entered **BATTLE** instead of **battle** at the prompt, you would have gotten the message

No matching string found.

When the While expression is done, the next group of expressions takes the old text line apart and replaces the old string with the new. First

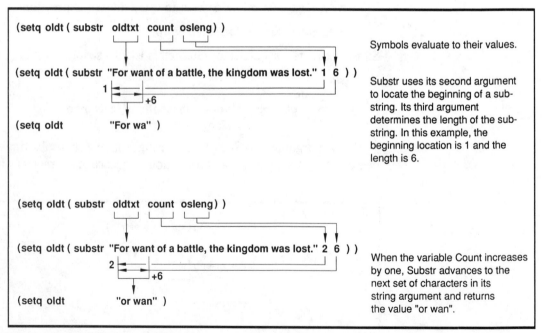

Figure 7.3: Using the Substr function

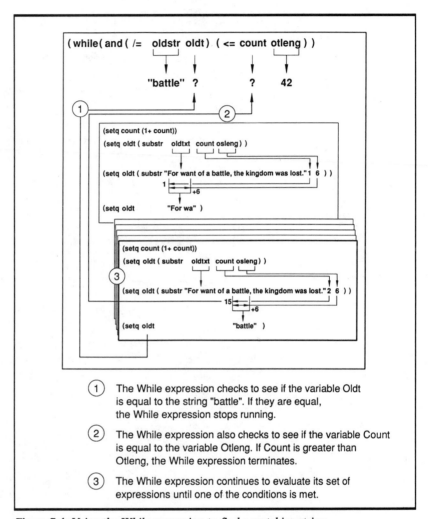

Figure 7.4: Using the While expression to find a matching string

the If function is used to test whether the Oldstring was indeed found:

(if (< = count otleng)

The If expression checks to see whether the variable Count is less than or equal to the length of the old text line. If Count is less than

Otleng, then the following set of expressions are evaluated:

```
(progn
    (setq old1 (substr oldtxt 1 (1- count)))
    (setq old2 (substr oldtxt ( + count osleng) otleng))
    (setq newtxt (strcat old1 newstr old2))
    (revtxt)
)
```

The Progn function allows the group of expressions that follow to appear as one expression to the If function. The first expression of this group

```
(setq old1 (substr oldtxt 1 (1- count)))
```

separates out the first part of the old text line just before the old string. This is done using the Substr function and the Count variable to find the beginning of the old string (see Figure 7.5).

The next expression

```
(setq old2 (substr oldtxt ( + count osleng) otleng))
```

separates out the last part of the old text line, starting just after the old string. Again this is done with the Substr function and the Count variable. This time, Count is added to Osleng to find the beginning of the last portion of the old string. Otleng is used for the substring length. Even though its value is greater than the length of the substring we want, AutoLISP will read the substring to the end of Oldtxt (see Figure 7.6).

Finally, the expression

```
(setq newtxt (strcat old1 newstr old2))
```

combines the first and last part of the old text line with the new string to form the replacement text line (see Figure 7.7).

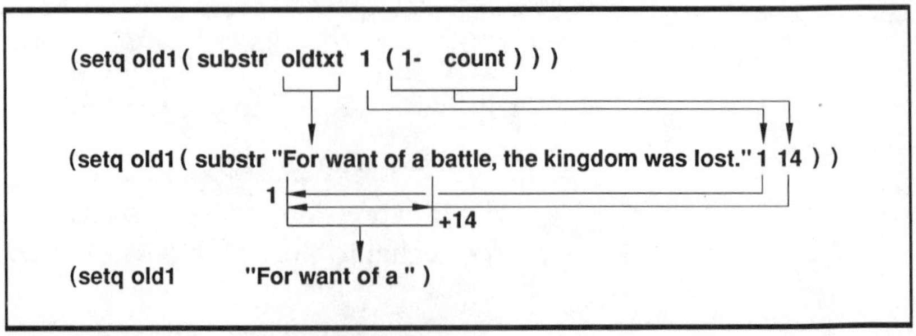

Figure 7.5: Finding the string before Oldstr

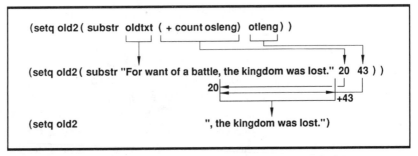

Figure 7.6: *Finding the string after Oldstr*

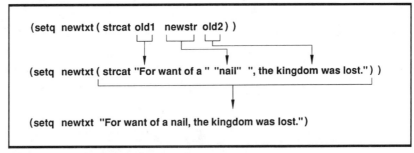

Figure 7.7: *Constructing the replacement string*

The last expression in this group

(revtxt)

is a user-defined function that does the work of replacing the old text with the new:

```
(defun revtxt ( )
   (setq newtxt (cons 1 newtxt))
   (entmod (subst newtxt txtstr oldobj))
)
```

In the event that Count is greater than Otleng, the following expression is evaluated:

(princ "\nNo matching string found.")

This expression prints the message:

No matching string found.

to the prompt line.

The very last expression of the program

(princ)

seems pretty useless at first glance. Princ without any arguments prints a blank to the prompt line. If this expression were not here, however, Auto-LISP would display the value of the last expression evaluated. Remember that AutoLISP constantly cycles through the read-evaluate-print process. Generally, the value of the last expression evaluated is printed to the prompt line. While this doesn't affect the workings of the program, it may prove to be an annoyance to the user or it may confuse someone not familiar with the program. Since Princ will print a blank at the prompt line when no arguments are supplied, it is often used without arguments at the end of a program simply to keep the appearance of the program clean. If you'd like, delete the Princ expression from the program, and reload and run the program again. You will find that a value will appear in the prompt line when it finishes running.

How to Convert Numbers to Strings and Strings to Numbers

There are times when it is necessary to convert a string value to a number or vice versa. Suppose, for example, that you want to be able to control the spacing of numbers generated by the Seq program that you created in Chapter 5. (Recall that this program produces a sequence of numbers spaced equally.) The user may determine the beginning and ending numbers and the location of the beginning number, but cannot determine the distance between numbers. You can use the Rtos function to help obtain a distance value and include it with the program. Figure 7.8 shows the Seq program modified to accept distance input. In the next exercise, you'll see how Rtos works with this program. Then you'll learn about some other functions that convert strings and numbers.

Converting a Number to a String with Rtos

Exit AutoCAD and open the AutoLISP file SEQ.LSP. Make the changes shown in boldface type in Figure 7.8. Save and exit the file and return to the Chapt7 drawing. Load the Seq program and do the

```
(defun C:SEQ (/ pt1 currnt last)
  (setq pt1    (getpoint "\nPick start point: "))
  (setq spc    (getdist pt1 "\nEnter number spacing: "))
  (setq currnt (getint "\nEnter first number: "))
  (setq last   (getint "\nEnter last number: "))
  (setq stspc  (rtos spc 2 2))
  (setq stspc  (strcat "@" stspc "" ))
  (command "text" pt1 "" "" currnt)
    (repeat (- last currnt)
      (setq currnt (1+ currnt))
      (command "text" stspc "" "" currnt)
    )
)
```

Figure 7.8: The modified sequential number program

following:

1. Enter **seq** at the command prompt.

2. At the prompt

    Pick start point:

    pick the point at coordinates 1, 3.

3. At the prompt

    Enter spacing:

    enter **.5.**

4. At the prompt

    Enter first number:

    enter **4.**

5. At the final prompt

    Enter last number:

    enter **12.**

The numbers 4 through 12 will appear beginning at your selected start point and spaced at 0.5-unit intervals.

Let's take a closer look at how the modified program works. The program starts by prompting the user to pick a starting point:

(setq pt1 (getpoint "\nPick start point: "))

A new prompt was added that obtains the spacing for the numbers:

(setq spc (getdist pt2 "\nEnter number spacing: "))

The spacing is saved as the symbol Spc. The program continues by prompting the user to enter starting and ending values:

(setq currnt (getint "\nEnter first number: "))
(setq last   (getint "\nEnter last number: "))

Next, the function Rtos is used to convert the value of Spc to a string:

(setq stspc (rtos spc 2 2))

The syntax for Rtos is

(rtos *real/integer value unit_style_code precision*)

The first argument to Rtos is the number being converted. It can be a real or an integer. The next argument is the unit style code. Table 7.1 shows a listing of these codes and their meanings. The code determines the style the number will be converted to. For example, if you want a number to be converted to feet and inches, you would use the code 4.

The third argument, precision, determines how many decimal places to convert. In the example, I used 2 for the unit style code and 2 for the number of decimal places to convert to a string.

The next expression combines the converted number with the strings "@" and "<0" to form a string that can be used with the command function

(setq stspc (strcat "@" stspc "<0"))

The next expression sets up the location of the beginning of the text:

(command "text" pt1 "" "" currnt)

Table 7.1: Unit Style Codes Used with Rtos

CODE	FORMAT
1	Scientific
2	Decimal
3	Feet and decimal inches
4	Feet and inches
5	Fractional units

This is done because in the next set of expressions, the string that locates the text provides a distance and direction rather than a point. The previous expressions locate a point which will cause the Text command in the next expression to place the text in the proper place:

```
(repeat (- last currnt)
    (setq currnt (1 + currnt))
    (command "text" stspc "" "" currnt)
)
)
```

In this last expression, the Repeat function is used to issue the Text command, enter the number, and advance to the next number repeatedly until the last number is in place (see Figure 7.9).

*C*onverting Data Types with Other Functions

Before you continue, you should briefly look at several other functions that offer data-type conversion. These functions are listed in Table 7.2.

Angtos works in a similar way to Rtos. It accepts a unit style code and a precision value. Its syntax is

(angtos *angle_value unit_style_code precision*)

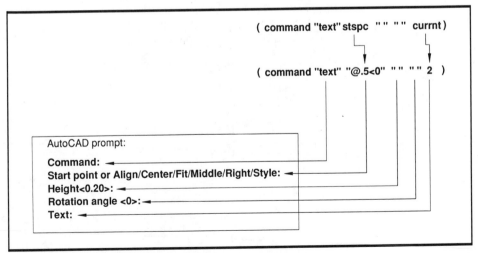

Figure 7.9: Writing the numbers into the AutoCAD file

Table 7.2: Other Functions for Data-Type Conversion

FUNCTION	USES
(Angtos *real*)	Converts real numbers (radians) into string values.
(Ascii *string*)	Converts a string into its ASCII character code.
(Atoi *string*)	Converts a string into an integer.
(Itoa *integer*)	Converts an integer into a string.
(Chr *integer*)	Converts an integer representing an ASCII character code into a string.

All of the other functions listed in Table 7.2 take a single item, the value to be converted, as their argument. For example, to convert the integer 55 into a string, enter the following expression:

(itoa 55)

The resulting value is "55".

The functions Ascii and Chr convert ASCII character codes. These are numeric values that represent letters, numbers, and symbols. Table 7.3 shows these codes and their meaning.

Table 7.3: ASCII Character Codes

CODE	MEANING
07	Beep
09	Tab
10	New line
13	Return
27	Escape
32	Space
33	!
34	"
35	#
36	$

Table 7.3: ASCII Character Codes (Continued)

CODE	MEANING
37	%
38	&
39	' (apostrophe)
40	(
41	)
42	*
43	+
44	, (comma)
45	- (hyphen)
46	. (period)
47	/ (forward slash)
48	0
49	1
50	2
51	3
52	4
53	5
54	6
55	7
56	8
57	9
58	: (colon)
59	; (semicolon)
60	<
61	=
62	>
63	?
64	@

Table 7.3: ASCII Character Codes (Continued)

CODE	MEANING
65	A
66	B
67	C
68	D
69	E
70	F
71	G
72	H
73	I
74	J
75	K
76	L
77	M
78	N
79	O
80	P
81	Q
82	R
83	S
84	T
85	U
86	V
87	W
88	X
89	Y
90	Z
91	[
92	\ (backslash)

Table 7.3: ASCII Character Codes (Continued)

CODE	MEANING
93	]
94	^ (caret)
95	_ (underscore)
96	' (reverse apostrophe)
97	a
98	b
99	c
100	d
101	e
102	f
103	g
104	h
105	i
106	j
107	k
108	l
109	m
110	n
111	o
112	p
113	q
114	r
115	s
116	t
117	u
118	v
119	w
120	x

Table 7.3: *ASCII Character Codes (Continued)*

CODE	MEANING
121	y
122	z
123	{
124	¦
125	}
126	~ (tilde)

*U*sing a Text-Import Program to Read ASCII Files

There are many reasons why you may want to have a program read an ASCII file. You may store commonly used notes in ASCII files on your hard disk that you would like to import into your drawing. Or you may want to store drawing information, such as layering setup or block lists, on disk for later retrieval.

The program shown in Figure 7.10 is a rudimentary text-import program. In this section, you will use it to examine the way AutoLISP reads external ASCII files.

```
(Defun C:IMPRT (/ sp dt stl qst)
(setq nme (getstring "\nName of text file to import: "))
(setq sp  (getpoint "\nText starting point: "))
(setq txt (open nme "r"))
(setq dt  (read-line txt))
(setq lns (getdist "\nEnter line spacing in drawing units: "))
(setq ls  (rtos lns 2 2))
(setq ls  (strcat "@" ls "<-90"))
(command "text" sp "" "" dt)
   (while (/= dt nil)
      (setq dt (read-line txt))
      (command "text" ls "" "" dt)
   )
(close txt)
(command "redraw")
)
```

Figure 7.10: *A text-import program*

Create a file named IMPRT.LSP and copy into it the program shown in Figure 7.10. Go back to the Chapt7 drawing and load the IMPRT.LSP file. Now follow these steps to run the program:

1. Enter **imprt** at the Command prompt.

2. At the prompt

   Name of text file to import:

   Enter **imprt.lsp**.

3. At the next prompt

   Text starting point:

   pick a point at coordinates 2, 8.

4. At the next prompt

   Enter line spacing in drawing units:

   enter **.4**.

The contents of the file IMPRT.LSP will be written into the drawing area using AutoCAD text (see Figure 7.11).

The Imprt program starts out by prompting the user to identify the file to be imported:

(setq nme (getstring "\nName of text file to import: "))

The entered name is saved as the variable Nme. Next, the program prompts the user for the starting point:

(setq sp (getpoint "\nText starting point: "))

This point is saved as Sp. The last prompt sets up the line spacing:

(setq lns (getdist sp "\nEnter line spacing in drawing units: "))

The spacing distance is assigned to the variable Lns. Note that Getdist allows the user to input a distance with either the keyboard or the cursor.

In the next line, the AutoLISP function Open is used to open the file to be imported:

(setq txt (open nme "r"))

This expression tells AutoLISP to open a file to be read and then assign that file to the variable Txt. From this point on, you can treat

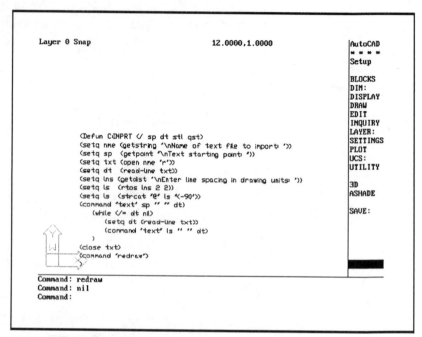

Figure 7.11: The text added to the drawing

the variable Txt as a read-only version of the file itself. This variable that assumes the identity of the file is called the *file descriptor*. You can assign an open file to a symbol and then treat that symbol as if it were the file itself.

The syntax for Open is

(open *filename read/write_code*)

The first argument is the name of the file to be opened. The second argument is a code that tells AutoLISP whether to allow read-only, write-only, or appending operations on the file. The following table shows the codes and their meaning:

Code	Use
"r"	Opens a file for reading only. If the file does not exist, any attempts to read from it will result in an error message.

"w"   Opens a file to write to. If the file already exists, its contents will be written over. If the file does not exist, it will be created.

"a"   Opens a file and appends to the end if it. If the file does not exist, it will be created.

It is important to note that the code is in lowercase letters. If you use uppercase letters, the Open function will not work.

The next line uses the AutoLISP function Read-line to read the first line of text from the open file:

```
(setq dt (read-line txt))
```

A line of text is read from the file represented by the symbol Txt and is assigned to the variable Dt. Read-line has only one argument, the file descriptor. When the file is first opened, AutoLISP goes to the beginning of the file. When Read-line reads the first line, AutoLISP moves to the second line and waits for further instructions to read the file. The next time the expression (read-line txt) is evaluated, AutoLISP reads the second line and then moves to the following line and waits for another Read-line function call.

The next two expressions set up the location of the beginning of the text in the drawing editor:

```
(setq ls (rtos lns 2 2))
(setq ls (strcat "@" ls "<-90"))
```

The numeric value entered at the line-spacing prompt is converted to a string and then concatenated with "@" and "<-90" to create a string that can be used in the Text command that follows. The next line writes the text from the first line of the file into the AutoCAD drawing:

```
(command "text" sp "" "" dt)
```

The following While expression continually reads lines from the open file and writes them to the AutoCAD drawing editor:

```
(while (/ = dt nil)
   (setq dt (read-line txt))
   (command "text" ls "" "" dt)
)
```

The Read-line function will return nil when it reaches the end of the file. At that point, the While expression will stop its iteration.

Finally, to take care of housekeeping, the program closes the open file:

(close txt)

This is a very important step in the file-reading process. If a file is not closed, the contents of that file can be lost.

I should mention that Imprt requires that the current text style have a height value of 0. If this is not the case, the program will not work properly. This is because the expression that actually writes the text into the drawing editor

(command "text" ls "" "" dt)

assumes that AutoCAD will prompt for a height value for the text. The height prompt occurs only when the current text style has a height value of 0. If the current text style has a height value other than 0, the height prompt will be skipped and the above expression will enter one too many carriage returns in the Text command sequence (see Figure 7.12).

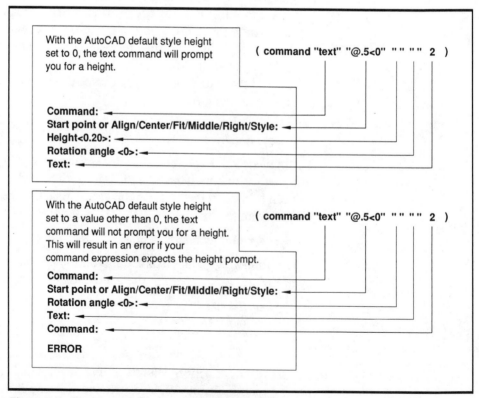

Figure 7.12: The Text command expects specific input

Using a Text-Export Program to Write ASCII Files to Disk

AutoLISP lets you create ASCII files. You can use this capability to store different types of information, ranging from the current drawing status to general notes that appear in a drawing. The Exprt program in Figure 7.13 demonstrates this capability.

The Exprt program starts by prompting the user to enter a name for the file to be saved to:

(setq fname (getstring "\nEnter name of file to save: "))

Then, just as with the Imprt program, the Open function opens the file:

(setq txt (open frame "w"))

In this case, the "w" code indicates that this file is to be written to. The next line obtains a group of objects for editing, using the Ssget function:

(setq selset (ssget))

This selection set is saved as the variable Selset. Next, a variable count is given the value 0 in preparation for the While expression that follows:

(setq count 0)

Next, the If expression checks to see that the user has indeed picked objects for editing:

(if (/ = selset nil)

```
;Program to export text from AutoCAD -- Exprt.lsp
(Defun C:EXPRT (/ fname txt selset count nme oldtx)
  (setq fname (getstring "\nEnter name of file to be saved: "))
    (setq txt (open fname "w"))                      ;open file, assign symbol
    (setq selset (ssget))                            ;get selection set
    (setq count 0)                                   ;set count to zero
    (if (/= selset nil)
      (while (< count (sslength selset))             ;while count < # of lines
        (setq nme (ssname selset count))             ;extract text string
        (setq oldtx (cdr (assoc 1 (entget nme))))
        (write-line oldtx txt)                       ;write string to file
        (setq count (1+ count))                      ;go to next line
      );end while
    );end if
(close txt)                                          ;close file
);end C:EXPRT
```

Figure 7.13: A text-export program

If the variable Selset does not return nil, then the While expression is evaluated. This While expression uses the Count variable to determine the number of times it must evaluate its set of expressions:

(while (< count (sslength selset))

The Sslength function returns the number of objects contained in a selection set. In this case, it returns the number of objects recorded in the variable Selset. This value is compared with the variable Count to determine whether or not to evaluate the expressions found under the While expression.

The next two expressions extract the text-string value from the first of the objects selected:

(setq entnme (ssname selset count))
(setq oldtx (cdr (assoc 1 (entget entnme))))

This extraction process involves several new functions which I will discuss in Chapter 9. For now, just accept that the end result is the assignment of the text value of the selected object to the variable Oldtx.

Now the actual writing to the file occurs:

(write-line oldtx txt)

Here the Write-line function reads the string held by Oldtx and writes it to the file represented by the variable Txt.

Write-line's syntax is

(write-line *string file_descriptor*)

The first argument is the string to be written, and the second argument is a variable assigned to the open file.

The next line increases the value of Count by 1:

(setq count (1+ count))

This expression counts the number of text strings, and therefore objects, that have been processed. Since the While test expression checks to see if the value of Count is less than the number of objects selected, once Count reaches a value equivalent to that number, the While expression stops processing.

Finally, the all-important Close expression appears:

)
   (close txt)
)

Just as with the Imprt program, Close must be used to properly close the file under DOS, otherwise its contents may become inaccessible.

Other AutoLISP File Reading and Writing Functions

Read-line and Write-line are two of several file read-and-write functions available in AutoLISP. Table 7.4 lists these functions along with a brief description of each.

The functions Prin1, Princ, and Print are nearly identical, with only slight differences. All three use the same syntax, as shown in the following:

(princ *string/string_variable optional_file_descriptor*)

The file descriptor is a symbol that has been assigned an open file.

The main difference between these three functions is in what they produce as values. The following shows an expression using Prin1, followed by the resulting value:

(prin1 "\nFor want of a nail...")
"\nFor want of a nail..."""\nFor want of a nail..."

Notice that the string argument to Prin1 was printed twice to the prompt line. This is because both Prin1 and AutoLISP printed something to the prompt. Prin1 prints a literal version of its string argument. AutoLISP's read-evaluate-print loop also prints the value of the last object evaluated. The net result is the appearance of the string twice on the same line.

Princ differs from Prin1 in that, instead of printing a literal version of its string argument, it will act on any control characters included in the string:

(princ "\nFor want of a nail...")
For want of a nail..."\nFor want of a nail..."

In the Prin1 example, the \n control character is printed and not acted upon. In the Princ example above, the \n control character causes the AutoCAD prompt to advance one line. Also, the string is printed without the quotation marks. Again, the AutoLISP interpreter prints the value of the string directly to the prompt line after Princ does its work.

Table 7.4: *File Reading and Writing Functions*

FUNCTION	DESCRIPTION
(Prin1 *symbol/expression*)	Prints any expression to the screen prompt. If a file descriptor is included as an argument, the expression is written to the file as well.
(Princ *symbol/expression*)	The same as Prin1 but executes control characters. Also, string quotation marks are dropped.
(Print *symbol/expression*)	The same as Prin1 but a new line is printed before its expression and a space is printed after.
(Read-char *file_descriptor*)	Reads a single character from the keyboard. If a file descriptor is included as an argument, it reads a character from the file. The value returned is in the form of an ASCII character code.
(Read-line *file_descriptor*)	Reads a string from the keyboard or a line of text from an open file.
(Write-char *integer file_descriptor*)	Writes a single character to the screen prompt or, if a file descriptor is provided, to an open file. The character argument is a number representing an ASCII character code.
(Write-line *string file_descriptor*)	Writes a string to the screen prompt or, if a file descriptor is provided, to an open file.

Table 7.5 shows a list of control characters and what they do. The last item on the table indicates characters referred to by their octal codes.

The Print function differs from the Prin1 function in that it advances the prompt one line before printing the string and then adds a space at the

Table 7.5: Control Characters

CHARACTER	USE
\e	Escape
\n	New line
\r	Return
\t	Tab
\007	Beep
nnn	Character whose octal code is *nnn*

end of the string:

(print "\nFor want of a nail...")

"\nFor want of a nail..." "\nFor want of a nail..."

Just as with Prin1, Print produces a literal version of its string argument.

*S*ummary

Although a good deal of your effort while using AutoLISP will concentrate on graphics and numeric computation, the ability to manipulate string data will also be an important part of your work. You have been introduced to those functions that enable you to work with strings.

You have also seen how these functions work together to perform some simple tasks like reading and writing text files. But you don't have to limit yourself to using these functions for text editing. Since any kind of information can be stored as a string, you may find ways to enhance your use of AutoCAD through the manipulation of string data. For example, you could import numeric data for graphing, charting, or other types of data analysis. As long as data is stored in an ASCII format, AutoLISP can read it. And with AutoLISP's data conversion functions, numeric data can be easily translated from ASCII files.

8

Making Programs Responsive to the User

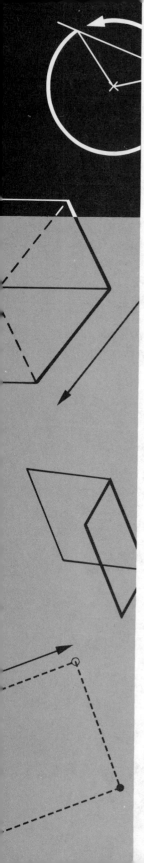

8

AutoLISP offers a number of ways to interact with AutoCAD and the user. You have already seen how AutoLISP can control system variables through the Setvar and Getvar functions, and you have seen the various ways your programs can obtain information from the user with the Get functions. You can also control the display of menus, status and coordinate readouts, graphic and text screens, and even the drawing area. By controlling the display, you can improve the way your programs interact with users.

In this chapter, you will explore some of the ways you can exploit AutoLISP and AutoCAD features to make your programs more responsive to the user.

Reading and Writing to the Screen

Many functions allow you to write prompts to the command prompt line. But you are not limited to control of the prompt. Several functions allow you to both read from and write to other parts of the AutoCAD drawing editor. In this section, you will examine these functions.

Reading the Cursor Dynamically

In Chapter 3 you used a function called Rxy. This function reads the cursor location relative to a reference point and writes the relative coordinate directly to the coordinate readout. This is done dynamically as the cursor moves. The function that allows this to occur is the Grread function. Grread's syntax is

(grread *optional_argument***)**

Grread is a general input-device reading function. It can read input from the keyboard, from buttons on your pointing device, or from the cursor location. Grread returns a list of two elements:

(*integer integer/coordinate_list*)

The first element is a code representing the type of input received. The second element is either an integer or list, depending on whether a point has been input, or whether a key or pointing-device button has been depressed. Table 8.1 shows a list of codes for the first element of the list returned by Grread and what the second element will be if this code is used.

Table 8.1: Input Codes for the Grread Function

INPUT CODE	MEANING
(2 *ASCII_code*)	Keyboard key pressed. The second element of the list will be an integer representing the ASCII code of the key character pressed.
(3 *coordinates*)	Cursor location picked using the pick button on the pointing device. The second element of the list will be a coordinate list.
(4 *cell_number*)	Screen menu cell picked. The second element of the list will be an integer representing the cell number. The cells are numbered from top to bottom.
(5 *coordinate*)	Dynamic cursor mode in which the location of the cursor is read as it moves across the screen. The second element of the list will be a coordinate list. This code is returned only if a non-nil argument is supplied to the Grread function.
(6 *button_number*)	Button on pointing device pressed. The second element of the list will be an integer representing the button number.

Table 8.1: Input Codes for the Grread Function (Continued)

INPUT CODE	MEANING
(7-10 *box_number*)	Tablet menu item selected. 7 equals tablet1 menu group, 8 equals tablet2 menu group, and so on. The second element of the list will be an integer representing the tablet box number.
(11 *box_number*)	Aux1 menu item selected. The second element of the list will be an integer representing the tablet item box number.
(12 *coordinates*)	If two Grread functions are used in sequence and the first returns a code 6, the second Grread will return a code 12 and its second element will be the coordinate of the cursor at the time the pointing device button was picked.
(13 *menu_cell_number*)	Screen menu item picked using keyboard cursor keys instead of the pointing device. The second element of the list will be the menu cell number.

Let's take a look at how Grread works. Open a new AutoCAD file and turn on the Snap mode. Enter the following at the AutoCAD command prompt:

(grread)

Now pick a point near the center of the screen using your mouse or digitizer puck. You will get a list similar to the following:

(3 (7.0 5.0 0.0))

The first element of the list is the integer 3. This tells us that the pick button on the pointing device was entered. The second element is a coordinate list showing the coordinate that was picked.

Now look at the expression in the Rxy function that uses Grread to read the cursor dynamically:

(setq pt (cadr (setq lt (grread t))))

The T argument tells Grread to read the cursor location dynamically, that is, read it regardless of whether a button has been pushed or not. Therefore, Grread reads the cursor location even as it moves. The value from Grread is assigned to the symbol Lt for later processing. This value in turn is applied to Cadr to obtain the coordinate list. Finally, the coordinate list is assigned to the symbol Pt (see Figure 8.1).

The following set of expressions takes the x and y components of the point Pt and subtracts them from the x and y components of the reference point Lpt1, which has been selected earlier by the user. It then multiplies the remaining x and y values together to get the area of the rectangle formed by these two points. Finally, these values are turned into strings that can be sent to the screen.

First, the If expression tests to see whether the code returned by Grread is 5. This checks to see if the coordinate was derived from the cursor in a drag mode.

(if (= (car lt) 5)(progn

Remember that Lt is the list from the Grread expression, so the Car of Lt is its first element, the input code.

The next line is the outermost nest of an expression that combines a set of strings together into one string using Strcat:

(setq x (strcat

This is followed by an expression that subtracts the x component of Lpt1, our reference point, from that of the current point, Pt:

(rtos (- (car pt) (car lpt1))) " x "

The resulting difference is converted into a string by Rtos. The " x "

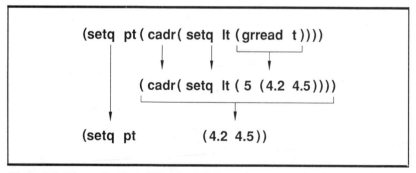

Figure 8.1: The evaluation of the Grread expression

element in this expression is the x that appears between the x and y value in the coordinate readout (see Figure 8.2).

The next expression subtracts the y component of Lpt1 from that of Pt and then converts the resulting difference into a string:

```
(rtos (- (cadr pt) (cadr lpt1))) " SI = "
```

The " SI = " at the end of this line appears after the coordinate list in the coordinate readout. SI stands for *square inch* (see Figure 8.2).

The next two expressions multiply the x- and y-value differences to get the area of the rectangle represented by Lpt1 and Pt:

```
(rtos (*(- (car pt) (car lpt1))
       (- (cadr pt) (cadr lpt1))
      )
   2 2)
```

The 2 2 in the fourth line are the unit style and precision arguments to the Rtos function found at the beginning of this set of expressions.

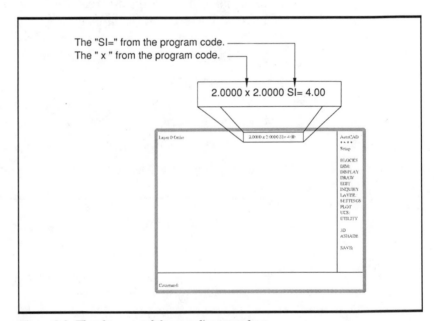

Figure 8.2: The elements of the coordinate readout

*W*riting Text to the Status and Menu Areas

In the last code segment, all the values of the preceding group of expressions are concatenated and then stored as the variable X, which is in turn given as an argument to Grtext:

(grtext -2 x)

Grtext writes the value of x to the coordinate readout. Grtext's syntax is

(grtext *cell_code string optional_highlight_code*)

The cell code is the number of the screen menu cell you want to write the string to. Screen menu cells are numbered from 0 to 1 less than the maximum number of cells available. If a −1 is used for the cell code, the string is written to the status area in the upper left corner of the screen. If the code is −2, as in the Rxy function, it is written to the coordinate readout area (see Figure 8.3).

Although Grtext allows you to display a string in the screen menu, you cannot read such a string by picking it with the cursor, as you

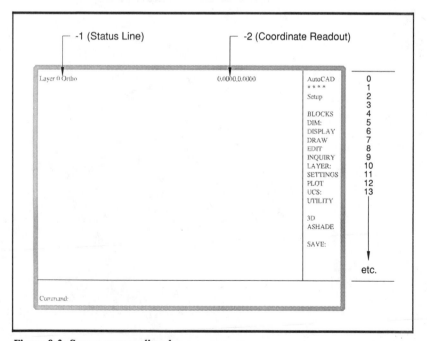

Figure 8.3: *Screen menu cell codes*

might think. Instead, if you pick the string, the underlying menu option that has been written over by the Grtext function is activated. If you want to override the underlying menu option, you can use Grread to find the cell number picked with the cursor. Once you know the cell number, you can write expressions that instruct AutoCAD to perform alternate tasks.

Near the end of the Rxy program, an expression sets the variable Pick to T or nil depending on the input code from the variable Lt:

(setq pick (= 3 (car lt)))

If the input code from Lt is 3, then Pick is set to T, otherwise it is set to nil. This expression controls the While expression. If you look at the beginning of the While expression, the use of this expression becomes more clear (see Figure 8.4).

The While expression continually evaluates its set of expressions as long as Pick is not equal to T. The last expression checks to see if the input code from Lt is 3. If it is, that means that a point has been

```
(defun RXY (/ pt lt x last pick lpt1)
(if (not pt1)(setq lpt1 (getvar "lastpoint"))(setq lpt1 pt1))
(while (/= pick t)
    (setq pt (cadr (setq lt (grread t))))
    (if (= (car lt) 5)(progn
        (setq x (strcat
            (rtos (- (car pt) (car lpt1))) " x "
            (rtos (- (cadr pt) (cadr lpt1))) " SI= "
            (rtos (*(- (car pt) (car lpt1))
                (- (cadr pt) (cadr lpt1))
            )
            2 2)
        )
    )
    (grtext -2 x)
    )
)
    (setq pick (= 3 (car lt)))
)
(cadr lt)
)
```

Figure 8.4: The Pick variable used to control the While expression

selected with the pick button. Pick is then set to T and the While expression stops running.

Calling Menus from AutoLISP

To make your program easier to use, you may want to have a menu that offers the various options of your AutoLISP program whenever the program runs. AutoLISP provides the Menucmd function for this purpose. Menucmd's syntax is

(menucmd *menu_specification*)

The menu specification is a code used to call a particular menu. The code resembles the ones used within the menu system to call other menus. The only difference between this code and its menu counterpart is that a Menucmd code is not preceded by a dollar sign. These codes are briefly described below.

Code	Description
bn = *menu name*	Calls button menus. The n is the number of the button menu group.
s = *menu name*	Calls screen menus.
pn = *menu name*	Calls pull-down menus. The n is the number of the pull-down menu group.

Figure 8.5 shows the Box program from Chapter 2 with the addition of the Menucmd function that calls the Osnap screen menu. If you load and run this program, the Osnap screen menu will appear at the first prompt.

```
(defun c:BOX ( /  pt1 pt2 pt3 pt4 )
(menucmd "s=osnapb")
(setq pt1 (getpoint "Pick first corner: "))
(setq pt3 (getcorner pt1 "Pick opposite corner: "))
(setq pt2 (list (car pt3) (cadr pt1)))
(setq pt4 (list (car pt1) (cadr pt3)))
(command "line" pt1 pt2 pt3 pt4 "c" )
)
```

Figure 8.5: The Box program modified to call a screen menu

Using Menucmd with the pull-down menus is a bit more involved. Figure 8.6 shows the same program, this time making a call to the Filters pull-down menu. If you load and run this program, the Filters pull-down menu will pop down.

Notice that a line was added in addition to the first Menucmd line:

(menucmd "p1 = *")

Just as you must include $p1 = * in a menu macro to display the Tools pull-down menu, you must also include the asterisk call in your Auto-LISP program following any pull-down menu call. This asterisk call is the mechanism that makes the menu pop down.

```
(defun c:BOX ( /   pt1 pt2 pt3 pt4 )
 (menucmd "p1=filters")
 (menucmd "p1=*")
 (setq pt1 (getpoint "Pick first corner: "))
 (setq pt3 (getcorner pt1 "Pick opposite corner: "))
 (setq pt2 (list (car pt3) (cadr pt1)))
 (setq pt4 (list (car pt1) (cadr pt3)))
 (command "line" pt1 pt2 pt3 pt4 "c" )
)
```

Figure 8.6: The Box program modified to call a pull-down menu

*D*rawing *Temporary Images on the Drawing Area*

There may be times when you will want an image drawn in the drawing area that is not part of the drawing database. Such a temporary image can be useful to help you locate points or place objects.

Figure 8.7 shows a program that performs zooms in a different way from the standard AutoCAD zoom. In this program, called Qzoom, the screen is divided visually into quadrants. You are prompted to pick a quadrant, at which point the quadrant is enlarged to fill the screen. Optionally, you can press ↵ at the "Pick quadrant" prompt and you will be prompted to pick a new view center. This option is essentially the same as a pan.

If you like, copy Qzoom into an AutoLISP file, and load and run it. The program is written with comments that divide it visually into

```
(defun mid (a b)
(list (/ (+ (car a) (car b) ) 2) (/ (+ (cadr a) (cadr b) ) 2))
)

(defun C:QZOOM (/ center height ratio width
                  wseg hseg ll ur ul lr newctr)

;find screen position
(setq center (getvar "viewctr"))
(setq height (getvar "viewsize"))
(setq ratio  (getvar "screensize"))
(setq width  (* height (/ (car ratio)(cadr ratio))))
(setq wseg   (/ width  2.0))
(setq hseg   (/ height 2.0))

;find screen corners
(Setq ll (list (- (car center) wseg)(- (cadr center) hseg)))
(Setq ur (list (+ (car center) wseg)(+ (cadr center) hseg)))
(Setq ul (list (- (car center) wseg)(+ (cadr center) hseg)))
(Setq lr (list (+ (car center) wseg)(- (cadr center) hseg)))

;draw screen quadrants
(grdraw center (polar center pi wseg) -1 1)
(grdraw center (polar center 0  wseg) -1 1)
(grdraw center (polar center (* pi 0.5) hseg) -1 1)
(grdraw center (polar center (* pi 1.5) hseg) -1 1)

;get new center and height
(setq newctr (getpoint "\nPick quadrant/<pan>: "))
 (cond
  ( (not newctr)
     (setq newctr (getpoint "\nPick new center: "))
     (setq hseg height)
  )
  ( (and (< (car newctr)(car center))(< (cadr newctr)(cadr center)))
     (setq newctr (mid center ll))
  )
  ( (and (< (car newctr)(car center))(> (cadr newctr)(cadr center)))
     (setq newctr (mid center ul))
  )
  ( (and (> (car newctr)(car center))(< (cadr newctr)(cadr center)))
     (setq newctr (mid center lr))
  )
  ( (and (> (car newctr)(car center))(> (cadr newctr)(cadr center)))
     (setq newctr (mid center ur))
  )
 )
(command "zoom" "c" newctr hseg)
)
```

Figure 8.7: *The Qzoom program*

groups. The first group establishes several variables. It finds the current view-center point, the view height in drawing units, and the view's height to width ratio. Based on this ratio, it finds the width of the current view in drawing units. It also finds the values for half the width and half the height (see Figure 8.8).

The next group establishes the four corner points of the current view. This is done by taking the center point of the view and adding and subtracting the x and y value for each corner (see Figure 8.9).

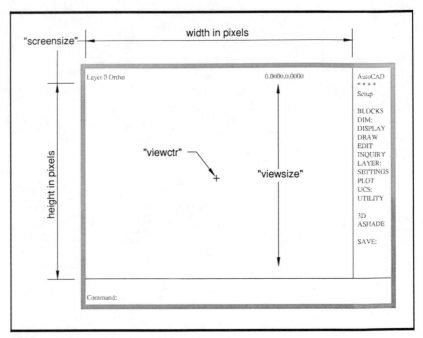

Figure 8.8: The current screen properties

The next group draws the lines that divide the screen into quadrants (Figure 8.10).

Looking at the first line, you can see the Grdraw function:

(grdraw center (polar center pi wseg) -1 1)

The syntax for Grdraw is

**(grdraw *from_point to_point color_code*
optional_highlight_code)**

The lines Grdraw draws act like blips. As soon as you issue any command that changes the display, including a redraw, the lines disappear. The first and second arguments to Grdraw determine the endpoints of the temporary line. The third argument is the color code. This code is an integer value that represents the color you want the line to have. When the color code is −1, the line will be drawn in a color that contrasts with its background. This ensures that the line will be seen. The fourth argument is optional. Whenever it is an integer other than 0, the line will be drawn highlighted. This usually means in a dotted pattern similar to that shown in a crossing window.

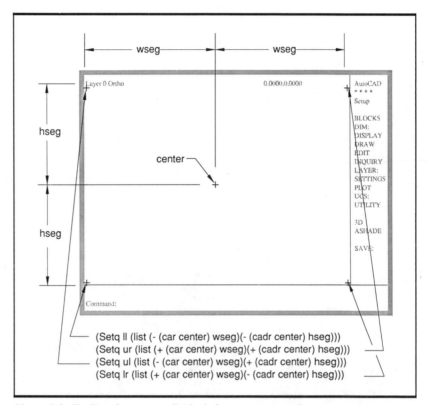

Figure 8.9: *Finding the current display's four corner coordinates*

In the Qzoom program, Grdraw draws lines from the center of the current view out toward the four sides of the screen. The -1 color code is used so the color of the lines contrasts with the background color. Finally, the highlight option is used by supplying a 1 as a fourth argument.

The last group of expressions does the work of reading the pick point from the user and determining which quadrant to enlarge.

Using Defaults in a Program

Virtually every AutoCAD command offers a default value. For example, the Line command will continue a line from the last point

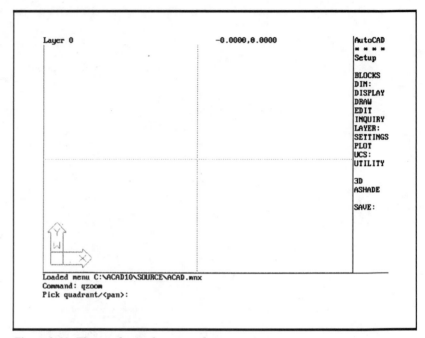

Figure 8.10: *The quadrants drawn on the screen*

selected if no point is selected at the "First point" prompt. Defaults can be a great time saver, especially when the user is in a hurry. In this section, you will see first hand how you can add defaults to your own programs.

*A*dding Default Responses to Your Program

The Qzoom program uses a default response. If the user presses ◄─┘ without picking a point, the program goes into a pan mode, allowing the user to select a new view center. This pan option makes the program easier to use and more flexible.

Many AutoCAD commands provide default values for options. For example, the Offset command will offer the last offset distance as a default value for the current offset distance. If you want to use that value, you only need to press ◄─┘ to go on to the next part of the command.

You can incorporate similar flexibility into your programs by using global variables. Figure 8.11 shows the sequential number program

```
(defun C:SEQ (/ pt1 currnt last spc)
 (if (not *seqpt)(setq *seqpt 2.0))              ;setup global default
 (setq pt1     (getpoint "\nPick start point: "))  ;get start point
 (princ "\nEnter number spacing <")              ;first part of prompt
 (princ *seqpt)                                  ;print default part of prompt
 (setq spc     (getdist pt1 ">: "))              ;finish prompt - get spac'g
 (setq currnt (getint "\nEnter first number: ")) ;get first number
 (setq last    (getint "\nEnter last number: ")) ;get second number
 (if (not spc)(setq spc *seqpt)(setq *seqpt spc)) ;set global variable
 (setq stspc   (rtos spc 2 2))                   ;convert spacing to string
 (setq stspc   (strcat "@" stspc "<0" ))         ;create spacing string
 (command "text" pt1 "" "" currnt)               ;place first number
   (repeat (- last currnt)                       ;start repeat 'till last
     (setq currnt (1+ currnt))                   ;add 1 to current number
     (command "text" stspc "" "" currnt)         ;place text
   )                                             ;end repeat
 )                                               ;end defun
```

Figure 8.11: The Seq program modified to include a default

created in Chapter 5 with code added to include a default value for the number spacing.

Make the changes to your copy of the Seq program so it looks like Figure 8.11. Open a new drawing in AutoCAD, load the newly modified Seq program, and then run it. The program will run as it has before, but it now offers a default value of 2.0 at the "Enter number spacing" prompt:

Enter number spacing <2.0>:

Press ◂┘ at this prompt. The default value of 2.0 will be applied to the number spacing. If you enter a different value, .5 for example, this new value becomes the default. The next time you run the program, .5 will appear as the default value for the number spacing:

Enter number spacing <0.5>:

Several expressions were added to make this default option possible. First there is a conditional expression that tests to see if a global variable called *seqpt is non-nil:

(defun Seq (/ pt1 currnt last spc)
(if (not *seqpt)(setq *seqpt 2.0))

If its value is nil, it is given the value of 2.0. This is just an arbitrary value. You can make it anything you like. (You may wonder why the global variable *seqpt starts with an asterisk. Names given to global variables don't have to be different from other symbols, but you can set them off by preceding them with an asterisk. This is a convention used in Common LISP that can be carried over to AutoLISP.)

Next, the user is prompted to pick a point, just as in the previous version of the program:

```
(setq pt1   (getpoint "\nPick start point: "))
```

The next set of expressions displays the default value to the Auto-CAD prompt:

```
(princ "\nEnter number spacing <")
(princ *seqpt)
(setq spc   (getdist pt1 ">: "))
```

The prompt is broken into three parts. The first expression prints everything before the default value. The second expression prints the default value. The third expression uses the Getdist function to obtain a new distance value from the user. The end of the prompt is included as the prompt string to the Getdist function. The net result is a single line appearing at the AutoCAD prompt (see Figure 8.12).

The next two lines are unchanged from the earlier version of the program:

```
(setq curmt (getint "\nEnter first number: "))
(setq last   (getint "\nEnter last number: "))
```

The next line is a new conditional expression that tests to see if a value was entered at the "Enter number spacing" prompt:

```
(if (not spc)(setq spc *seqpt)(setq *seqpt spc))
```

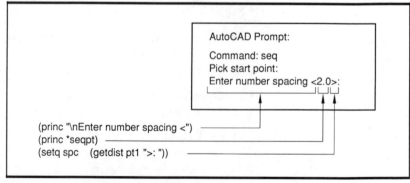

Figure 8.12: Using Princ to construct a prompt

This expression tests the variable Spc to see whether its value is non-nil. If it is nil, indicating the user pressed ◄─┘ without entering a value, Spc is assigned the value of the global variable *seqpt. This is the default value that appears in the prompt. If Spc does have a value, then its value is assigned to *seqpt thus making the value of Spc the new default value. The rest of the program is unchanged.

Creating a Function to Handle Defaults

If you find that many of your programs include defaults, it may be worthwhile to create a function that creates the default prompts for you. Figure 8.13 shows the Seq program with the Deflt function added to handle default prompts.

The function Deflt takes two arguments. The first is the beginning text of the prompt and the second is the default value:

(defun deflt (str1 def / lunts)
(setq lu (getvar "lunits"))
(strcat str1 " <" (rtos def lu 4) ">: ")
)

The arguments are concatenated to form a single string which is the value returned by the function. Since the default value is a real data

```
(defun deflt (str1 def)
 (setq lu (getvar "lunits"))
 (strcat str1 " <" (rtos def lu 4) ">: ")
)


(defun C:SEQ (/ pt1 currnt last spc)
 (if (not *seqpt)(setq *seqpt 2.0))              ;setup global default
 (setq pt1    (getpoint "\nPick start point: "))
 (setq spc    (getdist (deflt "\nEnter spacing" *seqpt)))
 (setq currnt (getint "\nEnter first number: "))
 (setq last   (getint "\nEnter last number: "))
 (if (not spc)(setq spc *seqpt)(setq *seqpt spc)) ;set global variable
 (setq stspc  (rtos spc 2 2))
 (setq stspc  (strcat "@" stspc "<0" ))
 (command "text" pt1 "" "" currnt)
   (repeat (- last currnt)
     (setq currnt (1+ currnt))
     (command "text" stspc "" "" currnt)
   )
 )
```

Figure 8.13: The Seq program with a default-handling function

type, it is converted to a string with the Rtos function. The Getvar expression at the beginning of the function finds the current unit style to control the unit style created by Rtos.

The Seq program uses this function in the expression

(setq spc   (getdist (deflt "\nEnter spacing" *seqpt)))

Here, the function is placed where the prompt string normally appears in a Getdist expression. When Deflt is evaluated, it returns the string

"\nEnter spacing <2.0000>: "

This string is then supplied to the Getdist function as the prompt string argument.

The Seq program still requires the two conditional expressions that were added earlier:

(if (not *seqpt)(setq *seqpt 2.0))
.
.
.
(if (not spc)(setq spc *seqpt)(setq *seqpt spc)) ;set global

So, without increasing the amount of code, you can make a simpler and more flexible system to add prompts to your programs. An added benefit is a more readable program.

*D*ealing with Aborted Functions

If you are writing programs for your own use, you may not be too concerned with how the program looks or behaves. But if you start to write programs for others to use, you should start thinking about ways of making your programs more error proof. For example, you should provide ways for the unfamiliar user to exit your program easily. Error handling, as it is often called, means writing your program to include code that anticipates any possible input errors the user might make. Fortunately, most of AutoLISP's Get functions have some error-handling capabilities built in. For example, if you enter a string when a Get function expects a coordinate point, you will get a message telling you that a point is expected.

Creating an Error-Checking Function

The most common error-handling problem you will encounter is an aborted program. You can get an idea of how an aborted program can affect a user's work by looking at the Break2 program from Chapter 6.

1. Open an AutoCAD file and load the Break2 program.

2. Enter **break2** at the command prompt.

3. At the prompt

   Select object:

   press the Ctrl-C key combination to abort the program.

Now whenever you use the cursor to select a point or object, you will get the Nearest Osnap cursor. This because you aborted the program before it was able to set the Osnap mode back to None (see Figure 8.14).

```
(defun c:break2 (/ pt1 pt2 pt3 pt4 pt0 ang1 dst1)
    (setvar "osmode" 512)
    (setq pt1 (getpoint " Select object: "))
    (setq pt2 (getpoint pt1 " Enter second point: "))
    (setvar "osmode" 128)
    (setq pt3 (getpoint pt1 " Select parallel line: "))
    (setvar "osmode" 0)
    (setq ang1 (angle pt1 pt3))
    (setq dst1 (distance pt1 pt3))
    (setq pt4 (polar pt2 ang1 dst1))
    (command
        "break" pt1 pt2
        "break" pt3 pt4
        "line" pt1 pt3 " "
        "line" pt2 pt4 " "
    )
)
```

Program is aborted at this point.
Osnap is not set back to None.

Figure 8.14: What happens when Break2 is aborted

To deal with such problems, you can use a special AutoLISP function called *error*. If a function is defined with the name *error*, it will be evaluated whenever an error occurs. Figure 8.15 shows the Break2 program with the addition of an error-checking function.

4. Open the BREAK2.LSP file and add the *error* function shown in Figure 8.15.

5. Save the file and go back to the AutoCAD drawing. Be sure that Osnap is set to None.

6. Load and start the Break2 program. Again, at the "Select object" prompt, press Ctrl-C.

Now, instead of leaving the Osnap mode set to Nearest, the *error* function resets it to None. It also prints the message

Function cancelled

Let's look at this function to see exactly how it works. The first line looks like a typical Defun expression:

(defun *error* (msg)

```
(defun *error* (msg)
 (setvar "osmode" 0)
 (princ msg)
 (princ)
)


(defun c:break2 (/ pt1 pt2 pt3 pt4 pt0 ang1 dst1)
 (setvar "osmode" 512)                            ;near osnap mode
 (setq pt1 (getpoint "\nSelect object: "))        ;get first break point
 (setq pt2 (getpoint pt1 "\nEnter second point: ")) ;get second break point
 (setvar "osmode" 128)                            ;perpend osnap mode
 (Setq pt3 (getpoint pt1 "\nSelect parallel line: "));get 2nd line
 (Setvar "osmode" 0)                              ;no osnap mode
 (setq ang1 (angle pt1 pt3))                      ;find angle btwn lines
 (setq dst1 (distance pt1 pt3))                   ;find dist. btwn lines
 (setq pt4 (polar pt2 ang1 dst1))                 ;derive pt4 on 2nd line
   (command
        "break" pt1 pt2                           ;break 1st line
        "break" pt3 pt4                           ;break 2nd line
        "line" pt1 pt3 ""                         ;close ends of lines
        "line" pt2 pt4 ""
   )
 )
```

Figure 8.15: The Break2 program with an error-checking function added

The argument list contains the symbol msg. *error* accepts an error message as its argument. This error message is the one that would appear normally without the *error* function. In the next line

(setvar "osmode" 0)

the Osnap mode is set back to None. Next, the error message supplied by AutoLISP is printed to the AutoCAD prompt:

(princ msg)

The last Princ prevents the error message from appearing twice in the prompt.

This will work very nicely if you always begin with Osnap set to None. But suppose your Osnap setting varies during your editing session and you want your function to return to the setting that was current at the time the program was run? Figure 8.16 shows the Break2 program again with some additional code that restores Osnap to its previous setting regardless of what it may have been.

The line

(setq *osnap (getvar "osmode"))

is added to the beginning of the program. This creates a global variable *osnap that stores the Osnap code that determines the current

```
(defun *error* (msg)
 (setvar "osmode" *osnap)
 (princ msg)
 (princ)
)


(defun c:break2 (/ pt1 pt2 pt3 pt4 pt0 ang1 dst1)
 (setq *osnap (getvar "osmode"))
 (setvar "osmode" 512)                                ;near osnap mode
 (setq pt1 (getpoint "\nSelect object: "))            ;get first break point
 (setq pt2 (getpoint pt1 "\nEnter second point: "))   ;get second break point
 (setvar "osmode" 128)                                ;perpend osnap mode
 (Setq pt3 (getpoint pt1 "\nSelect parallel line: ")) ;get 2nd line
 (Setvar "osmode" *osnap)                             ;no osnap mode
 (setq ang1 (angle pt1 pt3))                          ;find angle btwn lines
 (setq dst1 (distance pt1 pt3))                       ;find dist. btwn lines
 (setq pt4 (polar pt2 ang1 dst1))                     ;derive pt4 on 2nd line
    (command
         "break" pt1 pt2                              ;break 1st line
         "break" pt3 pt4                              ;break 2nd line
         "line" pt1 pt3 ""                            ;close ends of lines
         "line" pt2 pt4 ""
    )
 )
```

Figure 8.16: The Break2 program modified to handle any Osnap setting

Osnap setting. The expression that returned the Osnap mode to None,

(setvar "osmode" 0)

is replaced by one that sets the Osnap mode to whatever was saved as *osnap:

(setvar "osmode" *osnap)

This same expression appears in the *error* function so that, in the event of a cancellation by the user, the Osnap mode will be returned to its previous setting.

Organizing Code to Reduce Errors

The error-handling function just described could be incorporated into your ACAD.LSP file and be available for any AutoLISP error that might occur. You can also enlarge it to include other settings or variables that might require resetting. But the way a program is organized also can affect the impact an error has. For example, Figure 8.17 shows the Seq program with its expressions in a slightly different order.

The conditional expression

(if (not spc)(setq spc *seqpt)(setq *seqpt spc))

immediately follows the expression that prompts for the spacing distance:

(Sctq spc (getdist (deflt "\nEnter spacing" * seqpt)))

```
(defun deflt (str1 def)
(strcat str1 " <" (rtos def 2 4) ">: ")
)


(defun C:SEQ (/ pt1 currnt last spc)
(if (not *seqpt) (setq *seqpt 2.0))                    ;setup global default
(setq pt1     (getpoint "\nPick start point: "))
(setq spc     (getdist (deflt "\nEnter spacing" *seqpt)))
(if (not spc) (setq spc *seqpt) (setq *seqpt spc)) ;set global variable
(setq currnt (getint "\nEnter first number: "))
(setq last    (getint "\nEnter last number: "))
(setq stspc (rtos spc 2 2))
(setq stspc (strcat "@" stspc "<0" ))
(command "text" pt1 "" "" currnt)
  (repeat (- last currnt)
    (setq currnt (1+ currnt))
    (command "text" stspc "" "" currnt)
  )
)
```

Figure 8.17: The reorganized Seq program

This seems to be a natural place for this expression, since it immediately assigns the variable Spc or *seqpt to a value once the value of Spc has been obtained. But what happens if the user decides to cancel the program after this expression is evaluated? If the user inputs a new value for the number spacing, then the global variable *seqpt will hold that new value even though the program has been canceled. The next time the user runs the Seq program, the value that was entered previously will be the new default value.

This may or may not be a problem, but for many users, issuing a cancel means canceling the affects of any data entry made during the command. So to avoid having the global variable *seqpt changed when the program is canceled, the conditional expression is placed in a position after all the prompts. This way, the user can cancel the program while in the middle of a prompt with no effect to the *seqpt variable.

Debugging Programs

While I am on the subject of errors, let's discuss the debugging of your programs. As you begin to write programs on your own, you probably will not get them exactly right the first time. Often you will write a program and then run it, only to see an error message appear. Then you must review your program to try and find the offending expression. In this section you'll learn about some common programming errors, and how to use some AutoLISP debugging tools.

Common Programming Errors

Most of the time, errors are due to the wrong number of parentheses or the wrong placement of parentheses within a program. If this is the case, you usually get the error message

error: malformed list

or

error: extra right paren

There aren't any simple solutions to this problem other than checking your program very carefully for number and placement of parentheses. Usually the best thing to do is to print out your program. As you probably know by now, it is often easier to spot errors on paper than on your computer screen.

Another common error is to misspell symbols. This is especially a problem with similar characters such as lowercase l's and 1's, and 0's and O's. Errors of this sort are often hard to detect. Again, the best solution is to print out your program and take a careful look.

If you get the message

error: Insufficient string space

chances are you didn't provide a closing quotation mark after a string value, as in the following:

(menucmd "p1 = *)

(Also, keep in mind that prompt strings cannot exceed 100 characters.)

Finally, trying to apply a wrong data type to a function will result in an error. I have mentioned a common error that can arise when you give a variable a string value that happens to be a number:

(setq str1 "1")

Later, you might attempt to use this string as an integer in another function:

(1+ str1)

This results in a "bad argument type" error.

Appendix A contains the AutoLISP error messages and their meanings. You may want to refer to it as you debug your programs.

Using Variables as Debugging Tools

AutoLISP helps you find errors by printing to the screen the offending expression along with the error message. But sometimes this is not enough. If you find you are having problems with a program, you can check the variables in the program with the exclamation point to see what values they obtained before the program aborted. If you have an argument list, you may want to keep it empty until you finish debugging your program. That way, you can check the value of the program's variables. Otherwise, the values of the variables will be lost before you have a chance to check them.

If you have a particularly lengthy program, you can use Princ to print variables to the prompt line as the program runs. By placing the Princ function in strategic locations within your program, you can see dynamically what your variables are doing as the program runs. You can also use Princ to print messages telling you where within your program it is printing from.

Summary

You have learned how to read information from the screen, including reading the cursor dynamically, and how to write to the screen as well. You have also learned how to make your programs more error-proof, both by providing default entry options in the manner of Auto-CAD's functions and by creating error-handling routines. Finally, you have learned some approaches to debugging your programs. All of these techniques will enable you to develop programs that are thorough, effective, and easy to use.

9

Using Lists to Store Data

Featuring:

Getting data from a list

Using lists for comparisons

Searching lists

Manipulating the properties of AutoCAD entities

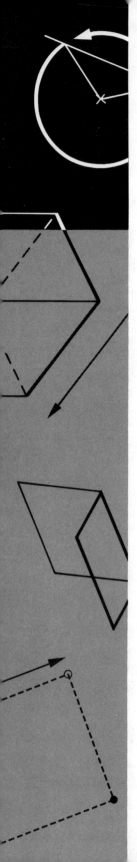

9

In previous chapters you learned that there are actually two classes of lists, those meant to be evaluated, which are called expressions or forms, and those that are repositories for data, such as coordinate lists. No matter what type of list you are dealing with, you can manipulate them to suit the needs of your program. In this chapter you will look at the general subject of lists and review some of the functions that allow you to manipulate them.

Using Lists as Data Repositories

So far, you have used lists to structure and build your programs. But lists can also be repositories for data. You have already seen how coordinate lists are used to store the x- and y-coordinate values of a point. Lists used for storing data can be much larger than that. Consider the Mdist program you saw in Chapter 5. It uses the Append function to constantly add values to a list. This list is then evaluated to obtain the sum of its contents (see Figure 9.1).

This is an example of a list that is both a repository of data and a form to be evaluated. This is because the list starts with the plus function. Each time a value is appended to it, the list is evaluated and returns the sum of its numeric elements.

```
(Defun C:MDIST (/ dstlst dst)
(setq dstlst '(+ 0))
  (while (setq dst (getdist "\nPick point or Return to exit: "))
         (Setq dstlst (append dstlst (list dst)))
         (princ (Eval dstlst))
  )
)
```

Figure 9.1: *The Mdist program*

Suppose you have a list that does not contain a function, but you want to apply some function to it. You can use one of several functions that allow you to access and manipulate lists in a variety of ways. You have already seen Car and Cdr. Table 9.1 shows a list of other functions with a brief description of their uses.

The following sections discuss ways you can use the functions listed in Table 9.1 to perform computations on lists.

Table 9.1: Functions Used with Lists

FUNCTION	USE
(mapcar *function list list* ...)	Apply elements of lists as arguments to a function. Each element in each list is processed until the end of the last list is reached.
(apply *function list*)	Apply the entire contents of a list to a function.
(foreach *symbol list expression*)	Reads an element of *list* and assigns the element to *symbol*. Then Foreach evaluates an expression containing that symbol. Each element in the list is read and assigned to *symbol*; then the expression is evaluated until the end of the list is reached.
(reverse *list*)	Reverses the order of elements in a list.
(cons *element list*)	Adds a new first element to a list. The element can be any legal data type.
(append *list list* ...)	Takes any number of lists and combines their elements into one list.
(last *list*)	Finds the last element of a list.
(length *list*)	Finds the number of elements in a list.
(member *element list*)	Finds the sublist of a list that starts with *element* and continues to the end of the list.
(nth *integer list*)	Finds the element of a list whose number is *integer*. The first item in a list has the number 0.

Getting Data from a List

In the Mdist program, a function was applied to a list to get the total of all the numbers in that list. Functions like plus, minus, multiply, and divide accept multiple numeric values for arguments. But what if you want to apply a list of elements to a function that will only take single elements for arguments?

Using Simple Lists to Store Data

You use Mapcar when you want to apply a list to a function, one argument at a time. It allows you to use a single function on a list of items. For example, suppose you want the sequential numbering program from Chapter 5 to place the numbers at points you manually select rather than in a straight line. Figure 9.2 shows a program that does this.

In the Seqrand program, the following While expression is used to allow the user to pick random point locations for the numbered sequence:

```
(while rand
    (setq rand (getpoint "\nSelect points in sequence: " ))
```

```
;Program to write sequential numbers -- Seqrand.lsp
(defun C:SEQRAND (/ rand currnt ptlst)
(setvar "cmdecho" 0)                              ;no echo to prompt
(setq rand T)                                     ;set up rand
(setq currnt (getint "\nEnter first number in sequence: "))
(while rand                                       ;while point is picked
    (setq rand (getpoint "\nSelect points in sequence: " ));get point
    (setq ptlst (append ptlst (list rand) ))      ;add point to list
)
(mapcar
    '(lambda (rand)                               ;define lambda expression
        (if rand                                  ;if point (rand) exists
          (progn
          (command "text" rand "" "" currnt)      ;place number at point rand
          (setq currnt (1+ currnt))               ;get next number
          )
        )
     )
  ptlst                                           ;list supplied to lambda
 )
(setvar "cmdecho" 1)                              ;echo to prompt on
(princ)
)
```

Figure 9.2: A program to place sequential numbers in nonlinear locations

```
      (setq ptlst (append ptlst (list rand) ))
   )
```

This While expression creates the list Ptlst comprising points entered by the user. The user sees the prompt

Select points in sequence:

each time he or she selects a point. Once the user is done, the Mapcar expression reads the list of points and applies them to a function that enters the sequence of numbers at those points:

```
(mapcar
   '(lambda (rand)
      (if (not (not rand))
         (progn
         (command "text" rand " " " " currnt)
         (setq currnt (1 + currnt))
         )
      )
   )
   ptlst
)
```

In this set of expressions, Mapcar applies the elements of the list Ptlst to a Lambda expression. Lambda is an AutoLISP function for situations in which the creation of a function with Defun would take up more memory than you wish to use. An example would be a large function such as the Setup facility on the AutoCAD menu. Setup is actually an AutoLISP program called SETUP.LSP that is normally only used once in the course of an editing session.

Lambda is nearly identical to Defun. The only difference between Lambda and Defun is that Defun requires a name for the function being defined and Lambda does not. Otherwise, their syntax is identical:

(lambda *argument_list set_of_expressions*)

As I mentioned, the AutoCAD SETUP.LSP program uses a Lambda function. Since Setup is a fairly large program that is usually run only once in the life of a drawing, it is not worth making it into a function. If it were a function created with Defun, once it had been used to set up a file, it would remain in the portion of memory allocated to Auto-LISP, taking up precious space.

Lambda allows the Setup function to exist long enough to do its job. When Setup is done, it returns any memory it has used to the AutoLISP environment.

Although the Setup function is a single large Lambda expression, Lambda expressions can also be used within other functions.

The Lambda expression in the Seqrand program writes the variable Currnt to the drawing with the AutoCAD Text command and uses the single argument Rand as a coordinate to place the text. The Lambda expression also adds 1 to the Currnt variable, incrementing the number being added to the drawing by 1.

Mapcar takes the list of points stored as Ptlst and, one at a time, applies each element of the list to the variable Rand in the Lambda expression. Rand is then used as the point input in the Text command. This is done repeatedly until all the elements have been applied. The If expression is added to the Lambda expression to check for the end of Ptlst.

Mapcar can apply more than one list to a function, as shown in the following expression:

```
(mapcar 'setvar
   '("cmdecho" "blipmode" "osnap" "expert")
   '(0 0 512 1)
)
```

Here Mapcar applies several AutoCAD system variables to the Setvar function. One element is taken from each list and applied to Setvar. Cmdecho is set to 0, Blipmode is set to 1, Osmode is set to 512 (Nearest), and Expert is set to 1.

*E*valuating Data from an Entire List at Once

Apply is similar to Mapcar in that it allows you to supply a list as an argument to a function. But rather than metering out each item in the list one by one, Apply provides the entire contents of a list as an argument all at once. As an example, you could use Apply in the Mdist function to add distances, as shown in Figure 9.3.

In this program, Apply is given the list of distances, Dstlst, which it applies to the plus function. If you load and run this program, you'll find that it works no differently from the earlier version of Mdist.

```
;Program to measure non-sequential distances
(defun MDIST (/ dstlst dst)
   ;while loop to obtain list of points-------------------------------------
   (while (setq dst (getdist "\nPick distance or Return to exit: "))
        (Setq dstlst (append dstlst (list dst)))    ;append new point to list
        (princ (apply '+ dstlst))                   ;print current total
   );end while;-------------------------------------------------------------
);end MDIST
```

Figure 9.3: *The Mdist function using Apply*

Using Complex Lists to Store Data

In Chapter 8, you created an error function that reset the Osmode system variable when an error occurred. The problem with that error function was that it was too specific. It could only restore the Osmode system variable to its previous setting. But you can create a function that will help you handle system-variable settings in a more general way, using the Length function.

The Length function allows you to find the length of a list. This function is often used in conjunction with the Repeat function to process a list. The following function converts a list of system variables to a list containing both the variables and their current setting:

```
(defun GETMODE (mod1)
   (setq *mod2 '( ))
   (repeat (length mod1)
   (setq *mod2
      (append *mod2
         (list (list (car mod1) (getvar (car mod1)))))
      )
   )
   (setq mod1 (cdr mod1))
)
```

Using this function, you can store the current system variable settings in a list. Figure 9.4 shows the Break2 program from Chapter 8 modified to include the Getmode function.

The following expression has been added to the Break2 program:

(getmode '("osmode" "orthomode" "cmdecho"))

Here, a list of system variables is supplied as an argument to the Getmode function. The first expression in the Getmode function (after the Defun line) creates a list that will be appended to. The second

```
;function to save system variable settings------------------------------------
(defun GETMODE (mod1)
   (setq *mod2 '())                    ;create global variable to store settings
   (repeat (length mod1)              ;find length of variable list and repeat
      (setq *mod2                     ;build *mod2 list
            (append *mod2
                 (list (list (car mod1) (getvar (car mod1))))
            )
      )
      (setq mod1 (cdr mod1))          ;go to next element in list
   );end repeat
)

;function to restore system variable settings---------------------------------
(defun SETMODE (mod1)
   (repeat (length mod1)                  ;find length of list and repeat
      (setvar (caar mod1) (cadar mod1))   ;extract setting info and reset
      (setq mod1 (cdr mod1))              ;go to next element in list
   );end repeat
)

;function for error trap ------------------------------------------------------
(defun *error* (msg)
  (setmode *mod2)                     ;reset system variables
  (princ msg)                         ;print error message
  (princ)
)


;program to break circle into two arcs-----------------------------------------
(defun C:BREAK2 (/ pt1 pt2 pt3 pt4 pt0 ang1 dst1)
   (getmode '("osmode" "orthomode" "cmdecho"))        ;saves system vars.
   (mapcar 'setvar '("osmode" "orthomode" "cmdecho")  ;set vars. for funct.
         '(512 0 0)
   )
   (setq pt1 (getpoint "\nSelect object: "))           ;get first break point
   (setq pt2 (getpoint pt1 "\nEnter second point: ")) ;get second break point
   (setvar "osmode" 128)                               ;perpend osnap mode
   (Setq pt3 (getpoint pt1 "\nSelect parallel line: "));get 2nd line
   (setq ang1 (angle pt1 pt3))                         ;find angle btwn lines
   (setq dst1 (distance pt1 pt3))                      ;find dist. btwn lines
   (setq pt4 (polar pt2 ang1 dst1))                    ;derive pt4 on 2nd line
      (command
            "break" pt1 pt2                             ;break 1st line
            "break" pt3 pt4                             ;break 2nd line
            "line" pt1 pt3 ""                           ;close ends of lines
            "line" pt2 pt4 ""
      )
   (setmode *mod2)                                      ;reset system vars.
)
```

Figure 9.4: The revised Break2 program

expression performs an iteration on a set of expressions using the Repeat function:

```
(setq *mod2 '( ))
(repeat (length mod1)
```

Repeat uses an integer argument to determine the number of times it needs to repeat the evaluation of its other arguments. Here, Length returns the length of Mod1, which is a local variable that stores the list of system variables.

Looking at the Getmode expression in the Break2 program, you can see that the argument to Getmode is a list of three elements:

```
("osmode" "orthomode" "cmdecho")
```

This argument becomes the variable Mod1 in the Getmode function. Since the Length function returns the number of elements in a list, the function

```
(length mod1)
```

returns 3, which tells the Repeat function how many times to repeat the evaluation of its expressions (see Figure 9.5).

Repeat then processes the following set of expressions three times:

```
(setq *mod2
    (append *mod2
        (list (list (car mod1) (getvar (car mod1)))))
    )
)
(setq mod1 (cdr mod1)))
```

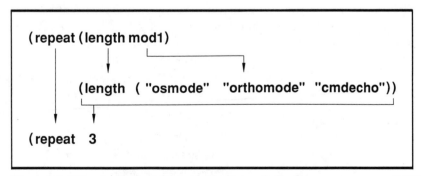

Figure 9.5: *Using Length and Repeat in the Getmode function*

This set of expressions takes an element of the list Mod1 and finds the current setting for that element:

(getvar (car mod1))

Then the setting value is combined with the setting name to form a two-element list:

(list (car mod1) (getvar (car mod1)))

This new list is then appended to the list *mod2 and *mod2 is reassigned the value of the new appended list:

(setq *mod2
    (append *mod2
       (list (list (car mod1)(getvar car mod1)))))

Finally, the first element of Mod1 is removed in preparation for the next iteration:

(setq mod1 (cdr mod1)))

Remember that Cdr returns a copy of a list with its first element removed. The whole process is then repeated again. When the Getmode is done, a global variable called *mod2 is created. That variable might look like this:

(("osmode" 0)("orthomode" 1)("cmdecho" 1))

In this list, each element is another list that contains the mode as its first element and its current setting as its second element.

    Once the desired settings have been saved, you can go on to change the settings to suit your program. In the case of the Break2 program, Osmode is set to 512, the Nearest setting, Orthomode is set to 0, which turns off the Orthomode, and Cmdecho is set to 0, which inhibits command echoing to the prompt line.

    When Break2 has done its work, you need a way to restore your saved settings. The Setmode function in Figure 9.4 will restore the settings saved by the Getmode function.

    This function also uses Length and Repeat to perform an iteration. In this case, the iterative function consists of two expressions:

(setvar (caar mod1) (cadar mod1))
(setq mod1 (cdr mod1))

The first of these expressions takes the first element of the list of saved settings and applies *its* two elements to Setvar. In our example, the result of this combination has the effect of this expression:

(setvar "osmode" 0)

The result is an expression that sets Osmode to 0. The next expression removes the first element from the list of settings, and then the process is repeated.

The Setmode function is placed at the end of the Break2 program to reset the system variables. It is also placed in the *error* function. As long as Getmode is used in a function to save system variables, the *error* function shown in Figure 9.4 will work to restore system variables in the event that the AutoLISP program is cancelled. With the addition of the Getmode and Setmode functions, you have a general module for maintaining system variables.

*U**sing Lists for Comparisons*

Like Mapcar, Foreach applies individual elements of a list to a function. But Foreach only accepts a single list. Foreach is often used to test elements of a list for a particular condition. For example, you could test a list of coordinates to sort out those above another datum point:

```
(foreach n
   '((4.00 1.00) (10.09 1.01) (11.96 6.80)
      (7.03 10.38) (2.11 6.79) (4.00 1.00))
  (if (> (cadr n) 2)(Setq newlist (append newlist (list n))))
  )
```

This function simply checks the y value of each coordinate list against the value 2. If that value is greater than 2, the coordinates are added to a new list that contains only those coordinates whose y values are greater than 2.

*L**ocating Elements in a List*

You won't always want to use all the elements of a list in your programs. In many instances, you will want to obtain a specific element from a list. There are two functions, Member and Nth, that can help you find specific elements in a list.

Searching through Lists

To see how these two functions work, look at the Clean program (Figure 9.6), which you first saw in Chapter 3.

Before analyzing this program, I must first explain what an Atomlist is. An Atomlist is a special list used to store data. It contains the names of all the built-in AutoLISP functions. It is also used to store any user-defined functions and symbols. You can view its contents by first flipping the screen to text mode, and then entering

!atomlist

You will see a screen like the one shown in Figure 9.7.

Notice that the list contains all of the Autolisp functions I have discussed so far and a few I have not. If you are using ACAD.LSP to load some of your own functions, they will also appear at the top of the list. Whenever you create a new function or symbol, it is added to the beginning of the Atomlist. Try entering the following:

(setq myfunc "My name")

Now enter **!atomlist**. You will see that Myfunc is added to the list. The more functions you add, the larger the Atomlist gets and more memory is used to store symbols and functions.

If the Clean function is included in your ACAD.LSP file, it will also be added to the Atomlist at startup time. Clean's purpose is twofold.

```
;program to clean symbols and functions from atomlist and close open files
;---------------------------------------------------------------------------
(defun C:CLEAN (/ i item)
  (setq i 0)                                              ;set up counter
    ;while not at the end of atomlist do...
    (while (not (equal (setq item (nth i atomlist)) nil))
      (if (= (type (eval item)) 'FILE)                   ;if item is a file
        (close (eval item))                              ;close the file
      );end IF
    (setq i (1+ i) )                                      ;add 1 t counter
    );end WHILE
  (setq atomlist (member 'C:CLEAN atomlist))             ;redefine atomlist
  'DONE                                                   ;without symbols
  )                                                       ;previous to C:CLEAN
```

Figure 9.6: The Clean program

```
Loaded menu C:\ACAD10\ACAD.mnx

Command: !atomlist
(ATOMLIST LOAD GETVAR YMIN YMAX - / ZGLOBE SETQ CADR COMMAND C:ZP DEFUN ZVAL3 CT
RFIN ZVCONT GETSTRING SW CAR XMIN XMAX = OR IF GDZ GD ZVAL YHI XHI YLOW XLOW PIC
K YBUF XBUF YCTR XCTR CTR ZVAL1 ZV C:ZV LIST > < + GETPOINT * <= /= PROGN MID DR
AW CADADR CAADR T GRREAD NOT WHILE B A DISTANCE GETCORNER COND AA DA GRDRAW CA B
A VDST GDC HDST Z W C:LOADMAC C:AR C:MR C:OS C:SC C:FL C:CH C:EX C:TR C:RT C:LN
C:BR C:CO C:ST C:MV C:ETA C:ER PT OB SSGET C:BRA C:SETV C:ET C:JOIN C:ADDVAL C:E
D C:ETS C:THK C:ASCRC INTERS GRTEXT GRCLEAR VPORTS TRANS HANDENT TBLSEARCH TBLNE
XT ENTUPD ENTMOD ENTSEL ENTLAST ENTNEXT ENTDEL ENTGET SSMEMB SSDEL SSADD SSLENGT
H SSNAME ANGTOS RTOS OSNAP REDRAW GRAPHSCR TEXTSCR POLAR ANGLE INITGET GETKWORD
GETINT GETORIENT GETANGLE GETREAL GETDIST MENUCMD PROMPT FINDFILE GETENV SETVAR
 TERPRI PRINC PRIN1 PRINT WRITE-LINE READ-LINE WRITE-CHAR READ-CHAR CLOSE OPEN S
TRCASE ITOA ATOF ATOI CHR ASCII SUBSTR STRCAT STRLEN PAUSE PI MINUSP ZEROP NUMBE
RP FLOAT FIX SQRT SIN LOG EXPT EXP COS ATAN 1- 1+ ABS MAX MIN AND >= ~ GCD BOOLE
 LSH LOGIOR LOGAND REM ASSOC MEMBER SUBST LENGTH REVERSE LAST APPEND CDDDDR CDDD
AR CDDADR CDDAAR CDADDR CDADAR CDAADR CDAAAR CADDDR CADDAR CADADR CAADDR CAADAR
CAAADR CAAAAR CDDDR CDDAR CDADR CDAAR CADDR CADAR CAAAR CDDR CDAR CAAR CDR CONS
LISTP TYPE NULL EQUAL EQ BOUNDP ATOM NTH PAGETB PICKSET ENAME REAL FILE STR INT
SYM SUBR MAPCAR APPLY LAMBDA EVAL *ERROR* QUIT EXIT _VER VER UNTRACE TRACE FOREA
CH REPEAT FUNCTION QUOTE READ SET MEM VMON ALLOC EXPAND GC)

Command:
```

Figure 9.7: *A typical Atomlist*

First, it closes any files that may have been inadvertently left open. As I mentioned, this can result in a loss of data for the open file. Second, Clean clears the Atomlist of any function that was added after it, thereby recapturing memory space.

In order to find and close any open files, Clean uses the While function in conjunction with the If and Type functions. First, a counter is set to 0. The symbol I is used as a counting device:

(setq i 0)

Next, a While expression checks to see if an item of the Atomlist is equal to nil. The Nth function is used to read each element of the Atomlist.

(nth i atomlist)

Nth's syntax is

(nth *integer list*)

where *integer* is the numeric position of an element in *list*. In Clean, Nth returns the element whose position within the Atomlist is represented by I. The variable I is a counter to which 1 is added each time the While function loops through the expressions it contains. The net result is that each element of the Atomlist is compared to nil. The While function continues to loop through its expressions until such a condition is met (Figure 9.8).

Notice that the element returned by Nth is assigned to the variable Item. This allows the next If to test the element to see whether it is a file descriptor:

(if (= (type (eval item)) 'FILE)

The Eval function forces an extra evaluation of the variable Item to extract its value. Eval can be used to find the value of a nested symbol, that is, a symbol whose value is also a symbol. Remember that the variable Item is used to store another variable. You want to know the data type of the value held by this variable, not Item's value. By using Eval on a variable, you are essentially saying "Evaluate this variable twice," since AutoLISP automatically evaluates everything once.

The Type function in this example returns the data type of the value of Item. If Eval were not used, Type would return the data type of the symbol Item rather than the data type of Item's value (see Figure 9.9).

```
(defun C:CLEAN (/ i item)
 (setq i 0)
  (while (not (equal (setq item (nth i atomlist)) nil))
    (if (= (type (eval item)) 'FILE)
      (close (eval item))
    );end IF
    (setq i (1+ i) )
    )
  (setq atomlist (member 'C:CLEAN atomlist))
  'DONE
  )
```

Figure 9.8: The While loop in Clean

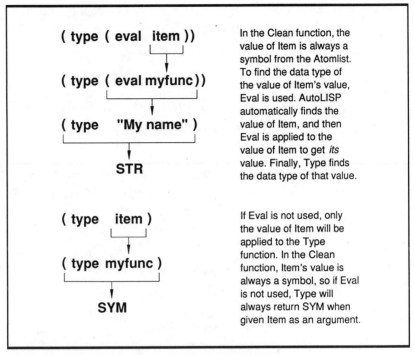

Figure 9.9: Using Eval to force one level of evaluation

The following table gives a list of the values returned by Type and their meanings:

Value	Meaning
REAL	Real number
FILE	File descriptor
STR	String
INT	Integer
SYM	Symbol
LIST	List or user-defined function
SUBR	AutoLISP function
PICKSET	Selection set
ENAME	Entity name
PAGETB	Function paging table

If an item turns out to be a file descriptor, then the next line closes that file:

(close (eval item))

Using Elements of Lists as Markers

Once Clean has finished closing any open files, it proceeds to redefine the Atomlist:

(setq atomlist (member 'C:CLEAN atomlist)

Here, the function Member is used to create a list whose elements are all the elements of the Atomlist beginning with Clean. Member returns a list that is a sublist of another list.

The syntax for Member is

(member *atom/list list*)

Member's first argument is an atom or list. This first argument identifies an element in the list from which the sublist is to be extracted and tells Member where to begin the sublist. The second argument is the actual list from which the sublist is to be extracted. Member returns a list containing all the elements of the second argument, starting with the element signified by the first argument.

The Setq expression above then assigns that sublist to the Atomlist. The symbol Clean acts like a marker within the list telling the Member function where to begin the sublist. The net affect is that of clearing the Atomlist of all the symbols and functions that were added after Clean (see Figure 9.10).

Finding the Properties of AutoCAD Entities

One of the most powerful features of AutoLISP is its ability to access the properties of drawing entities. You can find properties such as the endpoint coordinates of lines, their layer, color, and linetypes, and the string value of text. You can also modify these properties directly.

Entity properties are accessed using two AutoLISP data types—entity names and selection sets. Entity names are similar to symbols in

```
Command: !atomlist
(ATOMLIST LOAD GETVAR YMIN YMAX - / ZGLOBE SETQ CADR COMMAND C:ZP DEFUN ZVAL3 CT
RFIN ZVCONT GETSTRING SW CAR XMIN XMAX = OR IF GD2 GD ZVAL YHI XHI YLOW XLOW PIC
K YBUF XBUF YCTR XCTR CTR ZVAL1 ZV C:ZV LIST > < + GETPOINT * <= /= PROGN MID DR
AW CADADR CAADR T GRREAD NOT WHILE B A DISTANCE GETCORNER COND AA DA GRDRAW CA B
A VDST GDC HDST Z W C:LOADMAC C:AR C:MR C:OS C:SC C:FL C:CH C:EX C:TR C:RT C:LN
C:BR C:CO C:ST C:MV C:ETA C:ER PT OB SSGET C:BRA C:SETV C:ET C:JOIN C:CLEAN C:E
D C:ETS C:THK C:ASCRC INTERS GRTEXT GRCLEAR VPORTS TRANS HANDENT TBLSEARCH TBLNE
XT ENTUPD ENTMOD ENTSEL ENTLAST ENTNEXT ENTDEL ENTGET SSMEMB SSDEL SSADD SSLENGT
H SSNAME ANGTOS RTOS OSNAP REDRAW GRAPHSCR TEXTSCR POLAR ANGLE INITGET GETKWORD
GETINT GETORIENT GETANGLE GETREAL GETDIST MENUCMD PROMPT FINDFILE GETENV SETVAR
 TERPRI PRINC PRIN1 PRINT WRITE-LINE READ-LINE WRITE-CHAR READ-CHAR CLOSE OPEN S
TRCASE ITOA ATOF ATOI CHR ASCII SUBSTR STRCAT STRLEN PAUSE PI MINUSP ZEROP NUMBE
RP FLOAT FIX SQRT SIN LOG EXPT EXP COS ATAN 1- 1+ ABS MAX MIN AND >= ~ GCD BOOLE
 LSH LOGIOR LOGAND REM ASSOC MEMBER SUBST LENGTH REVERSE LAST APPEND CDDDDR CDDD
AR CDDADR CDDAAR CDADDR CDADAR CDAADR CDAAAR CADDDR CADDAR CADAAR CAADDR CAADAR
CAAADR CAAAAR CDDDR CDDAR CDADR CDAAR CADDR CADAR CAAAR CDDR CDAR CAAR CDR CONS
LISTP TYPE NULL EQUAL EQ BOUNDP ATOM NTH PAGETB PICKSET ENAME REAL FILE STR INT
SYM SUBR MAPCAR APPLY LAMBDA EVAL *ERROR* QUIT EXIT _VER VER UNTRACE TRACE FOREA
CH REPEAT FUNCTION QUOTE READ SET MEM VMON ALLOC EXPAND GC)

Command:
```

Figure 9.10: *The shaded area showing the symbols removed from the Atomlist with Member*

that they are symbolic representations of entities. An entity name is actually a device used to point to a record in a drawing database. This database record holds all the information regarding the particular entity. Once you know an entity name, you can retrieve the information stored in the entity's record.

Using Selection Sets and Entity Names

A selection set is a collection of entity names. Selection sets can contain just one entity name or several. Each name in the selection set has a unique number assigned to it from zero to the number of names in the set minus one.

To find out how you access this entity information, let's look at the Chtxt program used in Chapter 7 (Figure 9.11). As you may recall, this program allows you to edit a line of text without having to enter

```
;function to find text string from text entity---------------------------
(defun gettxt ()
(setvar "osmode" 64)                                  ;set osnap to insert
(setq pt1 (getpoint "\nPick text to edit: "))         ;get point on text
(Setvar "osmode" 0)                                   ;set osnap back to zero
(setq oldobj (entget (ssname (ssget pt1) 0) ))        ;get entity zero from prop.
(setq txtstr (assoc 1 oldobj))                        ;get list containing string
(cdr txtstr)                                           ;extract string from prop.
)

;function to update text string of text entity---------------------------
(defun revtxt ()
(setq newtxt (cons 1 newtxt))                         ;create replacement propty.
(entmod (subst newtxt txtstr oldobj))                 ;update database
)

;program to edit single line of text-------------------------------------
(defun C:CHTXT (/ count oldstr newstr osleng otleng oldt old1
                 old2 newtxt pt1 oldobj txtstr oldt)
(setq count 0)                                        ;setup counter to zero
(setq oldtxt (gettxt))                                ;get old string from text
(setq otleng (strlen oldtxt))                         ;find length of old string
(setq oldstr (getstring T "\nEnter old string "))     ;get string to change
(Setq newstr (getstring T "\nEnter new string "))     ;get replacement string
(setq osleng (strlen oldstr))                         ;find length of substring-
  ;while string to replace is not found, do...           to be replaced
  (while (and (/= oldstr oldt)(<= count otleng))
    (setq count (1+ count))                           ;add 1 to counter
    (setq oldt (substr oldtxt count osleng))          ;get substring to compare
  );end WHILE
  ;if counting stops before end of old string is reached...
  (if (<= count otleng)
        (progn
           (setq old1 (substr oldtxt 1 (1- count))) ;get 1st half of old string
           (setq old2 (substr oldtxt (+ count osleng) otleng));get 2nd half
           (setq newtxt (strcat old1 newstr old2))  ;combine to make new string
           (revtxt)                                  ;update drawing
        )
        (princ "\nNo matching string found.")        ;else print message
  );end if
(PRINC)
);END C:CHTXT
```

Figure 9.11: The Chtxt program

the entire line. The fourth line in Chtxt does the work of actually extracting the text string from the database:

(setq oldtxt (gettxt))

Here, the program makes a call to a user-defined function called Gettxt. Gettxt first finds a single point Pt1 that locates the text to be edited:

(setvar "osmode" 64)
(setq pt1 (getpoint "\nPick text to edit: "))
(setvar "osmode" 0)

Next comes the real work of finding the entity. The following line uses several functions to extract the entity name from the drawing database:

(setq oldobj (entget (ssname (ssget pt1) 0)))

This innocent-looking set of expressions does a lot of work. It first creates a selection set of one object with

(ssget pt1)

You may recall from Chapter 4 that Ssget accepts a point location to find objects for a selection set. If you entered the expression above at the command prompt, and Pt1 had been previously defined as a point nearest an object, you would get the name of a selection set. Try the following exercise.

1. Open an AutoCAD file and place the following text in the drawing:

   For want of a battle, the kingdom was lost.

2. Enter the following expression:

   (setq pt1 (getpoint "\nPick the text: "))

3. Use the Insert Osnap override option from either the side or pull-down menu and pick the text.

4. Enter the following expression:

   (ssget pt1)

   You will get a message that looks similar to the following:

   <Selection set: 1>

This is a selection set. The number following the colon in the above example may be different depending on whether previous selections sets have been created. Once a selection set has been created, Ssname is used to find the entity name.

5. Enter the following:

   (ssname (ssget pt1) 0)

   Ssname returns the entity name of a single object in the selection set that looks similar to the following:

   <Entity name: 600000c8>

Just as with selection sets, the number that follows the colon will differ depending on the editing session.

The syntax for Ssname is

(ssname *selection_set integer*)

You can get the selection set from a symbol representing it or directly from the Ssget function, as in the preceding example. The integer argument tells Ssname which entity to select within the selection set. In this example, there was only one object, so you used the integer 0, which represents the first object in a selection set. If there were several objects in the selection set, say four, you could use an integer from 0 to 3.

At the next level, the function Entget performs the actual database extraction.

6. Enter the following:

(setq oldobj (entget (ssname (ssget pt1) 0)))

You get a list revealing the properties of the text (see Figure 9.12). This list obtained using Entget is called a property list. Entget's syntax is

(entget *entity name*)

```
Command: redraw

Command: dtext
Start point or Align/Center/Fit/Middle/Right/Style:
Height <0.2000>:

Rotation angle <0>:

Text: For want of a battle, the kingdom was lost.
Text:
Command: (setq pt1 (getpoint "\nPick the text: "))

Pick the text: insert
of (4.34948 5.84609 0.0)

Command: (setq oldobj (entget (ssname (ssget pt1) 0) ))
((-1 . <Entity name: 60000030>) (0 . "TEXT") (8 . "0") (10 4.34948 5.84609 0.0)

(40 . 0.2) (1 . "For want of a battle, the kingdom was lost.") (50 . 0.0) (41 .

1.0) (51 . 0.0) (7 . "STANDARD") (71 . 0) (72 . 0) (11 0.0 0.0 0.0) (210 0.0 0.0

1.0))

Command:
```

Figure 9.12: *The property list of the text*

Property lists consist of other lists each of whose first element is an integer code. The code represents a particular property like an object's layer, color, linetype, or object type.

Property lists are in a class of lists called *association lists.* Earlier in this chapter, you constructed a list of system variables. That list looked like the following:

(("osmode" 0)("orthomode" 1)("cmdecho" 1))

This is also an association list. Each element of the list is itself a list of two elements, the first of which can be considered a key-value.

Each list within an entity's property list starts with an integer code. That integer code is the key-value to that list, otherwise known as the *group code.* The group code is associated with a particular property. For example, the group code 1 is associated with the string value of a text entity. The group code 10 is associated with the insertion point of the text. Table 9.2 shows the group codes for text and their meanings.

If you are familiar with the AutoCAD DXF file format and coding system, then these group codes should be familiar. Appendix B gives a detailed listing of these and other group codes if you want to know more.

Now that the expression has retrieved the property list, you need a way to pull the information out of the list. A function for this purpose is found in the next line.

7. Enter the following:

(setq txtstr (assoc 1 oldobj))

In the previous expression the property list was assigned to the variable Oldobj. The above expression uses a new function called Assoc:

(assoc 1 oldobj)

This expression returns the list

(1 . "For want of a battle, the kingdom was lost.")

Remember that Oldobj is the variable for the property list of the text you selected earlier.

The syntax for Assoc is

(assoc *key-value association_list*)

Assoc looks through an association list, finds the list whose first element is the key-value, and then returns that list containing the key-value.

Table 9.2: Group Codes for Text and Their Meanings

CODE	MEANING
-1	Entity name
0	Entity type ("TEXT", "LINE", "ARC", etc.)
7	Text style
8	Layer
10	Insertion point
11	Center alignment point (for centered text)
21	Right alignment point (for right-justified text)
31	Second alignment point (for fit or aligned text)
40	Text height
41	X scale factor
50	Rotation angle
51	Oblique angle
71	Text mirror code (2, mirrored in x axis; 4, mirrored in y axis)
72	Text alignment code (0, left justified; 1, centered at baseline; 2, right justified; 3, text uses align option; 4, centered at middle; 5, text uses fit option)
210	3-D extrusion amount in x, y, or z direction

In the case of this property list example, Assoc looks through the property list Oldobj, finds the list whose first element is the group code 1, and then returns that list. The list returned by Assoc is assigned to the symbol Txtstr. Finally, Cdr is applied to Txtsrt to obtain the string value of the selected text.

8. Enter the following:

(cdr txtstr)

The string value associated with the group code 1 is retrieved. Figure 9.13 diagrams the entire operation.

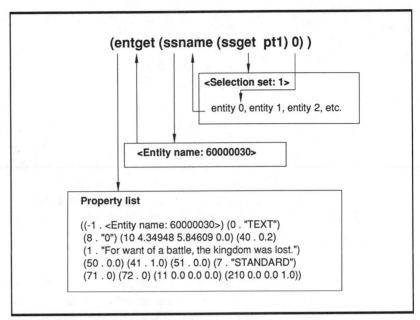

Figure 9.13: *A diagram of the property-list extraction*

In summary, to find a particular property of an entity, you must first create a selection set containing that entity with Ssget, extract the entity name from the selection set with Ssname, and then extract the property list using the entity name and the function Entget. Once you have the property list, you can apply Assoc to it to get the specific property you want, using group codes. Finally, apply Cdr to the singled-out property to get the value of the property.

*U*nderstanding the Structure of Property Lists

The first thing you might have noticed about the property list in the example above is that most of the sublists were two-element lists with a period separating the elements. This type of list is called a *dotted pair*. It is not a list in the true sense of the term, and many of the functions used to manipulate lists will not work on dotted pairs. For this reason, dotted pairs are usually considered a data type in themselves.

You can use Car and Cdr on dotted pairs just as you would on lists. For example, if you entered the following:

```
(car '(A . B))
```

the symbol A would be returned. You could also enter

(cdr '(A . B))

and the symbol B would be returned. As you can see, dotted pairs act slightly differently from regular lists. If Cdr is applied to a normal list, as in the following:

(cdr '(A B))

a list, (B), is returned. But in the case of a dotted pair, the second element of the dotted pair is returned by itself, not as part of a list.

You can create a dotted pair using the Cons function. Normally, Cons must have two arguments. The first argument is the element to be added to the beginning of a list and the second is the list to be added to. Enter the following:

(cons 'A '(B))

The list (A B) is returned. You could think of Cons as the opposite of Cdr since instead of returning a list with its first element removed, Cons returns a list with a new first element added. But if the second argument to Cons is not a list, then a dotted pair is created. Enter the following:

(cons 'A 'B)

The dotted pair (A . B) is returned.

The Cons function and dotted pairs reflect the inner workings of AutoLISP, and it would be too difficult and time-consuming to explain these items thoroughly. At the end of Chapter 11, I mention a few sources for more information on the general subject of LISP that can shed light on Cons and dotted pairs. For now, let's continue by looking at a function that allows you to directly modify the AutoCAD drawing database.

Changing the Properties of AutoCAD Entities

Now that you have seen how entity properties are found, it is a short step to actually modifying properties. To update an entity record in the drawing database, you redefine the entity's property list and then use the function Entmod to update the drawing database. Look at the EDTXT.LSP file again and consider the Revtxt function:

```
(defun revtxt ( )
(setq newtxt (cons 1 newtxt))
(entmod (subst newtxt txtstr oldobj))
)
```

The first thing Revtxt does is use the Cons function to create a dotted pair. The Cons expression uses the integer 1 for the first element and the string value held by Newtxt for the second. Newtxt is a string value representing the new text that is to replace the old text in the property list Oldobj. As I mentioned earlier, Cons creates a dotted pair when both its arguments are atoms. The new dotted pair looks like this:

(1 . "For want of a nail, the kingdom was lost.")

Notice that the structure of this list is identical to that of the list Txtstr, which was retrieved from the text property list earlier.

The last line of the Revtxt function does two things. First it uses the function Subst to substitute the value of Newtxt for the value of Txtstr in the property list Oldobj:

(subst newtxt txtstr oldobj)

Subst requires three arguments. The first is the replacing item, the second is the item to be replaced, and the third is the list in which the item to be replaced is found. So Subst's syntax is as follows:

(subst *replacing_item item_to_be_replaced list_containing_item*)

Subst returns a list with the substitution made.

Next, the function Entmod updates the drawing database. It looks at the entity name of the list that is passed to it as an argument. This list must be in the form of a property list. It then looks in the drawing database for the entity name that corresponds to the one in the list. When it finds the corresponding entity in the drawing database, it replaces that database record with the information in Entmod's property list argument. The user sees the result as a new line of text.

Getting Entity Names and Coordinates Together

You can rewrite Gettxt with a function that doesn't require that you obtain a selection set. Entsel will find a single entity name directly without you first having to use Ssget to create a selection set. Since Entsel only allows the user to pick a single object, it is best suited to situations in which a program or function doesn't require multiple selections of objects.

Here is an example of Gettxt using Entsel:

```
(defun gettxt ( )
(setq oldobj (entget (car (entsel "\nSelect object: "))))
(setq txtstr (assoc 1 oldobj))
(cdr txtstr)
)
```

Entsel acts like a Get function by allowing you to provide a prompt string. Instead of returning a number, string, or point, Entsel returns a list of two elements. The first element is an entity name, and the second is a list of coordinates specifying the point picked to select the entity, for example:

```
(<Entity name: 60000012> (4.0 3.0 0.0))
```

Since Gettxt is only concerned with the entity name, Car is used on the value returned:

```
(car (entsel "\nSelect object: "))
```

This expression replaces the Ssget and Ssname functions used previously:

```
(ssname (ssget pt1) 0)
```

Also, since Entsel pauses to allow the user to select an object, the Getpoint expression can be eliminated along with the Setvar function.

*S*ummary

You have seen how lists can be used to manipulate data both as forms and as simple lists of information. AutoLISP makes no distinction between a list that is an expression to be evaluated and a list that is used to store data; it will try to evaluate both types of lists as if they are expressions. Once you understand the methods for manipulating lists, you can begin to develop some powerful programs.

In the next chapter, you will look in more detail at how you can access information directly from AutoCAD. You will also look at how to access the property of complex objects such as blocks and polylines.

10

Editing AutoCAD Entities

Featuring:

Editing multiple objects efficiently

Speeding up your programs

Filtering entities based on properties

Searching AutoCAD's system tables

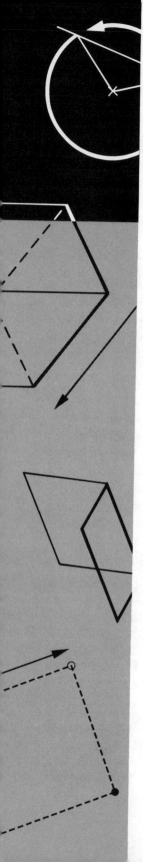

10

In the last chapter you learned about the Ssname and Entget functions that, together with Ssget, allow you to extract information about an object from the drawing database. In this chapter, you will learn how to edit several entities at once. You'll see how to use functions that can improve your computer's processing speed. You also will look at how to obtain information regarding a drawing's table information, which consists of layers and their settings, viewport, UCSs, and other system options.

*A*ccessing the Drawing Database

There are several functions that allow you to access the AutoCAD drawing database directly. Table 10.1 lists the functions and gives a brief description of each. You have already seen first-hand how a few of these functions work. In this and the following chapter, you will explore the use of several more of these very powerful editing tools.

*E*diting Multiple Objects

The Chtxt program you looked at in the last chapter used Ssget to obtain a single object. However, Ssget is really better suited to obtaining multiple sets of objects. You can use groups of objects collected together as selection sets to perform some operation on them all at once.

To examine methods for editing multiple entities, you will look at a program that offers an alternate to the AutoCAD Extend command. Though Extend allows you to extend several objects, you have to pick each object individually. Picking objects individually allows for greater flexibility in the type of object you can extend and the location of the extension. However, there are times when you will want to perform a more repetitive multiple extend operation such as extending several lines to another line.

Table 10.1: Functions Used to Access Drawing Database

FUNCTION	DESCRIPTION
(entnext *entity_name*)	If used with no argument, Entnext will return the entity name of the first entity in the database. If an entity name is given as an argument, Entnext returns the first subentity of *entity_name*. A subentity is an entity contained in a complex entity, such as a polyline vertex or a block attribute.
(entlast)	Returns the entity name of the last entity added to the drawing database.
(entsel *prompt*)	Prompts the user to select an entity and then returns a list whose first element is the entity's name and whose second element is the pick point used to select the entity. A prompt can be optionally added. If no prompt is added, the prompt "Select object" is used automatically.
(handent *handle*)	Returns an entity name given an entity's handle.
(entdel *entity_name*)	Deletes *entity_name*. If the entity has previously been deleted in the current editing session, then the entity named will be restored.
(entget *entity_name*)	Returns the property list of *entity_name*.
(entmod *property_list*)	Updates the drawing database record of the entity whose entity name appears in the *property_list*. The entity name is the − 1 group code sublist of the *property_list*.
(entupd *entity_name*)	Updates the display of polyline vertices and block attributes that have been modified using Entmod.

You can use AutoLISP's Ssget function to help you simplify the processing of multiple entities. Figure 10.1 shows a sketch of how a multiple-extend program might work manually and Figure 10.2 shows the actual program derived from that sketch.

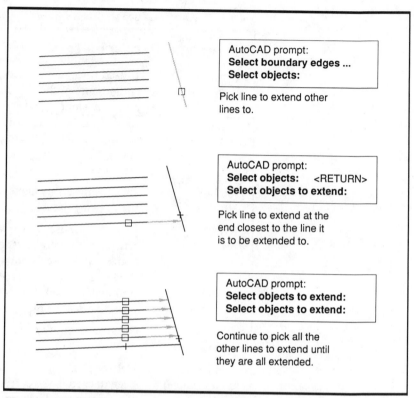

Figure 10.1: A sketch of a multiple-extend process

```
;Program to extend multiple lines - Mlext.lsp --------------------------------

(defun c:MLEXT (/ x y sset1 count pt1 pt2 int obj elst)
(graphscr)                                              ;shift to graphics
(princ "\nSelect Boundary edge...")                     ;print prompt
(setq obj (car (entsel)))                               ;Get entity name
(setq x (getpoint "\nPick axis crossing lines to extend: "))
(setq y (getpoint x "\nPick endpoint: "))               ;get axis crossing lines
        (setq sset1 (ssget "c" x y))                    ;get entities to extend
        (setq count 0)                                  ;set counter
          (if (/= sset1 nil)                            ;test for selection set
            (while (< count (sslength sset1))           ;while still select. set
              (setq elst (entget (ssname sset1 count))  ;get entity name
                    pt1  (cdr (assoc 10 elst))          ;get one endpoint
                    pt2  (cdr (assoc 11 elst))          ;get other endpoint
                    int  (inters x y pt1 pt2)           ;find intersection
              );end setq                                     of axis and line
              (command "extend" obj "" int "")          ;command to extend line
              (setq count (1+ count))                   ;go to next line count
            );end while
          );end if
);end defun
```

Figure 10.2: The MLEXT.LSP file

In this section you'll copy this program and create an AutoCAD drawing. Then you'll run the program and see how it works.

1. Open a file called MLEXT.LSP and copy the program in Figure 10.2 into your file. Once you are done, save and exit the MLEXT.LSP file.

2. Start AutoCAD and open a new drawing called Chapt10. Remember to add the equal sign at the end of the file name.

3. Draw the drawing shown in Figure 10.3. The figure indicates the coordinate location of the endpoints so you can duplicate the drawing exactly. Do not include the text indicating the coordinates.

4. Save this drawing—you'll use it again later in this chapter.

5. Load the MLEXT.LSP file and enter **mlext** at the command prompt.

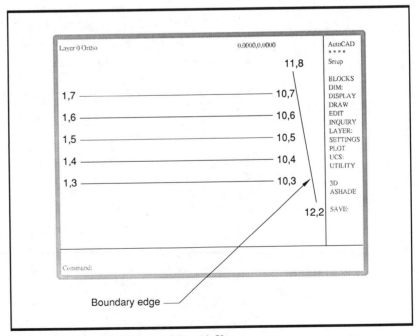

Figure 10.3: Lines drawn in the Chapt10 file

6. When you see the prompt

> **Select boundary edges...**
> **Select object:**

pick the line labeled Boundary Edge in Figure 10.3.

7. At the next prompt

> **Pick axis crossing lines to extend:**

pick a point at coordinates 8, 2. You can use the Snap mode and dynamic coordinate readout to help you locate this point.

8. At the next prompt

> **Pick endpoint:**

pick a point at coordinates 8, 9. The lines that are crossed by the axis are extended to the Boundary Edge line.

Let's look at how this program works. The first expression you come to is

> **(graphscr)**

This simply flips the display to the graphics screen in case the user is currently in Text mode. Another function called Textscr does just the opposite.

Next, Mlext finds the boundary line the other lines will be extended to:

> **(princ "\nSelect boundary edge...")**
> **(setq obj (car (entsel)))**

Here Entsel obtains the entity name. Since Entsel returns a two-element list containing the name and the pick coordinate, Car is used to extract the entity name from the list. Also note the use of a prompt similar to the one used by the Extend command.

The next several lines create a selection set of lines to extend:

> **(setq x (getpoint "\nPick axis crossing lines to extend: "))**
> **(setq y (getpoint x "\nPick endpoint: "))**
> **(setq sset1 (Ssget "c" x y))**

Here two points are obtained that indicate an axis along which the lines to be extended lie. These points will be used later to help find other pick points. Ssget is used with the Crossing option to create a selection set. The two points defining the axis are used as the two corner points of the crossing window.

The next two lines do some setup work:

```
(setq count 0)
    (if (/ = sset1 nil)
```

The first of these two lines sets a counting variable to zero. The next line checks to make sure a set of objects has indeed been selected and a selection set created.

Once these things have been established, the actual work is done:

```
(while (< count (sslength sset1))
    (setq elst (entget (ssname sset1 count)))
    (setq pt1  (cdr (assoc 10 elst)))
    (setq pt2  (cdr (assoc 11 elst)))
    (setq int  (inters x y pt1 pt2))
    (command "extend" obj "  " int "  ")
    (setq count (1 +  count))
);end while
```

This While expression is evaluated until the counter variable Count reaches the total number of entities in the selection set Sset1. Each time the expression is evaluated, Count is increased by one until Count equals the length of the selection set. Let's look at what each iteration of the While expression does.

*A*ccessing Individual Entities in a Selection Set

First, the While expression checks to see if the counting variable Count is less than the total number of elements in the selection set Sset1. This is done through the Sslength function:

```
(while (< count (sslength sset1))
```

Sslength simply returns the number of entities in its selection-set argument. The argument can be the actual selection set or a symbol representing it. In this example, the symbol Sset1 is used. If Count is less than the number of entities, the expressions that follow are evaluated.

Next, the variable Elst is given the entity name of an entity in the selection set:

```
(setq elst (entget (ssname sset1 count)))
```

The Count variable is used by Ssname to determine which entity in the selection set Sset1 is to be examined. Entget then extracts the property list for that entity. Finally this entity list is assigned to the variable Elst.

Next, the two endpoints of the entities are extracted:

```
(setq pt1 (cdr (assoc 10 elst)))
(setq pt2 (cdr (assoc 11 elst)))
```

Here the Assoc function extracts the two endpoint coordinates from the property list. The group codes 10 and 11 are used by Assoc to locate the sublist in Elst containing the coordinates in question. (See Appendix B for a full list of group codes and their meaning.) These coordinates are assigned to variables Pt1 and Pt2.

*M*odifying Entities in a Selection Set

Once the endpoint's coordinates are known, a function called Inters finds the intersection point of the current entity being examined and the entity crossing axis derived in the beginning of the function:

```
(setq int  (inters x y pt1 pt2))
```

Inters is a function that finds the intersecting point of two pairs of coordinates. Inters syntax is

```
(inters x1 y1 x2 y2 )
```

where x1 and y1 are the x and y coordinates of one axis, and x2 and y2 are the coordinates of the second axis. Inters returns a list containing the coordinates of the intersection of the two axes. In the Mlext program, this list is assigned to the variable Int.

Finally, the Command function is used to invoke the Extend command and extend the current entity:

```
(command "extend" obj "  " int "  ")
```

The first thing that the Extend command asks for is the line to extend to. Here, Obj is used to indicate that line. The pair of quotation marks issues a ⏎ to end the selection process. Then a point value is entered to indicate both the line to be extended and the location of the end to be extended. In this case, the intersection point of the line and the extend axis is used for this purpose. Finally, another ⏎ is issued to end the Extend command.

The last line in the While expression increases the value of count by one in order to get the next entity in the selection set.

(setq count (1+ count))

If count is still less than the number of entities in the selection set, the process repeats itself.

Since the Extend and Trim commands work in a nearly identical way, you can create a program that performs both multiple extends and multiple trims on lines by changing just a few elements in the Mlext program. Figure 10.4 shows such a program called Etline. The elements that are changed from Mlext are shown in boldface type.

```
;program to extend or trim multiple lines --Etline.lsp----------------------

(defun c:ETLINE (/ x y u sset1 count pt1 pt2 int obj)
(graphscr)                                          ;shift to graphics
(initget "Extend Trim")                             ;set keywords
(setq EorT (getkword "\Extend or <Trim>: "))        ;select operation
(if (equal EorT "")(setq EorT "Trim"))              ;test operation choice
(princ "\nSelect boundary edge...")                 ;print prompt
(setq obj (car (entsel)))                           ;Get entity name
(setq x (getpoint "\nPick axis crossing lines to edit: "))
(setq y (getpoint x "\nPick endpoint: "))           ;get axis crossing lines
        (setq sset1 (ssget "c" x y))                ;get entities to extend
        (setq count 0)                              ;set counter
           (if (/= sset1 nil)                        ;test for selection set
              (while ( count (sslength sset1))       ;while still select. set
                  (setq elst (entget (ssname sset1 count))  ;get entity name
                        pt1  (cdr (assoc 10 elst))   ;get one endpoint
                        pt2  (cdr (assoc 11 elst))   ;get other endpoint
                        int  (inters x y pt1 pt2)    ;find intersection
                  );end setq                               of axis and line
                  (if (equal EorT "Extend")          ;Test for extend choice
                   (command "extend" obj "" int "")  ;extend line or...
                   (command "trim" obj "" int "")    ;trim line
                  );end if
                  (setq count (1+ count))            ;go to next line count
              );end while
           );end if
);end progn
```

Figure 10.4: The Etline program to perform both extend and trim functions

*I*mproving Processing Speed

When you begin to write programs that act on several entities, processing speed begins to become an issue. There are two things you can do to improve the speed of such programs. The first is simple—set the

Cmdecho system variable to 0. The second is to modify the drawing database directly rather than rely on AutoCAD commands to make the changes for you. In this section, you will look at both options.

Using Cmdecho to Speed Up Your Programs

You may have noticed that when you ran the Mlext program, the commands and responses appeared for each line that was extended. The program is actually slowed by having to wait for AutoCAD to print its responses to the prompt line. You can actually double the speed of the Mlext program by adding the following expression at the beginning of the program:

(setvar "cmdecho" 0)

Cmdecho is an AutoCAD system variable that controls the echo to the command prompt. When set to 0, it will suppress any AutoCAD command prompts that would normally occur when AutoLISP invokes an AutoCAD command.

Open the MLEXT.LSP file you created earlier in this chapter and add the above line to the program. Also include the following line at the end of your program to set the Cmdecho variable back to 1.

(setvar "cmdecho" 1)

Your file should look like Figure 10.5. This figure shows the Mlext program with the changes indicated by boldface type.

Now retrieve the Chapt10 drawing file and recreate the drawing in Figure 10.3. Load and run the Mlext program as you did previously. Notice that it runs much faster and that the prompts for the Extend command no longer appear. Setting Cmdecho to 0 will improve the speed of any program that executes AutoCAD commands repetitively.

Increasing Speed through Direct Database Access

Another method for improving speed is to make your program modify the drawing database directly instead of going through an AutoCAD command. Figure 10.6 shows a version of the Mlext program (Mlext2) that does this.

```
;Program to extend multiple lines - Mlext.lsp -------------------------------

(defun c:MLEXT (/ x y sset1 count pt1 pt2 int obj elst)
(graphscr)                                              ;shift to graphics
(setvar "cmdecho" 0)                                    ;echo to prompt off
(princ "\nSelect Boundary edge...")                     ;print prompt
(setq obj (car (entsel)))                               ;Get entity name
(setq x (getpoint "\nPick axis crossing lines to extend: "))
(setq y (getpoint x "\nPick endpoint: "))               ;get axis crossing lines
        (setq sset1 (ssget "c" x y))                    ;get entities to extend
        (setq count 0)                                  ;set counter
            (if (/= sset1 nil)                           ;test for selection set
                (while ( count (sslength sset1))         ;while still select. set
                    (setq elst (entget (ssname sset1 count))  ;get entity name
                          pt1  (cdr (assoc 10 elst))     ;get one endpoint
                          pt2  (cdr (assoc 11 elst))     ;get other endpoint
                          int  (inters x y pt1 pt2)      ;find intersection
                    );end setq                              of axis and line
                    (command "extend" obj "" int "")     ;command to extend line
                    (setq count (1+ count))              ;go to next line count
                );end while
            );end if
(setvar "cmdecho" 1)                                    ;echo to prompt back on
);end defun
```

Figure 10.5: *The MLEXT.LSP file modified to increase processing speed*

```
;Function to find closest of two points-------------------------------------
(defun far ( fx fy dlxf / dst1 dst2 intx)
    (setq dst1 (distance dlxf fx))                      ;find distnce to one pt
    (setq dst2 (distance dlxf fy))                      ;find distnce to other pt
    ;If 1st pt.is farther than 2nd pt then eval 1st pt........
    (if (> dst1 dst2) fx fy )
)


;Proram to extend multiple lines -- Mlext2.lsp
;--------------------------------------------------------------------------
(defun c:MLEXT2 (/ sset1 count pt1 pt2 int OBJ objx objy
                elst int far1 sub1 sub2)
 (graphscr)
 ;Get entity list of line to be extended to then find endpoints.........
 (princ "\nSelect boundary edge...")                    ;print prompt
 (Setq obj (entget (car (entsel)))                      ;get boundary
        objx (cdr (assoc 10 obj))                       ;get 1st endpoint
        objy (cdr (assoc 11 obj))                       ;get 2nd endpoint
        sset1 (ssget)                                   ;get lines to trim
        count 0                                         ;set count to zero
 )
    ;IF lines have been picked........
    (if (/= sset1 nil)
        ;As long as count is less than number of objects in selection set...
        (while (< count (sslength sset1))
            ;Get intersect of two lines and find farthest endpt of line ...
            (setq elst (entget (ssname sset1 count))    ;get entity list
                  pt1  (cdr (setq sub1 (assoc 10 elst)))  ;get 1st endpoint
                  pt2  (cdr (setq sub2 (assoc 11 elst)))  ;get 2nd endpoint
                  int  (inters objx objy pt1 pt2 nil)   ;find intercts
                  far1 (far pt1 pt2 int)                ;find far point
            )
            ;IF pt1 equals point farthest from intersect.........
            (if (= far1 pt1)
                (entmod (subst (cons 11 int) sub2 elst))  ;update pt2
                (entmod (subst (cons 10 int) sub1 elst))  ;else update pt1
            );end IF 2
            (setq count (1+ count))                     ;add one to count
        );end WHILE
    );end IF 1
);END of defun
```

Figure 10.6: *The Mlext2 program that directly modifies the drawing database*

In this section you'll enter the modified program, and then use the Chapt10 drawing to see how the program works.

1. Exit the Chapt10 drawing and open an AutoLISP file called MLEXT2.LSP.

2. Copy the program in Figure 10.6 into the file, and then save it and exit.

3. Return to the Chapt10 drawing. Once again, reconstruct the drawing shown in Figure 10.3.

4. Load and run Mlext2.

5. At the first prompt

   Select boundary edges...
   Select object:

   pick the Boundary Edge line indicated in Figure 10.3.

6. At the next prompt

   Select objects:

   enter **C** to use a crossing window.

7. Pick the two points to select all of the horizontal lines. The lines will extend to the Boundary Edge line.

Notice that the extension operation occurred much faster than before. Since the program doesn't have to go through the extra step of processing the AutoCAD Extend command, the operation occurs much faster. Let's look at how the program was changed to accomplish the speed gain.

You might first notice the function Far added to the program file. I will explain this function a bit later. The beginning of the program shows some immediate changes:

```
(defun c:MLEXT2 (/ sset1 count pt1 pt2 int obj objx objy
                    elst int far1 sub1 sub2)
(graphscr)
(princ "\nSelect boundary edge...")
(setq obj (entget (car (entsel))))
(setq objx (cdr (assoc 10 obj)))
(setq objy (cdr (assoc 11 obj)))
```

Instead of simply obtaining the entity name of the Boundary Edge line, the program extracts the endpoint coordinates of that line and stores them as the variables Objx and Objy. These endpoints are used later in conjunction with the Inters function to find the exact point to which a line must be extended.

Next, Ssget without any arguments obtains a selection set of the lines to be changed:

```
(setq sset1 (Ssget))
```

Remember that this way, Ssget allows the user to choose the method of selection just as any "Select object" prompt would. The user can use a standard or crossing window, pick objects individually, or remove or add individual objects to the selection set. In the exercise, you entered **C** for a crossing window to select the lines.

This is followed by an If conditional expression to test whether entities have been selected:

```
(if (/ = sset1 nil)
```

The following While expression then does the work of updating the drawing database for each line that was selected. Just as with the Mlext program, the While expression checks to see if the value of Count is less than the number of entities in the selection set. It then finds the entity list for one of the lines and derives the two endpoints of that line:

```
(while (< count (sslength sset1))
    (setq elst (entget (ssname sset1 count)))
    (setq pt1  (cdr (setq sub1 (assoc 10 elst))))
    (setq pt2  (cdr (setq sub2 (assoc 11 elst))))
```

This part is no different from Mlext. But the next line is slightly different from its corresponding line in Mlext:

```
(setq int  (inters objx objy pt1 pt2 nil))
```

Here, Inters is used to find the intersection between the line currently being examined and the boundary-edge line. The variables Objx and Objy are the first two arguments to Inters. These are the two endpoints of the boundary-edge line derived earlier in the program. The variables Pt1 and Pt2 are the endpoints of the line currently being examined. A fifth argument, nil, causes Inters to find the intersection of the two pairs of coordinates even if they don't actually cross (see Figure 10.7). Inters treats the two lines as if they extended infinitely in

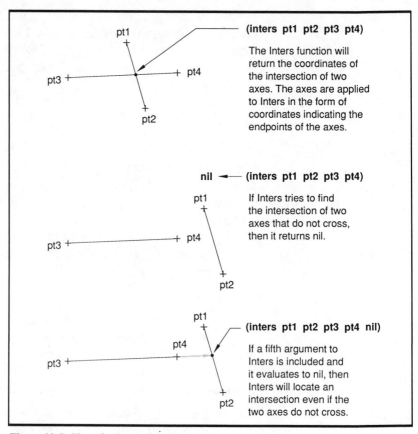

Figure 10.7: How the Inters function works

both directions in order to find a point common to both lines. This feature is needed since the line being edited and the boundary-edge line don't actually cross.

The next expression calls the user-defined function Far:

```
(setq far1 (far pt1 pt2 int))
```

This function finds which of two points is farthest from a third point. The first two arguments to Far are the points to be compared against the third argument, which is the reference point. Far then returns the point that is farthest from the reference point. The result is that Far finds the endpoint of the line that is the farthest from the intersection. I will discuss how Far works later.

Once the program finds the farthest of the two endpoints, the next three lines actually make the changes to the database.

```
(if ( = far1 pt1)
    (entmod (subst (cons 11 int) sub2 elst))
    (entmod (subst (cons 10 int) sub1 elst))
);end IF 2
```

The conditional If expression checks to see if the farthest endpoint of the current line is equal to Pt1. This test determines which endpoint of the current entity should be modified. The program should modify the endpoint closest to the intersection of the line and the boundary edge. If Pt1 is equal to Far1, and is therefore the farthest endpoint, then the sublist representing Pt2 is modified. If Pt1 proves not to be the farthest endpoint, then the sublist associated with Pt1 itself is modified.

Remember that Subst replaces one list for another within an association list. Then Entmod updates the drawing database record to reflect the new property list that is passed to it as an argument. The result is the extension of the line to the boundary edge.

The next line of the program adds one to the Counter variable and then the whole procedure repeats until all the entities in the selection set have been processed. Since this program circumvents the AutoCAD Extend command and directly modifies the drawing database, it executes the changes to the lines entities much faster. However, this extra speed did require some additional programming.

Now, let's briefly look at the Far function. It is a fairly simple function that first obtains the distance between a reference point and two other points, and then returns the value of the point that yields the greater distance. The value of Far's three arguments are passed to the variables Fx, Fy, and Dlfx. Fx and Fy are the points in question and Dlfx is the reference point:

```
(defun far ( fx fy dlxf / dst1 dst2 intx)
```

The function then finds the distance between Fx and Dlfx and assigns the value to Dst1:

```
(setq dst1 (distance dlxf fx))
```

The same procedure is applied to Fy:

```
(setq dst2 (distance dlxf fy))
```

Finally, the conditional If expression tests to see which distance is greater and returns a point value depending on the outcome:

(if (> dst1 dst2) fx fy)

Filtering Entities for Specific Properties

There are a number of other functions available that allow you to manipulate selection sets. Table 10.2 lists them and gives a brief description of what they do. You have already seen two of these functions, Sslength and Ssname, in previous examples. Let's see how you can use Ssadd to filter out object selections.

Filtering a Selection Set

Figure 10.8 shows a program that filters out entities in a selection set based on layers. This function is useful when several objects of different layers lie on top of each other and you want to select just the object on a specific layer.

Let's see first-hand how this function works.

1. Open a file call LFILTER.LSP and copy the Lfilter program in Figure 10.8. Save and exit the file.

```
;function to filter entities by layer -- Lfilter.lsp-------------------------
(defun LFILTER (/ lay sset count ent newent)
   (setq lay (cons 8 (strcase (getstring "\nEnter layer name: "))))
   (setq sset (ssget))                               ;get entities
   (setq count 0)                                    ;set counter to zero
   (while (< count (sslength sset))                  ;while still select. set
      (setq lay2 (assoc 8 (entget(setq ent(ssname sset count)))))) ;get layer
         (if (equal lay lay2)                        ;if layer matches entity
            (if (not newent)                         ;if new not select. set
               (setq newent (ssadd ent))             ;make new select. set
               (setq newent (ssadd ent newent))  ;else add to select. set
            );end if
         );end if
      (setq count (1+ count))
   );end while
   (if (= 1 (sslength newent))(ssname newent 0) newent) ;return select. set or
);end defun                                              entity name
```

Figure 10.8: The layer filtering program

Table 10.2: *Functions for Manipulating Selection Sets*

FUNCTION	DESCRIPTION
(ssadd *entity_name selection_set*)	Creates a selection set. If used with no arguments, it creates a selection set with no entities. If only an entity name given as an argument, then it creates a selection set which contains that entity. If an entity name and a selection-set name is given, then the entity is added to the selection set.
(ssdel *entity_name selection_set*)	Deletes an entity from a selection set and returns the name of the selection set. If the entity is not a member of the selection set, then it returns nil.
(sslength *selection set*)	Returns the number of entities in a selection set.
(ssmemb *entity_name selection_set*)	Checks to see if an entity is a member of a selection set. If it is, then Ssmemb returns the name of the selection set. If not, Ssmemb returns nil.
(ssname *selection_set nth entity*)	Returns the entity name of a single entity in a selection set. The second argument to Ssname corresponds to the entity's number within the selection set. The entity numbers begin with zero and go to the total number of entities in the selection set minus one.

2. Return to the AutoCAD Chapt10 drawing and erase any objects in the file.

3. Create the layers listed below. Be sure to assign the linetypes indicated for each layer.

Layer Name	Line Type
Hidden	hidden
Center	center
Dashed	dashed

4. Draw the lines shown in Figure 10.9 and assign each line to the layer shown directly to the right of each line. Use the coordinate and spacing information indicated in the drawing to place the lines.

5. Load the Lfilter program and then issue the Erase command.

6. At the "Select object" prompt enter

   (lfilter)

   You will get the prompt

   Enter layer name:

7. Enter **hidden**. You will get the next prompt

   Select objects:

8. Enter **C** to use a crossing window and pick the points 2, 1.25 for the lower-left corner of the window and 8, 8.25 for the upper-right. The lines that pass through the crossing window will ghost. Press ↵ after picking the points. The lines will

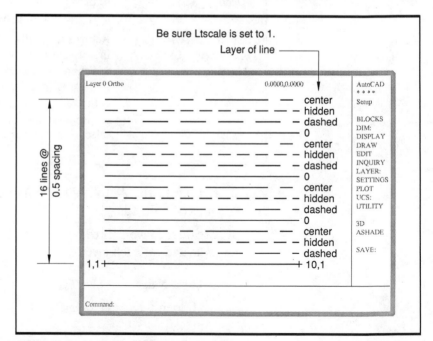

Figure 10.9: *A test drawing for Lfilter*

unghost and then the prompt will return the number of entities found. The entities you just selected with the crossing window that are on the layer Hidden will ghost.

9. Press ⏎. You have just erased only the items in your crossing window that were on the layer Hidden.

10. Issue the Oops command in preparation for the exercise in the next section.

Now that you know what Lfilter does, let's look at how it works. First, it creates a dotted pair representing the layer sublist in an entity property list:

```
(defun LFILTER (/ lay sset count ent newent)
  (setq lay (cons 8
    (strcase (getstring "\nEnter layer name: ")))))
```

When you are prompted for a layer, the name you enter is first converted to all uppercase with the Strcase function. This is done because the value associated with the layer group code in a property list is always in uppercase.

In order to compare data, you must make sure that the values you use in the comparison are in the same format. Since AutoLISP is case sensitive when it comes to string values, you must make sure that the value the user enters matches the case of the layer name in the property list. The Strcase function will convert a string to all lowercase if a second argument is present and is not nil. If there is no second argument or if the second argument is nil, Strcase converts the string to all uppercase.

Next the Cons function creates a dotted pair using 8 as the first element; 8 is the group code for layer names. The dotted pair looks like this:

```
(8 . "HIDDEN")
```

Finally, the newly created dotted pair is assigned to the variable Lay, which will later be used as a filtering value.

The next line obtains the selection set to be filtered:

```
(setq sset (Ssget))
```

Here, Ssget is used without any argument to allow the user to select objects using any of the usual AutoCAD selection options. This selection set is assigned to the variable Sset.

Next comes the While expression, which compares the 8 group-code sublist of each entity in the selection against the variable Lay. If it finds a match, the entity is added to a new selection set Newent. Let's look at this While expression in detail.

First, the counter is set to zero and the conditional test is set up:

```
(setq count 0)
(while (< count (sslength sset))
```

Then the 8 group-code sublist from the first entity in the selection set is extracted and assigned to the variable Lay2:

```
(setq lay2 (assoc 8 (entget(setq ent(ssname sset count)))))
```

Next, the variables Lay and Lay2 are compared:

```
(if (equal lay lay2)
```

If there is a match, signifying that the entity is on layer Hidden, then the program checks to see if the selection set Newent exists:

```
(if (not newent)
    (setq newent (ssadd ent))
    (setq newent (ssadd ent newent))
```

If Newent does not exist, then Ssadd creates a new selection set containing the entity whose layer group-code sublist matches (8 . "HIDDEN") and then assigns that selection set to the variable Newent. If Newent does exist, Ssadd adds the entity to the selection set Newent and redefines Newent. This last conditional If is required since Ssadd must be given different arguments depending on whether it is to create a new selection set or just add an entity to an existing selection set.

Finally, the counter is increased by one and the While conditional loop repeats itself:

```
        );end if
    );end if
    (setq count (1+ count))
);end while
```

Once the new selection set containing the filtered entities is complete, the last expression returns either the selection set of entities, or if there is only one entity in the selection set, the entity name.

```
(if (= 1 (sslength newent))(ssname newent 0) newent)
);end defun
```

The function Sslength is used with the equals predicate to see if Newent contains only one element. If it does, then Ssname is used to extract the entity name of the element from the selection set Newent. Otherwise, the entire selection set Newent is returned. This last step is added to allow the user to use Lfilter for situations in which only one item will be accepted for input, such as the Offset or Fillet commands.

In this sample program, layers are used to filter entities, but you can use any entity property as a filter. You can filter entities by linetype, color, or any other property available from the property list. Consult Appendix B for a list of group codes and their associated properties.

Selecting Entities Based on Properties

Another method for filtering can be found built into the Ssget function. Ssget allows you to select objects based on a filter list. A *filter list* is an association list much like a property list. The Getlayer function shown in Figure 10.10 simply selects the entire contents of a layer that the user specifies.

Let's see what it does:

1. Save and exit the Chapt10 file.

2. Open a file called GETLAYER.LSP and copy Figure 10.10 into the file. Save and exit the file.

3. Return to the Chapt10 drawing file and load Getlayer.

4. Issue the Erase command. At the Select object prompt, enter

    (getlayer)

```
;function to select all entities on a layer-----------------------------------
(defun GETLAYER (/ lay)
 (setq lay (list (cons 8
    (strcase (getstring "\nEnter layer name: ")))))
 (ssget "X" lay)
```

Figure 10.10: *The Getlayer function*

5. At the prompt

Enter layer name:

enter **center**. All the objects on layer Center ghost.

6. Press ◄──┘. All the objects on layer Center are erased.

Getlayer does its work by using the "X" argument to Ssget. This argument allows Ssget to create a selection set based on an association list of properties. In the case of Getlayer, the list is one element long. First, Getlayer prompts the user for a layer:

```
(defun GETLAYER (/ lay)
  (setq lay (list (cons 8
    (strcase (getstring "\nEnter layer name: ")))))
```

The layer name is used to construct a dotted pair much like the one in the Lfilter function. This dotted pair is included in a list with the List function. The result is a list containing a single dotted pair:

```
((8 . "CENTER"))
```

This list is assigned to the variable Lay, which is in turn applied to Ssget to create the selection set:

```
    (ssget "X" lay)
)
```

Here the "X" argument is used to tell Ssget to use a filter list to create the selection set. Ssget then searches the drawing database to find all the entities that have properties that matches the filter list.

Getlayer can be simplified to one expression, eliminating the need for the Lay variable:

```
(Ssget "X" (list (cons 8
  (strcase (getstring "\nEnter layer name: ")))))
```

But the Lay variable helps explain how this function works.

A filter list can have more than one property sublist element much like an entity property list. But Ssget will only accept certain group codes in the filter list. Table 10.3 shows those group codes and their associated properties.

Table 10.3: Group Codes Accepted in a Filter List by Ssget

GROUP CODE	ASSOCIATED PROPERTIES
0	Entity type
2	Block name
6	Linetype name
7	Text style name
8	Layer name
38	Elevation
39	Thickness
62	Color number: 0, by block; 256, by layer
66	Block contains attributes
210	3-D extrusion-direction vector

*A*ccessing AutoCAD's System Tables

The Tblnext and Tblsearch functions help you gather information about layers, linetypes, views, text styles, blocks, UCSs, and viewports. Each one of these AutoCAD tools is represented in a table that contains the tool's status. Tblnext and Tblsearch return this table information in the form of association lists similar to entity property lists. But unlike entity property lists, lists returned by Tblnext and Tblsearch cannot be modified. However, you can modify the settings associated with a Tblnext or Tblsearch listing using the standard AutoCAD commands.

*U*sing Tblnext

To use Tblnext, enter the following at the command prompt:

(tblnext "layer")

You will get an association list similar to the following:

((0 . "LAYER") (2 . "0") (70 . 0)(62 . 7) (6 . "CONTINUOUS"))

The individual dotted pairs can be extracted from this list using Assoc just as with any other association list or property list. Enter the Tblnext expression above again and you will get an association list of the next layer. Each time Tblnext is used, it advances to the next table setting until it reaches the last item in the particular table you are searching. Once it reaches the end, Tblnext returns nil. To reset Tblnext to read from the beginning of the table again, you must include a second argument that evaluates to a non-nil value, as in the following:

(tblnext "layer" T)

If you enter this expression, you will get the same list as the one you got the first time you used Tblnext. The second argument could be any expression that evaluates to non-nil. Once you get a list, you can manipulate it in the same way as any other association list.

Using Tblsearch

Tblsearch works slightly differently. Instead of stepping through each table item, Tblsearch will go to a specific table item which you name. Enter the following:

(tblsearch "layer" "hidden")

You will get the association list pertaining to the layer Hidden.

((0 . "LAYER") (2 . "HIDDEN") (70 . 0)(62 . 7) (6 . "HIDDEN"))

If you include a non-nil third argument to Tblsearch and then use Tblnext, it will start from the next item after the one obtained from Tblsearch. Note that Tblsearch will accept lowercase strings.

Though I used layer settings as an example for Tblnext and Tblsearch, you can apply any of the table settings mentioned at the beginning of this section.

Figure 10.11 shows a program that uses Tblnext to store layer settings in an external file. This program can be useful if you use a single multilayered drawing for several types of output. For example, an architect might have a drawing that serves as both an electrical layout plan and a mechanical floor plan with different layers turned on or off depending on which type of plan you want to edit or print. You can

```
;Program to save layer settings in a file -- Lrecord.lsp
;------------------------------------------------------------------------------
(defun c:lrecord (/ fname lafile record)
  (setq fname (getstring  "\nEnter name of layer file: "));get name of file
  (setq lafile(open fname "w"))                          ;open file, file desc.
  (setq record (tblnext "layer" T))                      ;get first layer set.
  (while record                                          ;while record not nil
    (prin1 record lafile)                                ;print record to file
    (princ "\n" lafile)                                  ;print to next line
    (setq record (tblnext "layer"))                      ;get next layer
  );end while
  (close lafile)                                         ;close layer file
);end defun

;Program to restore layer settings saved by lrecord
;------------------------------------------------------------------------------
(defun c:lrestore (/ clayer fname lafile flayer lname oldcset)
  (setvar "cmdecho" 0)                                   ;turn off prompt echo
  (setvar "regenmode" 0)                                 ;turn off autoregen
  (Setq clayer (getvar "clayer"))                        ;find current layer
  (setq fname (getstring "\nEnter name of layer file: ")) ;get layer file name
  (setq lafile(open fname "r"))                          ;open layer file
  (setq flayer (read (read-line lafile)))                ;read first line
  (while flayer                                          ;while lines to read
    (setq lname (cdr (assoc 2 flayer)))                  ;get layer name
    (setq oldcset (assoc 62 flayer))                     ;get color setting
    (if (and (< (cdr oldcset) 0) (equal lname clayer))   ;if col. is off/currnt
      (command "layer" "C" (cdr oldcset) lname "Y" "")   ;insert "Y" response
      (command "layer" "C" (cdr oldcset) lname "")       ;else normal
    );end if
    (Setq oldcset (assoc 70 flayer))                     ;find if frozen
    (if (= (cdr oldcset) 65)                             ;if frozen then...
      (if (equal lname clayer)                           ;if current layer
        (command"layer" "freeze" lname "y" "")           ;insert "y" response
        (command"layer" "freeze" lname "")               ;else normal
      );end if
      (command "layer" "thaw" lname "")                  ;else thaw layer

    );end if
    (setq flayer (read-line lafile))                     ;read next in file
    (if flayer (setq flayer (read flayer)))              ;strip quotes
  );end while
  (close lafile)                                         ;close file
  (setvar "regenmode" 1)                                 ;reset autoregen on
);end defun
```

Figure 10.11: *A program to store layer settings*

store your different layer settings for the electrical and mechanical plans and then restore one group of settings or the other depending on which plan you intend to work on.

The Lrecord program shown at the top of the Figure 10.11 simply creates a file and copies each layer association list into it. Lrecord uses the Prin1 function to perform the copying because Prin1 does not affect the list in any way. If you used Princ, the strings within the list would be stripped of their quotation marks. Also, Write-line could not be used because it expects a string argument. Both Princ and Prin1 will write any data type to a file.

The Lrestore program simply reads each line back from a file created by Lrecord. Since the Read-line function returns a string, the

Read function is used to strip the outermost level of quotation marks from the string to return the association list:

(setq flayer (read (read-line lafile)))

The layer data is then extracted from this list and applied to the Layer command, which sets the layer back to the saved settings. The If conditional test determines whether the layer to be restored is the current layer. A different command expression is evaluated depending on whether the layer in question is current or not. This is done because the Layer command issues an extra prompt if a layer to be turned off or frozen is the current layer.

```
(if (and (< (cdr oldcset) 0) (equal lname clayer))
    (command "layer" "C" (cdr oldcset) lname "Y" " ")
    (command "layer" "C" (cdr oldcset) lname " " ")
)
```

*S*ummary

You have seen a variety of ways to select, edit, and manipulate Auto-CAD entities. Selection sets and entity filters can provide a powerful means for automating AutoCAD. Tasks that would normally take several minutes to perform manually can be reduced to a few seconds with the proper application of selection sets and repetitive expressions.

You have also seen how changes in the way you write your program can affect your program's speed. Though the speed of your programs may not be an issue to you now, as your experience with AutoLISP accumulates, your requirements for speed will also increase.

In the next chapter, I will continue discussing entity access by looking at how you can edit polylines and attributes with AutoLISP.

11

Accessing Complex AutoCAD Entities

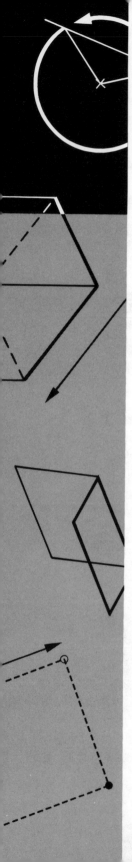

11

In this chapter, you will look at several programs that not only introduce you to new AutoLISP functions but also review many of the functions discussed in earlier chapters. In the process, you will learn how to access complex entity types such as attributes within blocks and polylines. You will also look at ways to store data as a permanent record within a drawing.

*A*ccessing Polyline Vertices

Polylines are complex entities that comprise many entities. Though they range from straight lines to three-dimensional Bezier-spline polylines, even the most complex polyline can be broken into three basic components—vertices, lines, and arcs. AutoCAD stores polylines as compound entities made up of several levels of information. To help you grasp this idea, think of this storage structure as an onion; as you peel off one layer, another layer is revealed. The first level, the one accessed by Entget, gives general information about the polyline. In this section, you will look at ways to access deeper levels of information using AutoLISP.

Let's take a look at a typical polyline property list first hand.

1. Open a drawing called Chapt11 and draw the polyline rectangle shown in Figure 11.1. Use the coordinates shown in the figure to locate the corners.

2. Enter the following expression at the command prompt:

   (entget (car (entsel)))

3. The selection cursor box appears and you get the "Select object" prompt. Pick the polyline you just drew. The following

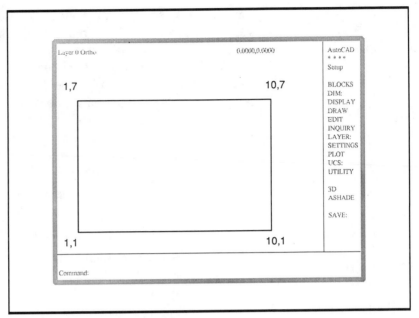

Figure 11.1: Test drawing for exercise

polyline property list appears. (This list is vertical for clarity; you will see the list shown as a continuous string on your text screen.)

```
((-1 . <Entity name: 60000120>)
(0 . "POLYLINE")
(8 . "TEXT")
(66 . 1)
(10 0.0 0.0 0.0)
(70 . 1)
(40 . 0)
(41 . 0)
(210 0.0 0.0 1.0)
(71 . 0)
(72 . 0)
(73 . 0)
(74 . 0)
(75 . 0))
```

You should now see the entity name, entity type, and layer listed, but where the point group code 10 should indicate some coordinate location, only zeros appear. You would also expect to see a list of at least four coordinate values, but instead you see unfamiliar 40 and 70 group codes, all showing zeros.

This doesn't mean that you are unable to access more specific information about polylines. You just need to dig a little deeper. I mentioned earlier that it helps to think of the polyline data as being stored in levels like layers of an onion. The listing above represents the outermost level. To get to the next level, you need to use the Entnext function.

4. Enter the next expression:

(entget (entnext (car (entsel))))

At the "Select objects" prompt, pick the polyline again. You will get a listing like the following:

((-1 . <Entity name: 60000120>)
(0 . "VERTEX")
(8 . "0")
(10 1.0 1.0 0.0)
(40 . 0)
(41 . 0)
(42 . 0)
(70 . 0)
(50 . 0))

This new property list gives you some new information. The entity name is different from the previous list, and the entity type is "VERTEX" instead of "POLYLINE". The layer information is the same except for the first point value, group code 10, which displays the coordinates for the first corner of the box, 1.0 1.0 0.0. For purposes of our discussion, we'll call this vertex entity a polyline subentity, or simply a subentity.

Now you know how to get more detailed information about a polyline by introducing Entnext into the expression to extract subentity information. You have "peeled off" the first layer of the onion to reveal the next layer of information—the first vertex of the polyline. To reveal the others, continue adding more Entnext functions.

5. Enter the following:

(entget (entnext (entnext (car (entsel)))))

6. When the "Select object" prompt appears, pick the polyline box. Another new property list appears:

```
((-1 . <Entity name: 60000120>)
(0 . "VERTEX")
(8 . "0")
(10 10.0 1.0 0.0)
(40 . 0)
(41 . 0)
(42 . 0)
(70 . 4)
(50 . 0))
```

Now you should see a list that describes the second vertex of the polyline. The entity name you get may be different from the one shown above. Note that the group code 10 value shows coordinates 10.0 1.0 0.0, which is the next vertex in the polyline.

Getting a Property List for Each Vertex

It would be inconvenient to have to keep expanding your expression by adding more Entnext functions to extract each subentity's property lists. If you have a polyline that has 40 vertices or more, it would take an enormous program to extract all of its vertices. Fortunately, you can use a function that performs iterations to retrieve the property list of each vertex. By using the same variable name to which you assign each vertex entity name, you eliminate the need to add continual nests of the Entnext function. Figure 11.2 shows a diagram of how this iteration works. Figure 11.3 shows the Addvert program, which first uses this iteration to extract a list of polyline vertices (Getver), and then inserts a vertex into the polyline. This figure also includes a function called Btwn that checks to see if a point lies between two other points. We will look at Getver first.

Getver takes an entity name as an argument. Presumably the entity in question is a polyline. It proceeds to obtain the first vertex entity name from that entity:

```
(defun getver (EntNme / SubEnt VerLst vertex)
    (setq SubEnt (entnext EntNme))
```

This vertex entity name is assigned to the symbol SubEnt. Next, a list

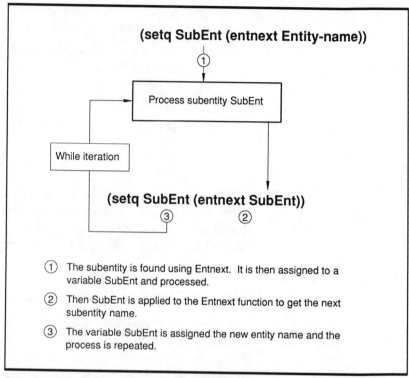

Figure 11.2: Using iteration to extract subentity information

is created to hold the vertex coordinates:

```
(setq VerLst '( ))
```

The following While expression then goes to each vertex property list and extracts the coordinate value. It first extracts the coordinate from the current vertex entity:

```
(while SubEnt
    (setq vertex (cdr (assoc 10 (entget SubEnt)))))
```

Next, it appends that coordinate value to the vertex list VerLst.

```
(setq VerLst (append VerLst (list vertex)))
```

Finally, the variable SubEnt is assigned the vertex entity name of the next vertex, and the process is repeated:

```
    (setq SubEnt (entnext SubEnt))
)
```

```
;Function to create list of polyline vertices---------------------------------

(defun getver (EntNme / SubEnt VerLst vertex)
 (setq SubEnt (entnext EntNme))                       ;get first vertex
 (setq VerLst '())                                    ;setup vertex list
 (while SubEnt
   (setq vertex (cdr (assoc 10 (entget SubEnt))))     ;get first vertex point
   (setq VerLst (append VerLst (list vertex)))        ;add vertex to verlst
   (setq SubEnt (entnext SubEnt))                     ;go to next vertex
 )
 VerLst                                               ;return vertex list
)

;Function to check if point lies between endpoints of line--------------------

(defun btwn (a b c)
(setq ang1 (angle a b))                               ;find vertex to point ang.
(setq ang2 (angle a c))                               ;find vertex to vertex ang.
(if (EQUAL (RTOS ang1 2 2) (RTOS ang2 2 2)) b)        ;if equal return point.
)

;Program to insert Vertex in simple polyline
;-----------------------------------------------------------------------------
(defun C:ADDVERT (/ pEnt VerLst Newpt int NewVer ptyp)
  (setq pEnt (entsel "Pick vertex location: "))       ;Get new vertex and pline
  (setq VerLst (getver (car pEnt)))                   ;extract vertices
  (setq ptyp (assoc 70 (entget (car pEnt))))
  (setq Newpt  (osnap (cadr pEnt) "nearest"))         ;Get new vertex location
     (while (cadr VerLst)
        (setq NewVer
          (append NewVer (list (car VerLst)))         ;add vertex to new NewVer
        )
        (setq int                                     ;Check for between-ness
          (btwn (car VerLst) newpt (Cadr VerLst))
        )
        (if int                                       ;if between, add to NewVer
          (setq NewVer (append NewVer (list int)))
        )
        (setq VerLst (cdr VerLst))                    ;Remove vertx. from list
     );end while
  (setq NewVer (append NewVer (list (car VerLst))))   ;add last vertx. to NewVer
  (command "erase" (car pEnt) "")                     ;erase old pline
  (command "pline")                                   ;start pline command
  (foreach n NewVer (command n))                      ;insert points from NewVer
  (if (= (cdr ptyp) 1)
     (command "close")
     (command "")                                     ;end pline command
  )
)
```

Figure 11.3: A function that implements the diagram in Figure 11.2

When all the vertices have been obtained, the function returns the list of vertices:

```
    VerLst
  )
```

*A*dding a Vertex to a Polyline

Now that you know what Entnext is capable of, let's look at a practical application. The Addvert program (Figure 11.3) adds a vertex to a polyline. If you have ever had to add a vertex to a polyline using the

AutoCAD Pedit command, you know it can be a trying effort. This program simplifies the operation to one step. Figure 11.4 illustrates this program. Let's see first hand how it works.

1. Save and exit the Chapt11 drawing.

2. Open an AutoLISP file called ADDVERT.LSP, then copy Figure 11.3 into the file. Save and exit ADDVERT.LSP.

3. Return to the Chapt11 file and load ADDVERT.LSP.

4. Enter **addvert** at the command prompt.

5. At the prompt

    Pick vertex location:

    pick the square polyline at the coordinates 10, 6. The box disappears and a new box is drawn with an additional vertex at the point you picked.

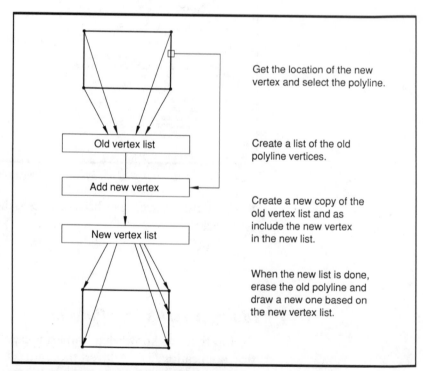

Figure 11.4: How Addvert works conceptually

The Addvert program reduces into one step a process that normally takes seven steps through the Pedit command. Let's see how it works in detail.

First, an object and a point are obtained using the Entsel function:

```
(defun C:ADDVERT (/ pEnt VerLst Newpt int NewVer ptyp)
  (setq pEnt (entsel "Pick vertex location: "))
```

As you may recall, Entsel pauses the program's processing and prompts the user to select an object. Once a user responds, it returns a list of two elements, the entity name and the coordinates used to pick the object.

The user-defined function on the next line, Getver, creates a new list containing only the vertex coordinates from the polyline entity picked. This list of vertices is assigned to the variable VerLst:

```
(setq VerLst (getver (car pEnt)))
```

You saw earlier how Getver works. It returns a list of polyline vertices. In the above expression, the list of vertices is assigned to the VerLst variable.

The next line obtains the associated value of the 70 group code from the polyline. The 70 group code identifies the type of polyline it is, whether it is closed, curve-fit, spline curved, etc. (see Appendix B for a full list of the 70 group code options):

```
(setq ptyp (assoc 70 (entget (car pEnt))))
```

This information will be used at the end of the program to determine how the polyline will be redrawn.

The next line uses the Osnap function to establish a point exactly on the polyline:

```
(setq Newpt  (osnap (cadr pEnt) "nearest"))
```

Here, the coordinate from the Entsel function used earlier is applied to the Osnap Nearest function to obtain a new point. This new point is exactly on the polyline.

Defining a New Polyline

The While expression that follows builds a new list of vertices from which a new polyline will be drawn. This list is actually a copy of the list created by the user-defined function Getver, with the new point added in the appropriate place.

The test expression in the While expression checks to see if the end of the list VerLst has been reached:

(while (cadr VerLst)

Next, the first element of VerLst is added to a list called NewVer:

(setq NewVer
  (append NewVer (list (car VerLst)))
)

This expression copies the first element of the original vertex list to the new list NewVer.

The next set of expressions tests to see if the new vertex Newpt lies between the first two points of the vertex list:

(setq int
  (btwn (car VerLst) newpt (Cadr VerLst))
)

Another user-defined function is used to actually perform the test. This function is called Btwn and it tests to see if one coordinate lies between two others. If Btwn finds that Newpt lies between the first and second point of VerLst, then Btwn returns the value of Newpt. Otherwise Btwn returns nil.

If the Btwn test function returns a coordinate, the next expression adds the new vertex to the NewVer list:

(if int
  (setq NewVer (append NewVer (list int)))
)

Finally, the first element of the vertex list is removed and the whole process is repeated:

(setq VerLst (cdr VerLst))
);end while

Once the While loop is done, VerLst is a list of one element. That last element is added to the NewVer list:

(setq NewVer (append NewVer (list (car VerLst))))

Drawing the New Polyline

The last several lines erase the old polyline and redraw it using the new vertex list. First the old line is erased:

(command "erase" (car pEnt) " ")

Then the Pline command is issued:

(command "pline")

Next, the Foreach function is used to input the vertices from the New-Ver list to the Pline command:

(foreach n NewVer (command n))

You may recall that Foreach is a function that reads elements from a list and applies them one-by-one to a variable, which is then used in an expression. The expression is evaluated repeatedly, one time for each element of the list. In this case, each vertex from the NewVer list is applied to a command function that supplies the vertex coordinate to the Pline command issued in the previous expression.

Once Foreach has completed evaluating every element of the NewVer list, the last expression ends the Pline command:

```
(if ( = (cdr Ptyp) 1)
    (command "close")
    (command " ")
)
```

The If conditional expression tests to see if the polyline is closed or not. If it is, then it enters the word "close" to close the polyline. If not, then a ◄─┘ is issued. You may recall that in the first part of the program, the 70 group code sublist was extracted from the polyline property list. This sublist was assigned to the variable Ptyp. Here, Ptyp is tested to see if its code value is 1. If it is 1, the polyline is closed, thereby causing the If expression to evaluate the (*command "close"*) expression. If this expression is left off, the new polyline box will have only three sides.

Testing for Polyline Types

The last expression above demonstrates a special concern when dealing with polylines. There are really several types of polylines, all of which must be handled differently. The Addvert program will only function properly when used on simple polylines made up of line segments. Polylines that are curve-fitted or splined will contain extra vertices that do not actually form part of the drawn polyline but are used as control points in defining curves and splines.

Fortunately, the 70 group code enables you to find out what type of vertex you are dealing with. Besides determining whether the polyline is closed or not, the 70 group code can test for other conditions. You could include a test for a spline vertex by comparing the 70 group code value of a vertex to 16. If it is 16, the value for a spline frame control point, then you know not to include the vertex in your vertex list. You can refer to Appendix B for more details on the group codes.

*H*ow Arcs Are Described in Polylines

Arcs in polylines are described using a bulge factor and two vertices. You can think of the *bulge factor* as the tangent of the angle described by the chord of the arc and a line drawn from one end of the arc to the arc's midpoint (see Figure 11.5). From this relationship, the following formula is derived:

bulge = h / (0.5 *cord) = 2h / cord

You can derive the geometry of the arc from these simple relationships. Figure 11.6 shows how to derive the arc's angle from the bulge factor.

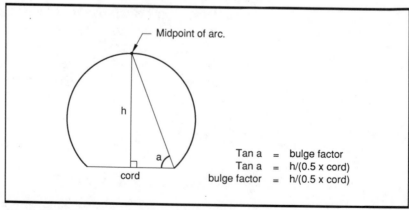

Figure 11.5: An arc's bulge factor

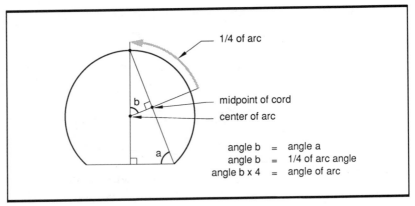

1/4 of arc

midpoint of cord

center of arc

angle b	=	angle a
angle b	=	1/4 of arc angle
angle b x 4	=	angle of arc

Figure 11.6: Finding the angle of an arc

I won't give an example here of a program to edit arcs in a polyline, as such a task can be quite involved. However, should you find the need to do so, you have the basics for building your own program to accomplish the task.

A ccessing Entity Handles and Block Attributes

In the last section, you saw how to extract information from a complex entity. You can use the same method to extract information from entity handles and block attributes. *Entity handles* are permanent names AutoCAD can give to entities in a drawing. The program you will examine in this section uses block attributes as well as entity handles and external files to help assign and store names to objects in your drawing. This section demonstrates how Entnext can be used to get attribute information from a block and how you can use attributes to permanently store information. First you will explore one possible way of using entity handles.

U sing Entity Handles

You know that every entity is given an alphanumeric entity name. This name is the key to accessing the entity's record in the drawing database. Unfortunately, this entity name changes from editing session to editing session. For example, during one editing session an object might have the entity name <Entity name: 600000d4>, while in another session the same entity could have the name <Entity name: 60000012>. Though this may not be of concern to you for the most part, you may still want to have a way of permanently identifying entities from one editing session to another.

Adding AutoCAD Entity Handles

Fortunately, with AutoCAD release 10 you can add a permanent, unchanging entity handle to each and every entity in your AutoCAD drawing. AutoCAD adds handles to the entities in a drawing when you issue the Handles command. When you turn on the Handles function, AutoCAD automatically assigns an alphanumeric name to every object in the drawing. (In a moment you'll see how you can assign your own names to entities.)

You can use the Handent function in conjunction with other functions to obtain entity handles from the drawing database. The handles are added to an entity's property list as a group code 5 property sublist. To get an entity's handle, you use the usual Assoc-Entget function combination to extract the sublist.

Let's take a look at this process by adding a handle to the Chapt11 drawing you created earlier in this chapter. Return to that drawing and enter **handles** at the command prompt. At the prompt

Handles are disabled.
ON/DESTROY:

enter **on.** Next, enter this expression:

(assoc 5(entget(car (entsel))))

At the "Select object" prompt, pick the polyline box. You will get a list similar to the following:

(5 . "29")

The second element of the group 5 property is the entity handle. Note that the handle is a numeric value in quotes, so it is really a string data type.

Assigning Names to Entities

You could write a simple routine to display an entity's handle, which you could record somewhere. Then, you could create another program to retrieve an object based on this handle. I've taken this idea a step further and have written a program (Namer) that allows you to assign any name you like to an entity and later select that object by entering the name you have assigned to it. Figure 11.7 shows this program and Figure 11.8 shows a diagram of how it works.

This program makes use of a block attribute as a storage medium for the names you assign to entities. Let's take a closer look.

First, you need to define the attribute used for storage.

```
;Function to turn a list into a string--------------------------------------

(defun ltos (lst / gfile strname)
(setq gfile (open "acad.grp" "w"))              ;open a file on disk
(prin1 lst gfile)                               ;print list to file
(close gfile)                                   ;close file
(setq gfile (open "acad.grp" "r"))              ;open file
(setq strname (read-line gfile))                ;read list from file
(close gfile)                                   ;close file
strname                                         ;return converted list
)

;Function to obtain name list stored in attribute---------------------------

(defun getatt (/ nament)
(setq nament (ssname(ssget "X" '((2 . "NAMESTOR")))0))   ;get attribute block
(read (cdr (assoc 1(entget (entnext nament)))))          ;get attribute value
)

;Function to clear stored names---------------------------------------------
(defun attclr ()
(setq nament (ssname (ssget "X" '((2 . "NAMESTOR")))0))  ;get attrib. block
(setq namevl (entget (entnext nament)))                  ;get attrib. ent. list
(setq namelt (assoc 1 namevl))                           ;get attrib. value
(entmod (subst (cons 1 "()") namelt namevl))             ;add list to attrib
)

;Program to assign a name to an entity
;--------------------------------------------------------------------------
(defun C:NAMER (/ group gname ename sname namevl namelt)
(setq ename  (cdr (assoc 5 (entget (car (entsel "\nPick object: "))))))
(setq gname  (list (strcase (getstring "\nEnter name of object: "))))
(setq group  (getatt))                          ;get names from attrib.
(setq gname  (append gname (list ename)))       ;new name + ent. name
(setq group  (append group (list gname)))       ;add names to list
(setq sname  (ltos group))                      ;convert list to strng
(setq namevl (entget (entnext (ssname (ssget "X" '((2 . "NAMESTOR")))0))))
(setq namelt (assoc 1 namevl))                  ;get attrib. value
(entmod (subst (cons 1 sname) namelt namevl))   ;add list to attrib
(entupd (cdr (assoc -1 namevl)))
(princ)
)

;Function to select an entity by its name-----------------------------------

(defun GETNAME (/ group gname )
(setq gname  (strcase (getstring "\nEnter name of entity: ")))
(setq group  (getatt))                          ;get names from attrib.
(handent (cadr (assoc gname group)))
)
```

Figure 11.7: The Namer program, which gives names to entities

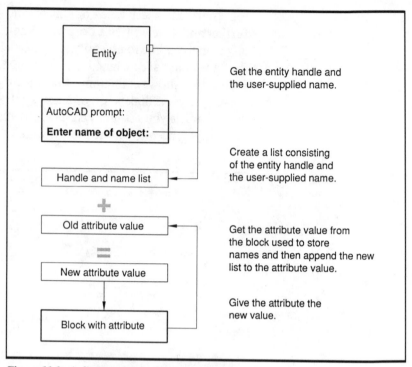

Figure 11.8: *A diagram of the Namer program*

1. Exit the Chapt11 drawing and open an AutoLISP file called NAMER.LSP. Copy the program shown in Figure 11.7 into your file, and then save and exit the file.

2. Return to the Chapt11 drawing and load NAMER.LSP.

3. Enter **attdef** to start the attribute definition command.

4. Enter the following responses to the Attdef prompts:

> **Attribute modes -- Invisible:N Constant:N Verify:N
>   Preset:N
> Enter (ICVP) to change, RETURN when done:** ↵
> **Attribute tag: name
> Attribute name: name
> Default attribute value: ( )
> Start point or Align/Center/Fit/Middle/Right/Style: 2,9
> Height (2.0):** ↵
> **Rotation angle <0>:** ↵

The word *name* will appear at coordinates 2, 9.

5. Now issue the Block command and enter the following responses to the block prompts:

> **Block name (or ?): namestor**
> **Insert base point: 2,9**

And at the prompt

> **select objects:**

pick the attribute defined in the previous step.

6. Issue the Insert command and enter the following responses to the insert prompts:

> **Block name (or ?): namestor**
> **Insertion point: 2,9**
> **X scale factor <1> / Corner / XYZ: ⏎**
> **Y scale factor (default = X): ⏎**
> **Rotation angle <0>: ⏎**
> **Enter attribute values**
> **name <( )>: ⏎**

You have just defined the attribute within which the program Namer will store your entity names. Now you are ready to use the program.

1. Enter **namer** at the command prompt. At the prompt

> **Pick object:**

pick the polyline box.

2. At the next prompt

> **Enter name of object:**

enter **square**. The computer will pause for a moment and then the command prompt will return. Also, the value of the attribute you inserted earlier will change to a list containing the name SQUARE and the entity handle associated with the name. The Namer program uses the attribute as a device in which to store the name you give the entity with its handle.

3. To see that the name SQUARE remains associated with the box, exit the Chapt11 drawing with the End command, and then open the file again.

4. Load the NAMER.LSP file again.

5. Now issue the Copy command. At the "Select object" prompt, enter

   (getname)

   You will get the prompt

   Enter name of entity:

   Enter **square**. The box will be highlighted, indicating that it has been selected.

6. At the "Base point" prompt, pick a point at coordinates 2, 2.

7. At the "Second point" prompt, pick a point at coordinates 3, 3. The box is copied at the displacement 1, 1.

The attribute used to store the name could have been made invisible so it doesn't intrude on the drawing, but it was intentionally left visible so you could actively see what is going on.

How the Entity-Naming Program Works

Namer works by first extracting the entity handle of the object selected and then creating an association list of the handle and the name entered by the user. This association list is permanently stored as the value of an attribute. The attribute value is altered using the Entmod function you saw in the last chapter. Let's take a detailed look at how Namer and Getname work.

Namer starts by obtaining the entity handle of the entity the user picks:

```
(defun C:NAMER (/ group gname ename sname nament
    namevl namelt)
(setq ename (cdr (assoc 5 (entget (car (entsel "\nPick object: "))))))
```

Here, Entsel is used to get the entity name of a single object. The Car function extracts the name from the value returned from Entsel, and then Entget retrieves the actual entity name. At the next level, the Assoc function is used to extract the 5 group code sublist from the entity. The actual entity handle is extracted from the group code with the Cdr function. This value is assigned to the variable Ename.

In the next expression, a list is created containing the name given to the entity by the user:

```
(setq gname (list (strcase (getstring "\nEnter name of object: "))))
```

The user is prompted to enter a name, which is converted to all uppercase letters with the Strcase function. Then it is converted into a list with the List function. Finally, the list is assigned to the variable Gname.

The next expression calls the user-defined function Getatt:

```
(setq group  (getatt))
```

This function extracts the attribute value from the block named Namestor. You may recall that the default attribute value of Namestor was "()". Getatt extracts this value, and the above expression assigns the value to the variable group. You'll look at how Getatt works a little later.

Next, the entity handle is appended to the list containing the name the user entered for the object. This appended list is then itself appended to the list named Group, which was obtained from the attribute:

```
(setq gname  (append gname (list ename)))
(setq group  (append group (list gname)))
```

The variable Group is the association list to which user-defined entity names are stored. It is the same list you see in the block attribute you inserted earlier.

The next line converts the list group into a string data type using a user-defined function called Ltos:

```
(setq sname  (ltos group))
```

Ltos simply writes the list represented by the symbol group to an external file then reads it back. The net effect is the conversion of a list into a string. This is done so the value of Group can be used to replace the current value of the attribute in the Namestor block. This is a situation in which data type consideration is important. Attribute values cannot be anything other than strings, so if our program were to try to substitute a list in place of a string, an error would occur.

Extracting Attribute Data

The next several lines obtain the property list of the Namestor block attribute and its attribute value in preparation for Entmod:

```
(setq namevl
    (entget (entnext (ssname (ssget "X" '((2 . "NAMESTOR")))0))))
```

Here, the Ssget "X" filter is used to select a specific entity, the block Namestor. In this situation, since the name of the block is a fixed value, include the name as a permanent part of the expression:

(ssget "X" '((2 . "NAMESTORE")))

This helps you keep track of what block you are using and also reduces the number of variables needed.

Once the block is found by Ssget, Ssname gets the block's entity names, and Entnext extracts the attribute's entity names. Entget extracts the attribute's property list, which is assigned to the Namevl variable. The expression that follows uses the Assoc function to extract the actual attribute value:

(setq namelt (assoc 1 namevl))

Figure 11.9 shows how this works.

Just as you used Entnext to extract the vertices of a polyline, you can use Entnext to obtain the attribute information from a block. If there is more than one attribute in a block, you step through the attributes the same way you step through the vertices of a polyline. The

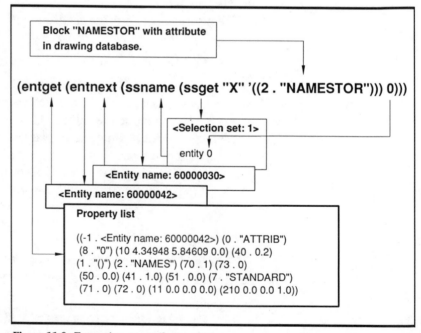

Figure 11.9: Extracting an attribute value

Getatt function works in a similar way to the expressions you have just examined.

Finally, Entmod updates the attribute to store the association list of the object name and entity handle:

```
(entmod (subst (cons 1 sname) namelt namevl))
(entupd (cdr (assoc -1 namevl)))
(princ)
```

The Subst function is used to substitute the newly appended name with the old attribute value in the attributes property list. Then Entmod updates the drawing database with the updated property list. The Entupd function updates the display of the attribute in the block. Entupd is only needed when attributes and curve-fitted polylines are being edited and you don't want to regenerate the entire drawing to update the display. You could think of it as a Regen for specific attribute and polyline entities.

The Getname function is actually quite simple compared to Namer.

```
(defun GETNAME (/ group gname getname handl nament newent)
(setq gname  (strcase (getstring "\nEnter name of entity: ")))
(setq group (getatt))
(handent (cadr (assoc gname group)))
)
```

Getname prompts the user for the name of the object to be selected. It then obtains the association list of names from the storing block attribute with the user-defined Getatt function. Finally, Getname extracts the entity handle from the association list using the name entered by the user as the key-value. The Handent function returns the entity name of the entity whose handle it receives as an argument.

Namer and Getname are fairly limited programs, as they have very little in the way of error checking. For example, if while using the Getname function you enter a name that does not exist, you'll get an AutoLISP error message. Also, if you attempt to save more than a dozen names, you will get the "out of string space" error message. This is due to the 100-character limit AutoLISP places on string data types. There is also no facility to check for duplicate user-supplied names. You may want to try adding some error-checking features yourself, or, if you feel confident, you can try to find a way to overcome the 100-character limit.

Summary

I hope this tutorial will continue to be helpful to you as a reference when you are stuck with a problem. Though I couldn't cover every AutoLISP function in detail (in particular, this book does not cover binary operations and a few other math functions), I did cover the major functions. You also were able to see how those functions are used within programs solving real-world problems.

As you gain programming experience, you may become interested in the theory behind the programming language. There are two excellent resources to help you further your understanding of the theoretical side of the LISP programming language on which AutoLISP is based. These are *Common LISPcraft* by Robert Wilensky, published by W.W. Norton & Company Inc., and *LISP: A Gentle Introduction to Symbolic Computation* by David S. Touretzky, published by Harper & Row, Publishers.

Programming can be the most frustrating experience you have ever encountered. But it also can be one of the most rewarding experiences a computer can offer. And once you master AutoLISP, you will actually begin to save time in your daily use of AutoCAD. But to get to that point, you must practice and become as familiar as possible with AutoLISP. The more familiar you are with it, the easier it will be to use and the quicker you will be able to write programs.

A

Error Messages

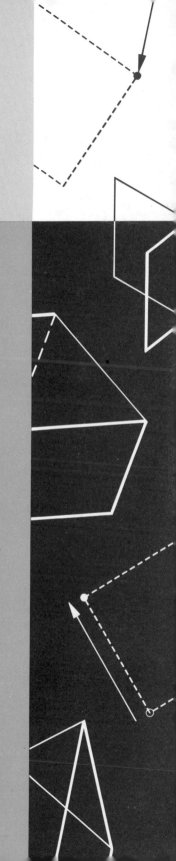

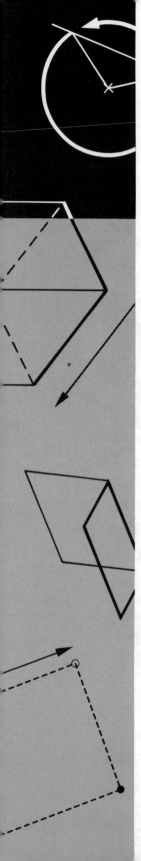

A

This appendix lists the error messages you are likely to encounter while writing your programs and a brief description of each. See Chapter 8 for a general discussion on debugging your programs.

atomlist modified after function swap

If Vmon is in use, and a function attempts to modify the Atomlist, you will get this message. You will also get this message if you attempt to use the Clean function in Chapter 3 in conjunction with Vmon.

AutoCAD rejected function

Either an argument to a function or the function itself is invalid. Some possible causes of this error are the attempted setting of a read-only system variable or attempted use of a Get function within a Command function.

bad argument type

An expression includes an incorrect argument type, for example, a string supplied as an argument to the Distance function.

bad association list

The argument supplied to Assoc is not an association list.

bad entmod list

The argument supplied to Entmod is not an entity list.

bad entmod list value

One of the sublists supplied to Entmod is not in the proper format for an entity list.

bad formal argument list

AutoLISP has detected an invalid argument list to a function.

bad function

The first element of a list is not a valid function. The list may be a data list and not a form.

bad list

A list is improperly formed. A possible cause is a real number between 1.0 and −1.0 that does not begin with a zero.

bad node

An invalid data type has been encountered by the Type function.

bad node type in list

An invalid data type has been encountered by the Foreach function.

bad point argument

A list of coordinates is improperly formed. A possible cause is a real number between 1.0 and −1.0 representing a coordinate that does not begin with a zero.

bad point value

See **bad point argument**.

bad ssget list

The association list passed to Ssget is improperly formed. Association lists are used with the "X" Ssget option.

bad ssget list value

An element of an association list passed to Ssget is improperly formed. Association lists are used with the "X" Ssget option.

base point required

Getcorner has been called without a reference or base point.

boole arg1 < 0 or > 15

The first argument to the Boole function must be an integer between 0 and 15.

can't evaluate expression

The expression is improperly formed. Check the placement of decimal points in reals or the syntax of expressions.

can't open (file) for input — LOAD failed

The file specified in the Load function could not be found. Make sure you specified the proper drive and directory.

can't reenter AutoLISP

You have attempted to access AutoLISP while AutoLISP is currently occupied with another program or function.

consol break

You have pressed Ctrl-C while a function is processing.

divide by zero

An expression has attempted to divide a value by zero. This is not allowed.

divide overflow

An expression has attempted to divide a value by a very small number, resulting in an invalid quotient.

extra right paren

There are too many right parentheses.

file not open

A file descriptor does not refer to an open file. Check any lists using the Open function to find the file descriptor or be sure the file has been opened.

file read — insufficient string space

AutoLISP's string space has been exhausted while attempting to read from a file. Single strings are limited to 100 characters.

file size limit exceeded

A file exceeds the maximum size allowed by the operating system. Applies to Unix-based systems only.

floating-point exception

This is a floating-point arithmetic error that applies to Unix-based systems only.

function canceled

You have pressed Ctrl-C in response to a prompt.

function undefined for argument

Arguments passed to Log or Sqrt are out of range.

function undefined for real

A real number has been passed to a function that requires an integer.

improper argument

Gcd has been passed zero or a negative number.

inappropriate object in function

An improperly formed user-defined function has been detected by Vmon.

incorrect number of arguments

> More than one object has been supplied to the Quote function.

incorrect number of arguments to a function

> The number of arguments supplied to a user-defined function does not match the number of arguments specified in the function's argument list.

incorrect request for command list data

> A command function cannot be executed due to the action of another function.

input aborted

> An error has been encountered while reading a file for input.

insufficient node space

> There is not enough heap space (LISPHEAP) to accommodate additional symbols or functions.

insufficient string space

> There is not enough heap space (LISPHEAP) to accommodate additional strings.

invalid argument

> A wrong data type has been supplied to a function.

invalid character

> An invalid character has been used in an expression. Check for letters being confused with numbers or vice versa. Also check for wrong character used for T or t.

invalid dotted pair

> A dotted pair is missing an element. A possible cause is a real number between 1.0 and −1.0 that does not begin with a zero.

invalid integer value

A number beyond the range for integers has been encountered. The range for integers on MS-DOS computers is −32,768 to +32,767. The integer range for 32-bit operating systems is −2,147,483,648 to +2,147,483,647.

LISPSTACK overflow

There is not enough stack space (LISPSTACK) to accommodate further computation. This can be caused by excessive function recursion or large argument lists in user-defined functions. To correct, increase the size of the LISPSTACK environment.

malformed list

A list read from a file has ended prematurely.

malformed string

A string read from a file has ended prematurely.

misplaced dot

A real number between 1.0 and −1.0 is missing its initial zero.

null function

An attempt has been made to evaluate a function that has no value.

too few arguments

Too few arguments have been supplied to an AutoLISP built-in function.

too many arguments

Too many arguments have been supplied to an AutoLISP built-in function.

B

Group Codes

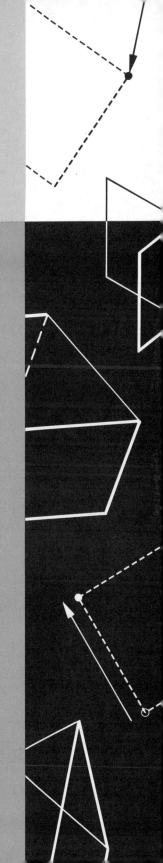

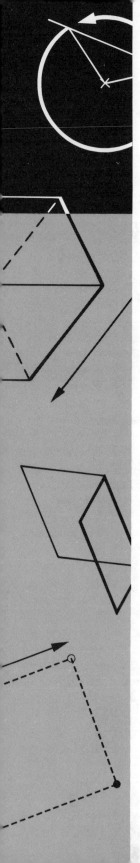

B

This appendix presents the group codes in six different tables. The first lists the codes and their associated values. The second shows the entity types and the group codes that are used with them. The four remaining tables explain the meaning of four group codes in detail—group codes 70, 71, 72, and 75.

Table of Group Codes

The table in this section shows the group codes and the meanings of their associated values. The associated value is a coordinate location, a single number, or a string. Here are some examples of group codes and values.

- *Strings* are entity names, entity types, or string values for text and attributes, as in this property list element:

    (1 . "CIRCLE")

- *Point coordinates* locate key points such as endpoints of lines, circles, arcs, and vectors, or text and block insertion points:

    (10 1.0 2.2 4.3)

- *Single numbers* that are reals can be scale factors, text heights, rotation angles, or distances:

    (40 . 45.0)

- *Integers* are usually bit or binary codes used to further convey information about the particular group code:

    (70 . 4)

Code	Associated Value Group
String Codes	
−1	Entity name (not a string)
0	Entity type ("TEXT", "LINE", "ARC", etc.)
1	Text string or attribute default value
2	Block or shape name or attribute tag
3	Attribute prompt string
5	Entity handle (Handles function must be on)
6	Linetype
7	Text style
8	Layer
Real Number Codes (Floating-Point)	
10	Block or text insertion point, start point, or center point
11	Text center alignment point (for centered text) or second point for lines, polyline segments, solids, and 3dfaces
12	Insertion point for continued or baseline dimensions, or third point for solids and 3dfaces
13–16	Definition point for dimensions, or fourth point for solids and 3dfaces (13 only)
21	Right alignment point (for right-justified text)
23–26	Definition point for dimensions
31	Second alignment point (for fit or aligned text)
33–36	Definition point for dimensions
40	Text height, radius of circle or arc, size of shapes, or polyline starting width
41	X scale factor or polyline ending width
42	Y scale factor for blocks, or bulge factor for polyline vertices
43	Z scale factor for blocks

44	Column spacing for Minsert blocks
45	Row spacing for Minsert blocks
50	Rotation angle or start angle for circles, arcs, and dimensions. Also x axis for UCS where entity is a point
51	Oblique angle for text and shapes, or end angle for circles and arcs

Integer Codes

62	Color if not Bylayer
66	The associated value is always 1. This code appears with polylines and indicates that vertices can be obtained using Entnext.
70	Column count for Minsert blocks. (See also "Group Code 70 Bit Codes" table in this appendix.)
71	Text mirror code. Also row count for Minsert blocks. (See also "Group Code 71 Bit Codes" table in this appendix.)
72	Text alignment code. See ("Group Code 72 Codes" table in this appendix.)
73	3dmesh smooth surface density in M direction, or field length in attributes. Corresponds to the Surftab1 system variable setting active at the time the 3dmesh entity was created.
74	3dmesh smooth surface density in N direction. Corresponds to the Surftab2 system variable setting active at the time the 3dmesh entity was created.
75	3D mesh smooth surface type. (See also "Group Code 75 Codes" table in this appendix.)

Real Number Codes (Floating-Point)

128	User-defined location for dimension text
210	Extrusion direction in x, y, and z coordinates

*E*ntity Types and Group Codes

This table shows the entity types and their group codes. As you can see, not all group codes are used with all entity types, nor do the group codes have the same meaning for all the entity types. Code 5 only appears if Handles has been turned on. Code 6 only appears if an entity is assigned a linetype other than Bylayer. Code 62 only appears if an entity is assigned a color other than Bylayer. By contrast, groups − 1, 0, and 1 always appear in property lists and they always have the same meaning.

Entity Type	Group Codes Used
Arc	− 1, 0, 1, 5, 6, 8, 10, 40, 50, 51, 62, 210
Attrib	− 1, 0, 1, 2, 5, 6, 7, 8, 10, 11, 21, 31, 40, 41, 50, 51, 62, 70, 71, 72, 73, 210
Block	− 1, 0, 1, 2, 5, 6, 8, 10, 41, 42, 43, 44, 45, 50, 62, 66, 70, 71
Circle	− 1, 0, 1, 5, 6, 8, 10, 40, 62, 210
Dimension	− 1, 0, 1, 2, 5, 6, 8, 10, 11, 13, 14, 15, 16, 40, 50, 51, 62, 210
Line	− 1, 0, 1, 5, 6, 8, 10, 11, 62, 210
Point	− 1, 0, 1, 5, 6, 8, 10, 50, 62, 210
Polyline	− 1, 0, 1, 5, 6, 8, 40, 41, 62, 66, 70, 71, 72, 73, 74, 75, 210
Vertex	− 1, 0, 1, 5, 6, 8, 10, 40, 41, 42, 50, 62, 70
Shape	− 1, 0, 1, 2, 5, 6, 8, 10, 40, 41, 50, 51, 62, 210
Solid	− 1, 0, 1, 5, 6, 8, 10, 11, 12, 13, 62, 210
Text	− 1, 0, 1, 2, 5, 6, 7, 8, 10, 11, 21, 31, 40, 41, 50, 51, 71, 72
Trace	− 1, 0, 1, 5, 6, 8, 10, 11, 12, 13, 62, 210
3dface	− 1, 0, 1, 5, 6, 8, 10, 11, 12, 13, 62, 70

Group Code 70 Bit Codes

The following table shows the meaning of the group code 70 bit codes. The meaning is different for different types of entities, so this table lists entity types and what the bit code means for each type.

Entity Type	Bit-Code Meaning
Blocks	1, anonymous block generated by hatching, dimensioning, or other internal operation; 2, block has attributes
Attributes	1, invisible attribute; 2, constant attribute; 4, verification required; 8, preset attribute
Polylines	1, closed polyline; 2, curve-fit polyline; 4, spline-fit polyline; 8, 3-D polyline; 16, 3-D polyline mesh (see group code 75); 32, 3-D polyline mesh closed in N direction
Vertex	1, extra vertex used for curve fitting; 2, curve-fit tangent definition; 4, not used; 8, spline vertex; 16, spline frame control point; 32, 3-D polyline vertex, 64; 3-D polyline mesh vertex
3dface	1, first edge is invisible; 2, second edge is invisible; 4, third edge is invisible; 8, fourth edge is invisible
Dimensions	0, rotated, horizontal, or vertical; 2, angular; 3, diameter; 4, radius; 128, text is in a location other than normal

Group Code 71 Bit Codes

This group deals only with text that has been mirrored.

Code	Meaning
2	Text is backward
4	Text is upside down

*G*roup Code 72 Codes

This group tells you how the text was placed. These codes correspond to the Align/Center/Fit/Middle options under the Text and Dtext commands.

Code	Meaning
0	Left-justified (default)
1	Centered at baseline
2	Right-justified
3	Aligned between two points (height varies)
4	Centered at middle
5	Fit between two points (height does not vary)

*G*roup Code 75 Codes

The 75 group code is exclusively used with 3-D surfaces. This group code reflects the Spline type system variable setting.

Code	Meaning
0	No smooth surface fit
5	Quadratic B-Spline surface fit
6	Cubic B-Spline surface fit
8	Bezier surface

C

AutoCAD Dimension Variables and System Variables

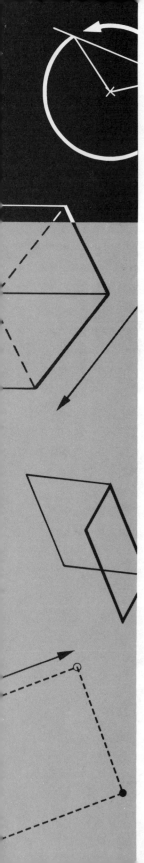

C

This appendix contains two tables of AutoCAD variables. The first describes variables that control the way AutoCAD draws dimensions. The second table lists all of the system variables you can access through the AutoCAD Setvar command.

*D*imension Variables

These variables control extension line and text location, tolerance specifications, arrow styles and sizes, and more.

Dimension Variable (Version)	Description
Dimalt(2.5)	When on, dimension texts for two measurement systems are inserted simultaneously (*alt*ernate). Dimaltf and Dimaltd must also be set appropriately. The alternate dimension is placed within brackets. Angular dimensions are not affected. This variable is commonly used when inches and metric units must be displayed at the same time in a dimension. The default setting is off.
Dimaltd(2.5)	When Dimalt is on, Dimaltd controls the number of decimal places the alternate dimension will have (*alt*ernate *d*ecimal places). The default value is 2.
Dimaltf(2.5)	When Dimalt is on, Dimaltf controls the multiplication factor for the alternate dimension (*alt*ernate *f*actor). The value held by Dimaltf will be multiplied by the standard dimension value to determine the alternate dimension. The

default value is 25.4, the number required to display metric units.

Dimapost(2.6) When Dimalt is on, you can use Dimapost to append text to the alternate dimension (*alternate post*). For example, if Dimapost is given the value "mm," the alternate dimension will appear as

*value*mm

instead of just

value

The default value is nul. To change a previously set value to nul, enter a period for the Dimapost new value.

Dimaso(2.6) When on, dimensions will be associative (*ass*ociative). When off, dimensions will consist of separate drawing entities with none of the associative dimension properties. The default is on.

Dimasz(1.4) Sets the size of dimension arrows or Dimblks (*a*rrow *si*ze. See Dimblk). If set to 0, a tick is drawn in place of an arrow. The default value is .18 units.

Dimblk(2.5) You can replace the standard AutoCAD dimension arrow with one of your own design by creating a drawing of your symbol and making it a block. You then give Dimblk the name of your symbol block. This block must be drawn corresponding to a one by one unit area and must be oriented as the right side arrow. The default value is nul.

Dimblk1(10) With Dimsah set to on, you can replace the standard AutoCAD dimension arrows with two different arrows using Dimblk1 and Dimblk2. Dimblk1 holds the name of the block defining the first dimension arrow

	while Dimblk2 holds the name of the second dimension arrow block.
Dimblk2(10)	See Dimblk1.
Dimcen(1.4)	Sets the size of center marks used during the Center, Diameter, and Radius dimension subcommands. A negative value draws center lines instead of the center mark cross, while a 0 value draws nothing. The default value is 0.09 units.
Dimdle(2.5)	With Dimtsz given a value greater than 0, dimension lines can extend past the extension lines by the amount specified in Dimdle (*d*imension *l*ine *e*xtension). This amount is not adjusted by Dimscale. The default value is 0.
Dimdli(1.4)	Sets the distance at which dimension lines are offset when you use the Baseline or Continue dimension subcommands (*d*imension *l*ine *i*ncrement). The default is 0.38 units.
Dimexe(1.4)	Sets the distance the extension lines are drawn past the dimension lines (*ex*tension line *exten*sion). The default value is 0.18 units.
Dimexo(1.4)	Sets the distance between the beginning of the extension line and the actual point selected at the *Extension line origin* prompt (*ex*tension line *o*ffset). The default value is 0.0625 units.
Dimlfac(2.5)	Sets the global scale factor for dimension values (*l*ength *fac*tor). Linear distances will be multiplied by the value held by Dimlfac. This multiple will be entered as the dimension text. The default value is 1.0. This can be useful when drawings are not drawn to scale.
Dimlim(1.4)	When set to on, dimension text is entered as two values representing a dimension range

rather than a single value. The range is determined by the values given to Dimtp (*p*lus tolerance) and Dimtm (*m*inus *t*olerance). The default value is off.

Dimpost(2.6)   Automatically appends text strings to dimension text. For example, if Dimpost is given the value "inches," dimension text will appear as

value inches

instead of just

value

The default value is nul. To change a previously set value to nul, enter a period for the Dimpost new value. If you use Dimpost in conjunction with appended dimension text, the Dimpost value is included as part of the default dimension text.

Dimrnd(2.5)   Sets the amount to which all dimensions are rounded. For example, if you set Dimrnd to 1, all dimensions will be integer values. The number of decimal places affected depends on the precision value set by the Units command. The default is 0.

Dimsah(10)   When set to on, allows the separate arrow blocks, Dimblk1 and Dimblk2, to replace the standard AutoCAD arrows (*s*eparate *a*rrow *h*eads). If Dimtsz is set to a value greater than 0, Dimsah has no effect.

Dimscale(1.4)   Sets the scale factor for dimension variables that control dimension lines and arrows and text size (unless current text style has a fixed height). If your drawing is not full scale, you should set this variable to reflect the drawing scale. For example, for a drawing whose scale is ¹/₄" equals 1', you should set Dimscale to 48. The default value is 1.0.

Dimse1(1.4)	When set to on, the first dimension line extension is not drawn (*suppress extension 1*). The default is off.
Dimse2(1.4)	When set to on, the second dimension line extension is not drawn (*suppress extension 2*). The default is off.
Dimsho(2.6)	When set to on, dimension text in associative dimensions will dynamically change to reflect the location of a dimension point as it is being moved (*show dimension*). The default is off.
Dimsoxd(10)	When set to on, dimension lines do not appear outside of the extension lines (*suppress outside extension dimension lines*). If Dimtix is also set to on and the space between the extension lines prohibits the display of a dimension line, no dimension line is drawn. The default is off.
Dimtad(1.4)	When set to on and Dimtih is off, dimension text in linear dimensions will be placed above the dimension line (*text above dimension line*). When off, the dimension line will be split in two and text will be placed in line with the dimension line. The default value is off.
Dimtih(1.4)	When set to on, dimension text placed between extension lines will always be horizontal (*text inside horizontal*). When set to off, text will be aligned with the dimension line. The default value is on.
Dimtix(10)	When set to on, dimension text will always be placed between extension lines (*text inside extension*). The default value is off.
Dimtm(1.4)	When Dimtol or Dimlin is on, Dimtm determines the minus tolerance value of the dimension text (*tolerance minus*).
Dimtofl(10)	With Dimtofl on, a dimension line is always drawn between extension lines even when text

	is drawn outside (*text* *o*utside—*f*orced *l*ine). The default is off.
Dimtoh(1.4)	With Dimtoh on, dimension text placed outside extension lines will always be horizontal (*text* *o*utside—*h*orizontal). When set to off, text outside extension lines will be aligned with dimension line. The default is on.
Dimtol(1.4)	With Dimtol on, tolerance values set by Dimtp and Dimtm are appended to the dimension text (*tol*erance). The default is off.
Dimtp(1.4)	When Dimtol or Dimlim is on, Dimtp determines the plus tolerance value of the dimension text (*t*olerance *p*lus).
Dimtsz(2.0)	Sets the size of tick marks drawn in place of the standard AutoCAD arrows (*t*ick *s*ize). When set to 0, the standard arrow is drawn. When greater than 0, tick marks are drawn and take precedence over Dimblk1 and Dimblk2. The default value is 0.
Dimtvp(10)	When Dimtad is off, Dimtvp allows you to specify the location of the dimension text in relation to the dimension line (*t*ext *v*ertical *p*osition). A positive value places the text above the dimension line while a negative value places the text below the dimension line. The dimension line will split to accommodate the text unless the Dimtvp value is greater than 1.
Dimtxt(1.4)	Sets the height of dimension text when the current text style height is set to 0. The default value is 0.18.
Dimzin(2.5)	Determines the display of inches when Architectural units are used. Set to 0, zero feet or zero inches will not be displayed. Set to 1, zero feet and zero inches will be displayed. Set to 2, zero inches will not be displayed. Set to 3, zero feet will not be displayed.

System Variables

These variables fall into three categories: adjustable variables, read-only variables, and variables accessible only through Setvar.

Adjustable Variables

You can adjust these variables either through the Setvar command or through the commands associated with the variable. For example, you can adjust the first three variables with the Units command, or with Setvar.

Variable	Description
Aflags	Controls the attribute mode settings: 1 = invisible, 2 = constant, 4 = verify, 8 = preset. For more than one setting, use the sum of the desired settings.
Angbase	Controls the direction of the 0 angle. Can also be set with the Units command.
Angdir	Controls the positive direction of angles: 0 = counterclockwise, 1 = clockwise. Can also be set with the Units command.
Aperture	Controls the Osnap cursor target height in pixels. Can also be set with the Aperture command.
Attmode	Controls the attribute display mode: 0 = off, 1 = normal, 2 = on. Can also be set with the Attdisp command.
Aunits	Controls angular units: 0 = decimal degrees, 1 = degrees-minutes-seconds, 2 = grads, 3 = radians, 4 = surveyors' units. Can also be set with the Units command.
Auprec	Controls the precision of angular units determined by decimal place. Can also be set with the Units command.
Axismode	Controls the axis mode: 0 = off, 1 = on. Can also be set with the Axis command.

Axisunit	Controls the X and Y axis spacing. Can also be set with the Axis command.
Blipmode	Controls the appearance of blips: 0 = off, 1 = on.
Chamfera	Controls first chamfer distance.
Chamferb	Controls second chamfer distance.
Coords	Controls coordinate readout: 0 = coordinates are displayed only when points are picked. 1 = absolute coordinates are dynamically displayed as cursor moves. 2 = distance and angle are displayed during commands that accept relative distance input. Also controlled by the F6 function key.
Dragmode	Controls dragging: 0 = no dragging, 1 = on if requested, 2 = automatic drag.
Elevation	Controls current three-dimensional elevation.
Filletrad	Controls fillet radius.
Fillmode	Controls fill status: 0 = off, 1 = on.
Gridmode	Controls grid: 0 = off, 1 = on.
Gridunit	Controls grid spacing.
Insbase	Controls insertion base point of current drawing.
Limcheck	Controls limit checking: 0 = no checking, 1 = checking.
Limmax	Controls the coordinate of drawing's upper-right limit.
Limmin	Controls the coordinate of drawing's lower-left limit.
Ltscale	Controls the line type scale factor.
Lunits	Controls unit styles: 1 = scientific, 2 = decimal, 3 = engineering, 4 = architectural, 5 = fractional.
Luprec	Controls unit accuracy by decimal place or size of denominator.
Orthomode	Controls the Ortho mode: 0 = off, 1 = on.

Osmode	Sets the current default Osnap mode: 0 = none, 1 = end point, 2 = midpoint, 4 = center, 8 = node, 16 = quadrant, 32 = intersection, 64 = insert, 128 = perpendicular, 256 = tangent, 512 = nearest, 1024 = quick. If more than one mode is required, enter the sum of those modes.
Qtextmode	Controls the Quick text mode: 0 = off, 1 = on.
Regenmode	Controls the Regenauto mode: 0 = off, 1 = on.
Sketchinc	Controls the sketch record increment.
Snapang	Controls snap and grid angle.
Snapbase	Controls snap, grid, and hatch pattern origin.
Snapisopair	Controls isometric plane: 0 = left, 1 = top, 2 = right.
Snapmode	Controls snap toggle: 0 = off, 1 = on.
Snapstyl	Controls snap style: 0 = standard, 1 = isometric.
Snapunit	Controls snap spacing given in x and y values.
Textsize	Controls default text height.
Thickness	Controls three-dimensional thickness of objects being drawn.
Tracewid	Controls trace width.

*R*ead-Only *Variables*

You can read these variables either through their associated commands or through Setvar. Rather than setting or adjusting some parameter of a drawing or of your AutoCAD system, they simply display the specified information.

Variable	Description
Acadver	Displays the AutoCAD version number.
Area	Displays the current area being computed.
Backz	Displays the distance from the Dview target to the back clipping plane.

Cdate	Displays calendar date/time read from DOS.
Cecolor	Displays current object color.
Celtype	Displays current object line type.
Clayer	Displays current layer.
Date	Displays Julian date/time.
Distance	Displays last distance read using Dist.
Dwgname	Displays drawing name.
Frontz	Displays the distance from the Dview target to the front clipping plane.
Handles	Displays the status of the Handles command. 0 = off, 1 = on.
Lastangle	Displays the end angle of last arc or line.
Lastpoint	Displays coordinates of last point entered. Same point referenced by at sign (@).
Lenslength	Displays the current lens focal length used during the Dview command Zoom option.
Menuname	Displays the current menu file name.
Perimeter	Displays the perimeter value currently being read by Area, List, or Dblist.
Popups	Displays the availability of the Advanced User Interface. 0 = not available, 1 = available.
Target	Displays the coordinate of the target point used in the Dview command.
Tdcreate	Displays time and date of drawing creation.
Tdindwg	Displays total editing time.
Tdupdate	Displays time and date of last save.
Tdusrtimer	Displays user-elapsed time.
Textstyle	Displays the current text style.
Ucsname	Displays the name of the current UCS.
Ucsorg	Displays the current UCS origin point.
Ucsxdir	Displays the X direction of the current UCS.
Ucsydir	Displays the Y direction of the current UCS.

Viewdir	Displays the view direction of the current view port.
Viewtwist	Displays the view twist angle for the current view port.
Vpointx	Displays the x value of the current three-dimensional viewpoint.
Vpointy	Displays the y value of the current three-dimensional viewpoint.
Vpointz	Displays the z value of the current three-dimensional viewpoint.
Worlducs	Displays the status of the World Coordinate System. 0 = WCS is not current, 1 = WCS is current.

Variables Accessible Only Through Setvar

You can access the following variables only through the Setvar command.

Adjustable Variables

You can alter these variables, but only through the Setvar command.

Variable	Description
Attdia	Controls the attribute dialog box for the Insert command: 0 = no dialog box, 1 = dialog box.
Attreq	Controls the prompt for attributes. 0 = no prompt or dialog box for attributes. Attributes use default values. 1 = normal prompt or dialog box upon attribute insertion.
Cmdecho	Used with AutoLISP to control what is displayed on the prompt line. See the AutoLISP manual for details.
Dragp1	Controls regen-drag input sampling rate.
Dragp2	Controls fast-drag input sampling rate. Higher values force the display of more of the dragged

image during cursor movement while lower values display less.

Expert	Controls prompts, depending on level of user's expertise. 0 issues normal prompts. 1 suppresses *About to Regen* and *Really want to turn the current light off?* prompts. 2 suppresses previous prompts plus *Block already defined* and *A drawing with this name already exists*. 3 suppresses previous prompts plus line type warnings. 4 suppresses previous prompts plus UCS and Vports *Save* warnings.
Flatland	Controls AutoCAD's handling of three-dimensional functions and objects as they relate to Object snaps, DXF formats, and AutoLISP. 0 = functions take advantage of version 10's advanced features, 1 = functions operate as they did prior to version 10.
Highlight	Controls object-selection ghosting: 0 = no ghosting, 1 = ghosting.
Menuecho	Controls the display of commands and prompts issued from the menu. A value of 1 suppresses display of commands entered from menu (can be toggled on or off with Ctrl-P); 2 suppresses display of commands and command prompts when command is issued from AutoLISP macro; 3 is a combination of options 1 and 2; 4 disables Ctrl-P menu echo toggle.
Mirrtext	Controls text mirroring: 0 = no text mirroring, 1 = text mirroring.
Pdmode	Controls the type of symbol used as a point during the Point command. Several point styles are available.
Pdsize	Controls the size of the symbol set by Pdmode.
Pickbox	Controls the size of the object-selection box. You can enter integer values to control the box height in pixels.

Skpoly	Controls whether the Sketch command uses regular lines or polylines. 0 = line, 1 = polyline.
Splframe	Controls the display of spline vertices, surface fit three-dimensional meshes, and invisible edges of 3dfaces. 0 = no display of Spline vertices of invisible 3dface edges. Displays only defining mesh or surface fit mesh. 1 = display of Spline vertices or invisible 3dface edges. Displays only surface fit mesh.
Splinesegs	Controls the number of line segments used for each spline patch.
Spline type	Controls the type of curved line generated by the Pedit Spline command. 5 = quadratic B-spline, 6 = Cubic B-spline.
Surftab1	Controls the number of mesh control points for the Rulesurf and Tabsurf commands and the number of mesh points in the M direction for the Revsurf and Edgesurf commands.
Surftab2	Controls the number of mesh control points in the N direction for the Revsurf and Edgesurf commands.
Surftype	Controls the type of surface fitting generated by the Pedit Smooth command. 5 = quadratic B-spline, 6 = cubic B-spline, and 8 = Bezier surface.
Surfu	The accuracy of the smoothed surface models in the M direction.
Surfv	The accuracy of the smoothed surface models in the N direction.
Texteval	Controls whether prompts for text and attribute input to commands are taken literally or as AutoLISP expressions. 0 = literal, 1 = text you input with left parens and exclamation points will be interpreted as AutoLISP expression. Dtext takes all input literally, regardless of this setting.

Ucsfollow | Controls whether changing the current UCS automatically displays the plan view of the new current UCS. 0 = displayed view does not change, 1 = automatic display of new current UCS in plan.

Useri*1-5* | Five variables for storing integers for custom applications.

Userr*1-5* | Five variables for storing real numbers for custom applications.

Worldview | Controls whether point input to the Dview and Vpoint commands is relative to the WCS or the current UCS. 0 = commands use the current UCS to interpret point value input, 1 = commands use UCS to interpret point value input.

Read-Only Variables

These variables can be read only through the Setvar command, unlike the variables in the first two sections of this table.

Variable	Description
Acadprefix	Displays the name of the directory saved in the DOS environment using the DOS command SET.
Dwgprefix	Displays drive and directory prefix for drawing file.
Extmax	Displays upper-right corner coordinate of drawing extent.
Extmin	Displays lower-left corner coordinate of drawing extent.
Screensize	Reads the size of the graphics screen in pixels.
Viewctr	Displays the center coordinate of the current view.
Viewsize	Displays the height of the current view in drawing units.

Acadprefix Displays the name of the directory saved in the DOS environment using the DOS command SET.

Tempprefix Displays the name of the directory where temporary AutoCAD files are saved.

Vsmax Displays the three-dimensional coordinate of the upper-right corner of the current viewport's virtual screen relative to the current UCS.

Vsmin Displays the three-dimensional coordinate of the lower-left corner of the current viewport's virtual screen relative to the current UCS.

Index

Selections from The SYBEX Library

COMPUTER-AIDED DESIGN AND DRAFTING

Visual Guide to AutoCAD
Genevieve Katz
325pp. Ref. 627-8

A visual step-by-step tutorial for AutoCAD beginners, this book gives the reader at a quick glance, the graphically presented information needed to understand and respond to commands. It covers more than 90 commands, from getting started to drawing composites using multiple commands. Through Release 10.

The ABC's of AutoCAD (Second Edition)
Alan R. Miller
375pp. Ref. 584-0

This brief but effective introduction to AutoCAD quickly gets users drafting and designing with this complex CADD package. The essential operations and capabilities of AutoCAD are neatly detailed, using a proven, step-by-step method that is tailored to the results-oriented beginner.

Mastering AutoCAD (Third Edition)
George Omura
825pp. Ref. 574-3

Now in its third edition, this tutorial guide to computer-aided design and drafting with AutoCAD is perfect for newcomers to CADD, as well as AutoCAD users seeking greater proficiency. An architectural project serves as an example throughout.

Advanced Techniques in AutoCAD (Second Edition)
Robert M. Thomas
425pp. Ref. 593-X

Develop custom applications using screen menus, command macros, and AutoLISP programming—no prior programming experience required. Topics include customizing the AutoCAD environment, advanced data extraction techniques, and much more.

AutoCAD Desktop Companion
SYBEX Ready Reference Series
Robert M. Thomas
1094pp. Ref.590-5

This is a complete reference work covering all the features, commands, and user options available under AutoCAD Release 10, including drawing basic and complex entities, editing, displaying, printing, plotting, and customizing drawings, manipulating the drawing database, and AutoLISP programming. Through Release 10.

AutoCAD Instant Reference
SYBEX Prompter Series
George Omura
390pp. Ref. 548-4, 4 ¾" × 8"

This pocket-sized reference is a quick guide to all AutoCAD features. Designed for easy use, all commands are organized with exact syntax, a brief description, options, tips, and references. Through Release 10.

The ABC's of Generic CADD
Alan R. Miller

278pp. Ref. 608-1

This outstanding guide to computer-aided design and drafting with Generic CADD assumes no previous experience with computers or CADD. This book will have users doing useful CADD work in record time, including basic drawing with the keyboard or a mouse, erasing and unerasing, making a copy of drawings on your printer, adding text and organizing your drawings using layers.

The ABC's of AutoLISP
George Omura

300pp. Ref. 620-0

This book is for users who want to unleash the full power of AutoCAD through the AutoLISP programming language. In non-technical terms, the reader is shown how to store point locations, create new commands, and manipulate coordinates and text. Packed with tips on common coding errors.

Mastering VersaCAD
David Bassett-Parkins

450pp. Ref. 617-0

For every level of VCAD user, this comprehensive tutorial treats each phase of project design including drawing, modifying, grouping, and filing. The reader will also learn VCAD project management and many tips, tricks, and shortcuts. Version 5.4.

Graphics Programming Under Windows
Brian Myers/Chris Doner

646pp. Ref. 448-8

Straightforward discussion, abundant examples, and a concise reference guide to graphics commands make this book a must for Windows programmers. Topics range from how Windows works to programming for business, animation, CAD, and desktop publishing. For Version 2.

LANGUAGES

Mastering Turbo Pascal 5 (Second Edition)
Douglas Hergert

628pp. Ref. 647-2

Explore the potential of the fast and efficient programming environment offered by Turbo Pascal 5 Version 5.5. Discover the powerful new advanced object-oriented programming, in addition to all the essential elements of a professional programming language; file-handling procedures; recursion; support for the 8087 numeric coprocessor chip; and user-defined units.

Introduction to Turbo BASIC
Douglas Hergert

523pp. Ref. 441-0

A complete tutorial and guide to this now highly professional language: Turbo BASIC, including important Turbo extras such as parameter passing, structured loops, long integers, recursion, and 8087 compatibility for high-speed numerical operation.

Introduction to Turbo Prolog (Second Edition)
Carl Townsend

325pp. Ref. 611-1

Written with beginning and intermediate users in mind, this thorough guide covers practical techniques for I/O, string and arithmetic operations, windows, graphics, sound, expert systems, natural language interfaces, and simulation systems. Includes exercises. For Version 2.0.

Mastering QuickBASIC
Rita Belserene

450pp. Ref. 589-1

Readers build professional programs with this extensive language tutorial. Fundamental commands are mixed with the author's tips and tricks so that users can create their own applications. Program templates are included for video displays, computer games, and working with databases and printers. For Version 4.5.

Turbo Pascal Toolbox (Second Edition)
Frank Dutton
425pp. Ref. 602-2

This collection of tested, efficient Turbo Pascal building blocks gives a boost to intermediate-level programmers, while teaching effective programming by example. Topics include accessing DOS, menus, bit maps, screen handling, and much more.

Introduction to Pascal: Including Turbo Pascal (Second Edition)
Rodnay Zaks
464pp. Ref. 533-6

This best-selling tutorial builds complete mastery of Pascal—from basic structured programming concepts, to advanced I/O, data structures, file operations, sets, pointers and lists, and more. Both ISO Standard and Turbo Pascal.

The ABC's of Quick C
Douglas Hergert
309pp. Ref. 557-3

This is the most unintimidating C language tutorial, designed especially for readers who have had little or no computer programming experience. The reader will learn programming essentials with step-by-step instructions for working with numbers, strings, arrays, pointers, structures, decisions, and loops. For Version 2.0.

Mastering QuickC
Stan Kelly-Bootle
602pp. Ref. 550-6

This extensive tutorial covers C language programming and features the latest version of QuickC. Veteran author Kelly-Bootle uses many examples to explain language and style, covering data types, storage classes, file I/O, the Graphics Toolbox, and the window-oriented debugger. For Version 2.0.

QuickC Instant Reference SYBEX Prompter Series
J. Daniel Gifford
394pp. Ref. 586-7, 4 ¾" × 8"

This concise guide to QuickC key words and library functions should be on every programmer's desk. Organized alphabetically for quick and easy access, it covers all the essential information such as format, syntax, arguments, and usage.

The ABC's of Turbo C
Douglas Hergert
310pp. Ref. 594-8

This unintimidating C language tutorial was written especially for those with little or no experience with computer programming. The ABC's teaches fundamental programming concepts and techniques with lots of program examples for working with numbers, strings, arrays, pointers, loops, decisions, and more. For Version 2.0.

Mastering Turbo C (Second Edition)
Stan Kelly-Bootle
609pp. Ref. 595-6

With a foreword by Borland International President Philippe Kahn, this new edition has been expanded to include full details on Version 2.0. Learn theory and practical programming, with tutorials on data types, real numbers and characters, controlling program flow, file I/O, and producing color charts and graphs. Through Version 2.

Systems Programming in Turbo C
Michael J. Young
365pp. Ref. 467-4

An introduction to advanced programming with Borland's Turbo C, and a goldmine of ready-made routines for the system programmer's library: DOS and BIOS interfacing, interrupt handling, windows, graphics, expanded memory, UNIX utilities, and more.

Systems Programming in Microsoft C
Michael J. Young
604pp. Ref. 570-0

This sourcebook of advanced C programming techniques is for anyone who wants to make the most of their C compiler or Microsoft QuickC. It includes a comprehensive, annotated library of systems functions, ready to compile and call.

Understanding C
Bruce H. Hunter
320pp. Ref. 123-3
A programmer's introduction to C, with special attention to implementations for microcomputers—both CP/M and MS-DOS. Topics include data types, storage management, pointers, random I/O, function libraries, compilers and more.

Mastering C
Craig Bolon
437pp. Ref. 326-0
This in-depth guide stresses planning, testing, efficiency and portability in C applications. Topics include data types, storage classes, arrays, pointers, data structures, control statements, I/O and the C function library.

SPREADSHEETS AND INTEGRATED SOFTWARE

Visual Guide to Lotus 1-2-3
Jeff Woodward
250pp. Ref. 641-3
Readers match what they see on the screen with the book's screen-by-screen action sequences. For new Lotus users, topics include computer fundamentals, opening and editing a worksheet, using graphs, macros, and printing typeset-quality reports. For Release 2.2.

The ABC's of 1-2-3 Release 2.2
Chris Gilbert/Laurie Williams
340pp. Ref. 623-5
New Lotus 1-2-3 users delight in this book's step-by-step approach to building trouble-free spreadsheets, displaying graphs, and efficiently building data-bases. The authors cover the ins and outs of the latest version including easier calculations, file linking, and better graphic presentation.

The ABC's of 1-2-3 Release 3
Judd Robbins
290pp. Ref. 519-0
The ideal book for beginners who are new to Lotus or new to Release 3. This step-by-step approach to the 1-2-3 spreadsheet software gets the reader up and running with spreadsheet, database, graphics, and macro functions.

The ABC's of 1-2-3 (Second Edition)
Chris Gilbert/Laurie Williams
245pp. Ref. 355-4
Online Today recommends it as "an easy and comfortable way to get started with the program." An essential tutorial for novices, it will remain on your desk as a valuable source of ongoing reference and support. For Release 2.

Mastering 1-2-3 Release 3
Carolyn Jorgensen
682pp. Ref. 517-4
For new Release 3 and experienced Release 2 users, "Mastering" starts with a basic spreadsheet, then introduces spreadsheet and database commands, functions, and macros, and then tells how to analyze 3D spreadsheets and make high-impact reports and graphs. Lotus add-ons are discussed and Fast Tracks are included.

Mastering 1-2-3 (Second Edition)
Carolyn Jorgensen
702pp. Ref. 528-X
Get the most from 1-2-3 Release 2 with this step-by-step guide emphasizing advanced features and practical uses. Topics include data sharing, macros, spreadsheet security, expanded memory, and graphics enhancements.

ABC's of AutoLISP Disk Offer

ABC'S OF AUTOLISP ON DISK is for those readers who do not have the time to enter all the programs listed in this book. It includes all the programs and AutoCAD drawing files needed to do the exercises. Also included is a program that strips comments from your programs so your programs load faster. Many additional AutoLISP programs are also included.

To order, just complete this form and send it to the address below along with a check or money order for the indicated amount.

**Omura Illustration, P.O. Box 6357 , Albany, CA 94706-0357
Phone : (415) 526-1113**

Name_____

Address_____

City/State/Zip_____

Country_____

ABC'S OF AUTOLISP ON DISK $30.00

In California, sales tax of destination: _____

Canada and Mexico add $3.00 U.S. for shipping.
Foreign orders other than Canada and Mexico add
$12.00 U.S. for shipping: _____

Domestic UPS 2nd day air add $7.00   _____

Total (make checks payable to Omura Illustration)   _____

Diskette type   ☐ 3.5"-720K   ☐ 5.25"-360K

AutoCAD version   ☐ 2.6   ☐ 9.0x   ☐ 10.0x

If you just want information on our other AutoCAD enhancement products,
ON-SCREEN AEC, V-Zoom, Editools, and AutoPS, check this box. ☐

SYBEX®

TO JOIN THE SYBEX MAILING LIST OR ORDER BOOKS
PLEASE COMPLETE THIS FORM

NAME _____ COMPANY _____

STREET _____ CITY _____

STATE _____ ZIP _____

☐ PLEASE MAIL ME MORE INFORMATION ABOUT **SYBEX** TITLES

ORDER FORM (There is no obligation to order)

PLEASE SEND ME THE FOLLOWING:

TITLE	QTY	PRICE
_____	____	____
_____	____	____
_____	____	____
_____	____	____

TOTAL BOOK ORDER   ____ $____

CUSTOMER SIGNATURE _____

SHIPPING AND HANDLING PLEASE ADD $2.00 PER BOOK VIA UPS   _____

FOR OVERSEAS SURFACE ADD $5.25 PER BOOK PLUS $4.40 REGISTRATION FEE   _____

FOR OVERSEAS AIRMAIL ADD $18.25 PER BOOK PLUS $4.40 REGISTRATION FEE   _____

CALIFORNIA RESIDENTS PLEASE ADD APPLICABLE SALES TAX   _____

TOTAL AMOUNT PAYABLE   _____

☐ CHECK ENCLOSED   ☐ VISA
☐ MASTERCARD   ☐ AMERICAN EXPRESS

ACCOUNT NUMBER _____

EXPIR. DATE _____ DAYTIME PHONE _____

CHECK AREA OF COMPUTER INTEREST:

☐ BUSINESS SOFTWARE

☐ TECHNICAL PROGRAMMING

☐ OTHER: _____

THE FACTOR THAT WAS MOST IMPORTANT IN YOUR SELECTION:

☐ THE SYBEX NAME

☐ QUALITY

☐ PRICE

☐ EXTRA FEATURES

☐ COMPREHENSIVENESS

☐ CLEAR WRITING

☐ OTHER _____

OTHER COMPUTER TITLES YOU WOULD LIKE TO SEE IN PRINT:

_____

_____

OCCUPATION

☐ PROGRAMMER   ☐ TEACHER

☐ SENIOR EXECUTIVE   ☐ HOMEMAKER

☐ COMPUTER CONSULTANT ☐ RETIRED

☐ SUPERVISOR   ☐ STUDENT

☐ MIDDLE MANAGEMENT   ☐ OTHER:

☐ ENGINEER/TECHNICAL   _____

☐ CLERICAL/SERVICE

☐ BUSINESS OWNER/SELF EMPLOYED

CHECK YOUR LEVEL OF COMPUTER USE

☐ NEW TO COMPUTERS

☐ INFREQUENT COMPUTER USER

☐ FREQUENT USER OF ONE SOFTWARE

   PACKAGE:

   NAME _____

☐ FREQUENT USER OF MANY SOFTWARE

   PACKAGES

☐ PROFESSIONAL PROGRAMMER

OTHER COMMENTS:

_____

_____

_____

_____

_____

_____

_____

PLEASE FOLD, SEAL, AND MAIL TO SYBEX

SYBEX, INC.
2021 CHALLENGER DR. #100
ALAMEDA, CALIFORNIA USA
94501

SEAL

SYBEX Computer Books are different.

Here is why . . .

At SYBEX, each book is designed with you in mind. Every manuscript is carefully selected and supervised by our editors, who are themselves computer experts. We publish the best authors, whose technical expertise is matched by an ability to write clearly and to communicate effectively. Programs are thoroughly tested for accuracy by our technical staff. Our computerized production department goes to great lengths to make sure that each book is well-designed.

In the pursuit of timeliness, SYBEX has achieved many publishing firsts. SYBEX was among the first to integrate personal computers used by authors and staff into the publishing process. SYBEX was the first to publish books on the CP/M operating system, microprocessor interfacing techniques, word processing, and many more topics.

Expertise in computers and dedication to the highest quality product have made SYBEX a world leader in computer book publishing. Translated into fourteen languages, SYBEX books have helped millions of people around the world to get the most from their computers. We hope we have helped you, too.

For a complete catalog of our publications:

SYBEX, Inc. 2021 Challenger Drive, #100, Alameda, CA 94501
Tel: (415) 523-8233/(800) 227-2346 Telex: 336311
Fax: (415) 523-2373

PROGRAMMING TASK	FUNCTION/TOPIC

File Operations

Create file	Open
Close file	Close
Read line from file	Read-line
Read character from file	Read-char
Write string line to file	Write-line
Write string character to file	Write-char
Strip quotation marks from file string	Read
Write data to file (literal)	Prin1
Write data to file (act on code)	Princ
Write data to file with return and space	Print

Drawing Entity Operations

Select a group of entities	Ssget
Select single entity	Entsel
Select last entity added to drawing	Entlast
Select entity from start of drawing	Entnext
Select subentity (Pline, attributes)	Entnext
Build/add entity to selection set	Ssadd
Delete entity from selection set	Ssdel
Find properties of entities	Assoc
Get property list of an entity	Entget
Get entity name of an entity	Ssname
Modify properties of entities	Entmod
Update the display of a subentity	Entupd
Substitute a property list item	Subst
Step through layer, style, etc. table	Tblnext
Find layer, style, etc. table	Tblsearch
Test if entity is in selection set	Ssmemb
Get selection set based on property	Ssget "X" filter
Get entity name based on entity handle	Handent